Writing Rumba

New World Studies

A. James Arnold, *Editor*

J. Michael Dash, David T. Haberly,
and Roberto Márquez,
Associate Editors

Joan Dayan, Dell H. Hymes,
Vera M. Kutzinski, Candace Slater,
and Iris M. Zavala,
Advisory Editors

Writing Rumba

THE AFROCUBANISTA MOVEMENT IN POETRY

Miguel Arnedo-Gómez

New World Studies
A. James Arnold, editor

University of Virginia Press
Charlottesville and London

University of Virginia Press
© 2006 by the Rector and Visitors of the University of Virginia
All rights reserved
Printed in the United States of America on acid-free paper

First published 2006

9 8 7 6 5 4 3 2

Library of Congress Cataloging-in-Publication Data
Arnedo-Gómez, Miguel, 1971–
   Writing rumba : the Afrocubanista movement in poetry / Miguel Arnedo-Gómez.
     p.   cm. — (New World studies)
   Includes bibliographical references and index.
   ISBN 0-8139-2541-X (cloth : alk. paper) — ISBN 0-8139-2542-8 (pbk. : alk. paper)
   1. Cuban poetry—20th century—History and criticism. 2. Cuban poetry—Black authors—History and criticism. 3. Blacks in literature. I. Title. II. Series.
PQ7380.A74 2006
861'.60935299607291—dc22

                                                                         2005030903

Para Samuel

Contents

	Acknowledgments	ix
	Introduction	1
1	Redefining the Mulatto Nation: The Rise of Afrocubanismo	21
2	"Rumbas, guarachas y solares": Afrocubanista Poetry and the Afro-Cuban Sectors	42
3	Transculturation and the Cuban Stew: Fernando Ortiz's Discourse on Cuban National Identity and Afrocubanista Poetry	65
4	Folklore and Afrocubanista Poetry in Ramón Guirao's *Órbita de la poesía afrocubana, 1928–1937*	86
5	The Black Rumbera	103
6	Afrocubanista Poetry and Afro-Cuban Performance	123
7	The Subversion of Afrocubanista Discourse	141
	Conclusion	165
	Notes	171
	Bibliography	191
	Index	213

Acknowledgments

THIS BOOK could never have been completed without the help and support of several people. I am deeply indebted to my excellent PhD supervisor, Patricia D'Allemand, and to her infectious passion for the study of Latin-American literature and culture. Verity Smith gave me emotional and intellectual support throughout the hardest times and provided encouraging feedback even for the earliest versions of my chapters (quite a feat). I would also like to express my gratitude to Catherine Davies, who persuaded me to submit my first article for publication and who always encouraged me by insisting on the importance of my research. Other people who also helped me in a variety of ways are Peter Wade, Adriana Méndez-Rodenas, Miguel Ángel Arnedo, Conrad James, John Perivolaris, Rob Rix, Omar García, Peter Evans, Alan Deyermond, Martin Duffle, Ralph Penny, Abigail Lee Six, Dave Pattman, Hamish Orr, Andy Warner, Rodolfo Hechavarría, Jane Whetnall, Cathie Brettschneider, Mark Mones, Sarah Leggott, Nicola Gilmour, Hansgerd Delbruck, Eugenio Matibag, Aline Helg, Narciso Hidalgo, Jean Stubbs, Dave Pattman, Toby Herschmann, Neil Bennun, Andrew Gideon Thomson, Olivia Funnell, Tristán White, Bill Bland, Mark Watkins, David Treece, Josep Antón Fernández, Vera Kutzinski, Sue Matthews, Claudia Bernardi, Pilar Rose-Alcorta, Xelo Sanmateu, Parvati Nair, Colleen R. Clark, and Alain Milhaud.

Some of the papers I have given at seminars and conferences were partly subsidized by three specific university departments and academic institutions in the UK. These are the Society of Latin-American Studies, the School of Modern Languages of Queen Mary (University of London), and the Forum for the Study of Cuba at the University of Wolverhampton.

This project could never have been completed without the help and support of the three most important people in my life: my parents, Miguel Ángel Arnedo and Ana Isabel Gómez, and my partner, Tabitha Phillips.

My parents agreed to finance my PhD studies and have suffered with me every time it became clear that I was still a long way from finishing. Despite this, they have proven their unconditional love and support by continuing to support me emotionally and financially until the very end. Since Tabitha met me, her life has been almost as closely intertwined with this book as my own. Her truly unconditional love and support throughout have been absolutely indispensable. Seeing her happiness and pride in my achievement at the end of this project makes everything worthwhile.

Some of the material included in chapters 3, 5, and 6 was part of three separate articles that I published in three British journals: *Bulletin of Latin American Research*, *Afro-Hispanic Review*, and *Modern Language Review*. I would like to thank these journals for giving me permission to reprint this material.

Writing Rumba

Introduction

IN THE 1920s and 1930s a series of Cuban artists and intellectuals took part in a movement of revalorization of Afro-Cuban culture widely known as *afrocubanismo*.[1] Cuban composers such as Alejandro García Caturla, Amadeo Roldán, and Gilberto Valdés introduced local African-influenced musical forms and rhythms, as well as black themes, into their compositions. Cuban painters such as Jaime Valls Díaz, Eduardo Abela, Antonio Gattorno, and Carlos Enríquez produced paintings that depicted or were inspired by black African-influenced cultural practices.[2] Literary afrocubanismo encompassed a variety of genres. According to Fredrick Habibe, one of the first narrative incursions into the world of Cuban blacks and African-influenced culture was the short story "La rumba" (The *Rumba*) by Roger de Lauria, which was published in 1927. Gerardo del Valle's "El bongó" (The Bongo Drum), a short story with black African-derived themes, came out in the same year, in the 20 November issue of the Cuban newspaper *Diario de la Marina*. Also in this year Alejo Carpentier wrote a novel entitled *Écue-yamba-ó*, in which the main characters were rural blacks of the period who followed African-influenced traditions (Habibe 1985, 20, 31; Carpentier 1982). Also worth mentioning are Lydia Cabrera's 1936 *Contes nègres de Cuba* (Black Stories from Cuba), a series of tales based upon the oral short stories that this author remembered hearing from her black servants in Cuba, and Rómulo Lachatañeré's 1938 *¡Oh, mío Yemayá! Cuentos y cantos negros* (Oh, My Yemayá! Black Songs and Stories), a collection of transcriptions of myths and legends of African origins that had been reconstructed by blacks in Cuba.

However, it was in the realm of poetry that the literary offshoot of afrocubanismo was most productive. On 8 April 1928, the Cuban newspaper *Diario de la Marina* (Daily of the Navy) published in its literary supplement a poem entitled "Bailadora de rumba" (The Rumba Dancer) by the white Cuban poet, essayist, and journalist Ramón Guirao (Guirao 1938, 53; Valdés-Cruz 1970, 57). As its title indicates, this short poem was a poetic rendition of a black woman dancing the rumba, more specifically, the rumba variety known as *guaguancó*. The rumba was an Afro-Cuban dance and music form that had been developed by Cuban blacks in lower-class urban neighborhoods (Moore 1997, 168; Manuel 1991, 49; Ortiz 1924a, 410). The publication of Guirao's "Bailadora de rumba" was closely followed by another poem depicting blacks dancing rumba: José Z. Tallet's "La rumba" (The Rumba), which was published in the August edition of the Cuban magazine *Atuey* (Guirao 1938, 68; Valdés-Cruz 1970, 58).

After the publication of these two poems in 1928, other poems about Cuban blacks and Afro-Cuban culture—by both white and black Cuban poets—began to appear in newspapers, magazines, and books. Several reviews and essays on this type of poetry were published as well, some in the form of critical introductions to anthologies of black-inspired poetry and others in Cuban journals and magazines such as *Revista Bimestre Cubana* (Bimonthly Cuban Journal) and *Estudios Afrocubanos* (Afro-Cuban Studies).

As Ramón Guirao explained in the introduction to his anthology of afrocubanista poetry, *Órbita de la poesía afrocubana, 1928–1937* (Orbit of Afro-Cuban Poetry), the participants of poetic afrocubanismo considered their movement a "closed cycle" by 1938 (xix). After this date, black-inspired poems by a few authors appeared only sporadically (Valdés-Cruz 1970, 82–83). Members of the movement in Cuban poetry that succeeded poetic afrocubanismo, the Grupo Orígenes (Origins Group), became critical of the poetry of the previous generation and moved toward a type of literature that avoided "localisms" and "folklorisms." It is only fair to add, however, that the members of the Grupo Orígenes did try to incorporate into their aesthetic program Lydia Cabrera's work on Cuban black African-influenced culture and Wilfredo Lams's Afro-Cuban inspired paintings (Barquet 1996, 7).

One of the main aims of this study of poetic afrocubanismo is to bring to light the movement's connections to the sociocultural specificities of 1920s and 1930s Cuba. Against the grain of a widespread tendency to interpret this movement as resulting from the influence of foreign artistic trends, I undertake a detailed examination of the Cuban social and cultural factors that gave rise to afrocubanismo. A related objective of this book is to establish the nature of the movement's connections to

1920s and 1930s Cuban blacks. This includes analyzing in detail the sociocultural composition of the black population at this time, the poets' interactions with contemporaneous black sectors and their cultural practices, and the poetry's links with the represented cultures. I also examine the thought of leading figures of the movement, with an emphasis on the links between their discourse and Cuban sociocultural specificities as well as afrocubanista representations of blacks and Afro-Cuban culture.

An important contribution of this book is to implant the study of Cuban black literature within Latin American cultural criticism. Adopting anthropological and sociological perspectives, this body of criticism explores the connections between Latin American literatures and Latin American sociocultural specificities.[3] Nevertheless, in terms of ethnic literatures, there has been a noticeable tendency to privilege the study of indigenous or *indigenista* (indigenist) literatures, to the detriment of black Latin American literatures.[4] In particular, not a great deal has been written on black Cuban literature within Latin American cultural criticism.[5] This neglect is due in part to the fact that, as Magaly Espinosa Delgado points out, the development of cultural criticism in Cuba has been hampered by the absence of a strong tradition of sociological and anthropological studies (1995, 223).

In order to make use of the most significant theoretical contributions in Latin American cultural criticism, this book draws upon the theories of critics whose work on ethnicity has centered on Andean or indigenista literature. Three scholars in particular are worth mentioning: Antonio Cornejo Polar, Ángel Rama, and Martín Lienhard. Cornejo Polar's work on indigenista literature moves away from the traditional emphasis in criticism on the extent to which the indigenista writer expresses the indigenous world "from the inside" (1978, 21). By accepting that the exteriority of indigenistas was an essential characteristic of the movement, rather than the sole criterion upon which to judge the "authenticity" of their representations, Cornejo Polar was able to offer an interpretation of the indigenista novel that accounts for its social and cultural articulations (1978, 1980). The influence of this aspect of the critic's work is particularly noticeable in the second chapter of my book. Another relevant contribution by Cornejo Polar is his study of the ways in which indigenista literature assimilates formal elements from indigenous cultures while at the same time reproducing the sociocultural fractures of the society in which it emerged. My book's debt to this perspective is particularly evident in the sixth chapter.[6]

Ángel Rama's work on transcultural narrative is equally important in this respect, since it also sheds light on the connections between the formal particularities of transcultural writings and Latin American regional cultures of indigenous origins. Also significant is Rama's emphasis on the counterhegemonic potential of these popular cultures, as evident in the literary works of Latin American writers such as José María Arguedas, Gabriel García Márquez, Juan Rulfo, and Augusto Roa Bastos (Rama 1982). In the present book, the seventh chapter in particular draws upon this aspect of Rama's writings.

Finally, Martín Lienhard's work on orality and its literary representations has provided a valuable theoretical base for this book's analysis of the afrocubanista treatment of nonwritten, oral, and performative Afro-Cuban cultural forms. The influence of his work is patent in chapter 6. Equally important in this same chapter is his notion of a "sociocultural sector," which is used to conceptualize the human groups that are represented in afrocubanista poetry (Lienhard 1992, 1994a, 1994b, 1996, 1997).

Another discipline that has informed this book's perspective is anthropology. The absence of an anthropological perspective in existing criticism on poetic afrocubanismo seems odd, since, as Amy Fass Emery points out, *negrismo* is part of the "anthropological imagination": the Latin American phenomenon of literary texts that encompass anthropology and literature (1996, 1). One element from anthropological theory that has been central to the present study is the notion that "race" cannot be defined in genetic or biological terms and is better understood as a social construction (Hall 1992, 297–98; Wade 1997, 13; Knight 1996, 72). "Race" is a variable concept subject to redefinition, which is why, as Hoetink explains, "one and the same person may be considered white in the Dominican Republic or Puerto Rico, and 'colored' in Jamaica, Martinique or Curacao" (1967, 12). Nevertheless, in this book, race is not understood as being somehow "unreal." The belief that races exist informs people's behavior, and this has serious and real consequences at the level of social reality (Wade 1997, 14). The term "black," thus, is understood here as a label that has been applied to dark-skinned Cuban blacks and mulattos on the basis of a series of phenotypical criteria that are construed in Cuba as signaling African ancestry. This understanding of the term respects the Cuban notion of *raza* or *clase de color,* a concept dating back to the 1860 official Cuban population census, which no longer divided free blacks into *pardos* and *morenos* but used only the term *gente de color* (Knight 1970, 93).

This book's approach also relies on an awareness of the classic distinction between etic and emic definitions of ethnicity in anthropology. From the former perspective, anthropologists used to ascribe identities to ethnic groups on the basis of the morphological characteristics of their cultures. However, subsequently it became a widely accepted principle in social anthropology that definitions of what are perceived as distinct groups of people should take into account the group definitions by their own members (Barth 1969, Eriksen 1993, 11; Wade 1995, 123; Jenkins 1986, 176; Verma 1984, 2). From this emic approach anthropologists do not try to provide an "objective" definition of what constitutes black culture. Instead, they ascertain what different groups understand black culture to be and analyze the different ways in which they define it. This study is based on an awareness of the problematic connotations of ascribing identities to ethnic groups or cultural forms solely on the basis of an etic perspective. Nevertheless, along the lines of Wade's approach to black music in Colombia, it also uses etic criteria in order to bring to light the presence of elements of African and/or Spanish origins in various Cuban cultural forms (Wade 1995). A general awareness of the emic/etic distinction is central to the book as a whole. However, it is especially important for the analysis in chapter 2 of definitions of blackness and discourses on ethnic identities among 1920s and 1930s Cuban blacks, and for the analysis in chapters 3 and 4 of Ortiz's and Guirao's discourses on mulatto culture and identity.

Critical Outline

In order to comprehend fully the significance of this book's approach to poetic afrocubanismo, it is necessary to provide an outline of the main tendencies in the existing criticism. From its inception afrocubanista poetry has often been conceptualized as a reflection of the fusion or union of black and white Cubans. Nicolás Guillén's introduction to his 1931 collection of afrocubanista poetry, *Sóngoro cosongo,* is one of the clearest examples of this interpretation: "Éstos son unos versos mulatos. Participan acaso de los mismos elementos que entran en la composición étnica de Cuba. . . . Y las dos razas que en la Isla salen a flor de agua, distantes en lo que se ve, se tienden un garfio submarino, como esos puentes hondos que unen en secreto dos continentes. Por lo pronto el espíritu de Cuba es mestizo. Y del espíritu hacia la piel nos vendrá el color definitivo. Algún día se dirá: 'color cubano.' Estos poemas quieren adelantar ese día" (These poems are mulatto. They are made of the same elements that make up the Cuban ethnicity. . . . And the two races on this island that rise up to the surface of the water extend an underwater hook to each other, like those deep bridges that, unbeknown to anyone, join together two different continents. For the moment, it is clear that the Cuban soul is mulatto. Our definitive color will come to our skin from our soul. One day, people will say "Cuban color." These poems want to make that day come sooner) (as cited in Madrigal 1990, 75).[7] In this same year Alberto Lamar Schweyer used Guillén's reference to the *mestizo* spirit of Cuba to define the nature of the poet's literary achievement. He argued that Guillén had found a way of expressing the African/Hispanic fusion that characterized Cuba:

> His merit, his brilliance is in seeing something that many other generations of poets have not yet seen: the Creole soul, which is half-cast, complex and new. He has not invented anything; he has merely found the way to bring into relief an old reality, fusing it in such a way as to make it lasting. In Nicolás Guillén everything is new. And yet, the themes are old because they come from that distant historical moment when the race of the Spanish conquistador mixed, fused and became united with the race that had been imported from Africa. (1931, 256–57)

After the end of afrocubanismo, the notion that afrocubanista poetry derives from the fusion of the black and the white became a dominant paradigm in a good deal of Cuban and Latin American criticism in general. In his 1942 article "La poesía afrocubana" (Afro-Cuban Poetry), José Juan Arrom explained the emergence of afrocubanista poetry by stating that "the Republic is becoming mulatto," and that in this period the two races were merging increasingly, both from a racial and an emotional point of view (1942, 379). Two years later H. R. Hays described the work of afrocubanista poets in the following way: "On that island, where a new people are developing what is almost a new race, pure Spanish traditions are already seen as a thing of the past. What is taking place alongside miscegenation is a synthesis of cultural elements. The new Cuban poets (and particularly Guillén) are aware of all these things. The same fusion of African and European elements is taking place in their work. A vital movement is resulting from their combination of technical sophistication and primitive emotion" (1944, 91–92). Similar ideas are present in Enrique Noble's argument that the image of the *mulata* in afrocubanista poetry and other Latin American genres of black poetry effectively symbolized the cultural, spiritual, and artistic "mulateo" that characterized the continent:

> Social poetry is a component of culture that portrays the people like they are. Latin American culture is a continuous re-elaboration of very different transculturations that are imbued in a constant process of cultural, spiritual and

artistic miscegenation. It is for this reason that the mulatto woman in Latin American poetry symbolizes a particular way of feeling and thinking, of living and cohabiting and of re-living until dying. It also reflects the noble process of Latin American cultural miscegenation: a noble, beautiful and civilizing embrace that eliminates racial difference. (1958, 6)

Rosa E. Valdés-Cruz reinforced this image of Latin American black poetry as resulting from racial and cultural mixture in her 1970 anthology, *La poesía negroide en América* (Negroid Poetry in America). She posited that Latin American writers interested in black culture in the 1920s and 1930s portrayed the phenomenon of mixture, adaptation, and transculturation that had always been part of their societies:

> The fashion for the black in Europe and the United States had an effect in Latin America and made artists and writers turn towards that element, which was not completely alien to them. What became fashionable was something that had always existed and had been palpitating in the blood of Latin America, where slavery had produced a phenomenon of mixture, adaptation and transculturation. Literature portrayed many characteristics of these old social formations. It re-created a literature that was not new (because it had started in the slavery period), but that was now receiving a modern literary treatment and was being written from a different human perspective, with an American theme and with an original form of expression. (1970, 12–13)

In a similar manner, in a 1976 article Salvador Bueno refers to the "interweaving and dovetailing between cultures that takes place in Latin America, and especially in Cuba." He concludes the article with the following description of Guillén's poems: "The Cuban identity palpitates in these poems. This identity is not white or black, it is not Spanish or African, but it comes from the white and the black, from the European and the African. It is transculturated in such a way that the result has been a new synthesis, something new that belongs to a new identity, the clear physiognomy and profile of the Cuban people" (1976, 91, 105). In the 1990s some Cuban critics continued to apply this interpretation to afrocubanista poetry. Nancy Morejón has recently been quoted as referring to the afrocubanista poetry of Marcelino Arozarena as a literature that draws from "that transculturated heritage in which the African and the Spanish become permanently fused into one" (as cited in Arozarena Himely and Pinto 1998, 5). For Jorge and Isabel Castellanos, afrocubanista poetry evinces "the eminently half-cast, mixed or mulatto character of the national spirit" (1994, 185).

By contrast, other Cuban critics have been much less enthusiastic about afrocubanista poetry. For instance, in a 1969 essay, black Cuban poet Gastón Baquero describes it, along with the anthropological studies of Afro-Cuban culture by Fernando Ortiz, as presenting an outdated image of Latin American blacks, whose culture, he argues, in reality had no African characteristics. The objective of these works, according to Baquero, was to reinforce the idea that blacks were inferior and to expel them from the Cuban nation (1969, 213–14). It is interesting to note that in the 1930s black Cuban intellectuals had already argued that black Cuban culture no longer contained any African elements. Alberto Arredondo, for example, used this argument to accuse afrocubanista symphonic compositions of conveying an inaccurate image of black Cubans as primitive savages (Moore 1997, 212–13).

Nevertheless, it is within the predominantly North American critical tendency known as Afro-Hispanism that afrocubanista poetry has been most severely criticized in the last twenty years or so. In this body of criticism, a critical approach to Latin American poetry on blacks written by white authors developed as the idea of a harmonious fusion of races and cultures in Latin America (the ideology of *mestizaje*) underwent increasing reevaluation in the 1960s and early 1970s. Studies of race relations at this time showed that widespread miscegenation in Latin America did not preclude racial prejudice. In fact, interracial procreation had often been conceived of as a way of eliminating blackness and black culture (Jackson 1976, xi–xvii, 1–4). UNESCO studies on race relations in Brazil reached similar conclusions (Skidmore 1998, 215–16; Winant 1999, 98–99). This history made it imperative to question ideas of mulatto national cultures and identities in Latin America. It became evident that, at least to some extent, these ideas reflect historical attempts to eliminate blacks through *mestizaje* because they exclude pure black cultures and identities. They also tend to present an image of national homogeneity and harmony that hides existing racial conflicts and cultural differences.

One of the first Afro-Hispanist critics to establish connections between these problematic connotations of *mestizaje* and literary representations of blacks in Latin American literature was Richard L. Jackson. As Rosemary Geisdorfer Feal explains, Jackson's 1976 *The Black Image in Latin American Literature* established "a scholarly base upon which a good deal of criticism in Afro-Hispanic studies is founded" (1988, 60). In this book Jackson set the direction of much Afro-Hispanist criticism by warning against the danger of defining *mestizaje* as ethnic and cultural fusion when in fact it was "often understood to mean the physical, spiritual and cultural rape of black people" (1976, 1). In a section entitled "Ethnic Lynching, or *Mestizaje* Properly Seen," he adds the following:

> Despite artistic expressions of black themes, blacks in Latin America have had to wage a constant battle against extinction through cultural fusion or acculturation and particularly through racial amalgamation. The strong process of miscegenation running throughout the history of Latin America would seem to refute the existence of a pattern of racial conflict in that part of the world. The two phenomena, however, are not mutually exclusive, especially if there is any truth in the assertion, put in its bluntest form, that whites try to get rid of blacks in . . . Latin America through racial amalgamation. . . . Just as cultural fusion and in some instances government pressures have not encouraged the development and existence of a separate black cultural heritage, the process of racial bleaching denies the Latin American black the recognisable African characteristics of his physical features and thus his black identity. (1976, 1–2)

On the basis of this understanding of miscegenation in Latin America, Afro-Hispanist Marvin Lewis identifies an assimilationist tendency in definitions of "black" Latin American poetry that fail to make a distinction between the literary production of blacks and that of whites. As an example of these definitions, Lewis cites the comment by afrocubanista poet Emilio Ballagas that "Afro-American poetry cannot be accurately termed 'black poetry' but rather 'mulatto poetry' since it expresses the contrast and assimilation of cultures. It is an expression of the sensibility of the black, the mulatto, and the white but through the sensibility of the American black, whose psyche has been modified by the experience of being taken to the new continent and the drama of slavery" (Ballagas 1973a, 72). Lewis's emphasis on the assimilationist connotations of Ballagas's definition highlights the importance of maintaining a critical stance toward interpretations of afrocubanista poetry as a reflection of black and white unity. It is clear that the desire of afrocubanista poets to promote an idea of black and white fusion, which is evident in Guillén's earlier-cited description of his poetry, often led them to gloss over existing racial conflicts and cultural differences between Cuban blacks and whites. Afrocubanista definitions of the poetry as a single mulatto genre are in part a manifestation of this desire to erase differences, for they are based on the questionable assumption that a historical process of harmonious cultural synthesis allowed white afrocubanistas to write like blacks.

Despite being problematic, these definitions continued to permeate the terminology used by many Latin American critics throughout the 1970s. For example, Lewis also brings attention to the assimilationist thrust of Rosa E. Valdés Cruz's introductory remarks to her previously cited anthology:

> Poetry about blacks has been described with a variety of terms, like "poesía negra" (black poetry), "*negrista* poetry" (blackist poetry), "poesía afrocubana" (Afro-Cuban poetry), "poesía mulata" (mulatto poetry), "poesía afroantillana" (Afro-Antillean poetry). We think the best term is "negroide," without meaning to be disrespectful. It seems to us to be the broadest and most appropriate term, as it encapsulates the poetic expressions of blacks, whites and mulattos, without the limitations of the other terms mentioned above, which would refer to the poetic production of one racial group (blacks), or to poetry written to entertain blacks ("negrista"), or to the poetry of one specific region ("afrocubana" or "afroantillana"). (Valdés Cruz 1970, 11)

There were a number of anthologies published during the 1970s that, like Valdés Cruz's own work, treated the poetic production of black and white Latin American authors as part of the same genre of *poesía negra* (black poetry), *poesía afroantillana* (Afro-Antillean poetry), and *poesía negrista* (blackist poetry). Examples are Hortensia Ruiz del Vizo's 1971 *Poesía negra del Caribe y otras áreas* (Black Poetry from the Caribbean and Other Areas), Jorge Luis Morales's 1976 *Poesía afroantillana y negrista* (Afro-Antillean and Blackist Poetry), and Mónica Mansour's 1973 *La poesía negrista*. Critics such as Ivo Domínguez and Leslie N. Wilson also describe the poetry of 1920s and 1930s black and white Caribbean poets of "black poetry" as part of the same movement (Domínguez 1977, 131; Wilson 1979, 89).

This book does not take issue with attempts to emphasize the distinctiveness of literature about blacks written by blacks as an alternative to this *mestizaje* perspective. The ways in which black writers experience the singularity of being black can mark their representations of blackness and make them distinguishable from representations of white writers. Nevertheless, in attempting to redress the assimilationist connotations of afrocubanismo and other Latin American literatures about blacks, Lewis and other Afro-Hispanists have also adopted the problematic approach of concentrating exclusively on the study of literature written by blacks. For instance, Lewis specifies that his object of study is "Afro-Hispanic poetry," which is "poetry by, about, and written to but not just for people of African descent in the Spanish[-]speaking world" (1983, 3). In line with this understanding, Lewis concentrates on the "examination of selected volumes of poetry by nine major writers of African descent in South America" (7). Ivonne Captain also considers the objective of

Afro-Hispanism to be the study of literature by black Latin American writers. She describes it as differing from criticism on the Caribbean or on negrista-like themes in that it treats "literature written by and claiming cultural significance for Afro-Hispanic people" (1994, 3).

This exclusive focus in Afro-Hispanism upon literature written by blacks is often justified on the basis of the notion that specific themes and concepts distinguish literature written by blacks from that written by whites. For instance, in *Black Literature and Humanism in Latin America,* Richard L. Jackson argues that "literature about blacks by blacks themselves, whether written in . . . Latin America or in Brazil, is clearly distinguishable in theme, focus, and purpose from Latin American literature about blacks by non-black authors" (1988b, xv). Marvin Lewis, on the other hand, enumerates the key concepts that underlie Afro-Hispanic literature: confrontation, dualism, identity, and liberation. For him, these can be found in Martha Cobb's study of negritude, negrista, and U.S. black poetry in which she outlines basic tendencies that, according to Lewis, are also applicable to "the South-American continent." This transposition is appropriate, he adds, even though Cobb's study was designed specifically for the Caribbean and the United States. Lewis describes this "thematic approach" as "an attempt to apply a critical framework to Afro-Hispanic literature built in part on the thematic model of the basic tenets of French *Négritude* and in part on the more recently defined literary characteristics of the black aesthetic, the cultural arm of Black Nationalism in the United States" (1983, 5). Lewis's characterization of this "thematic approach" is based on an argument made by Jackson in a 1978 paper entitled "Racial Identity and the Terminology of Literary Blackness in Spanish America" (1978, 48).

Jackson's writings on the afrocubanista poetic movement provide an example of how this thematic approach has been applied to afrocubanista poetry. Jackson divides afrocubanista poetry into "false black poetry," written by white negrista poets, and "authentic black poetry" or "poetry of *negritud*," written by black poets (1984, 5). For Jackson, what characterizes the former is the representation of qualities often associated with Cuban culture of African origins, such as song, dance, rhythm, and sexuality. He argues that negrista poets were only interested in "black folklore and rituals," in beating "black-drums in poetry" and making use of African-sounding words. Thus, according to him, they ignored the black man's suffering and failed to protest against racial prejudice and discrimination. By contrast, Jackson praises black Cuban poet Regino Pedroso, a contemporary of afrocubanista poets, because the themes of his poetry show that his "identification with his black brother is complete" and that "he wants the black man to develop social consciousness." Along similar lines the critic praises the collection of verse entitled *Canción negra sin color* (Black Song without Color) by the black poet Marcelino Arozarena. "This slim volume," he argues, "is an enlightening document not only of the black experience but also of the view that a black poet takes on social revolution and the universal brotherhood of man" (1976, 41–43, 121–23). In particular, Jackson praises Arozarena's "Evohé," in which the poet asks his black brothers to forget about "African gods such as *Ogún*" and, like Pedroso in "Hermano negro," to think about the Scottsboro case:

¡Evohé!
suelta el bongó,
no seas risa de turistas en rumbática secuencia:
. . . .
piensa un poco en Scottsboro y no en Ogún.
        (As cited in Jackson 1976, 123)

¡Evohé!
Let go of the bongo drum,
Don't be an object for the tourists' laughter with your *rumba* movements:
. . . .
think more about Scottsboro and less about Ogún.

Jackson further comments that "despite the strong African flavour of much of his verse, in poems like 'Canción negra sin color,' 'Justicia,' 'Evohé,' 'Negramaticantillana,' 'La canción de las zafras,' 'Cubandalusía,' and especially in 'Ya vamos viendo' Arozarena reveals himself to be a poet explicitly concerned with larger questions of man" (1976, 124).

Like Jackson, Edward Mullen bases his division of the afrocubanista poetic movement on the thematic differences between the poetry of white afrocubanistas and that of black afrocubanistas. He sees an initial phase marked by the production of picturesque and external representations of black culture. He argues that in these early poems by white writers, such as José Z. Tallet, sensuous images and onomatopoeic rhythms predominate. According to Mullen, a second phase that constituted a more serious depiction of the black experience starts with the work of the black writers Nicolás Guillén and Regino Pedroso (1988, 442–43).

The recurring themes in negrista poetry that these critics object to (Afro-Cuban religion and music and the sensuality of Afro-Cuban dance) are used to support other criticisms of negrista poetry in Afro-Hispanism. The poetry's emphasis on Afro-Cuban cultural practices is interpreted as a reflection of a superficial or dilettante approach similar to that which characterized the European revalorization of "exotic" and "primitive," non-Western cultures in the first decades of the twentieth century (Jackson 1984; 1988b, 21, 26–27). In addition, the recurring theme of the wanton sexuality of black Cuban women in negrista poetry is often seen by feminist critics as resulting from the sexist fantasies of negristas (Young 1977, 139; Williams 2000, 57, 61; RoseGreen-Williams 1993, 17). In feminist criticism this theme is equally used in support of the interpretation of the poetry as an appropriation of black culture and black bodies through which negrista poets furthered an ideology that degraded blacks and blackness (Kutzinski 1993, 180; RoseGreen-Williams 1993, 17; 1992, 126). These largely dismissive interpretations are undoubtedly part of the reason behind a shortage of in-depth analyses of the poetry written by white afrocubanistas. Indeed, most book-length studies of afrocubanismo in Afro-Hispanism concentrate on the poetry of black poet Nicolás Guillén.[8] It is worth noting, nevertheless, that the practice of focusing on the poetry of Guillén to the detriment of the rest of the afrocubanista corpus is not exclusive to North American Afro-Hispanism. Fundamental studies of Cuban literature, such as Gustavo Pérez Firmat's 1989 *The Cuban Condition*, the revised 1999 version *My Own Private Cuba: Essays on Cuban Literature and Culture*, and Antonio Benítez Rojo's 1992 *The Repeating Island*, pay little attention to the poetic production of any other afrocubanista poets. In fact, the present book is the first book-length study of the afrocubanista poetic movement as a whole.

Guillén was a major figure in afrocubanismo. With his three collections of poetry, *Motivos de son* (1930), *Sóngoro cosongo: Poemas mulatos* (1931), and *West Indies, Ltd.* (1934), Guillén wrote more poems dealing with black issues than any other poet. Guillén took up black poetry with his 1930 collection *Motivos de son* with a stronger intention to express his particular vision of racial and social issues and national identity than most white afrocubanistas, who tended to focus on re-creating through poetry different aspects of Afro-Cuban music, dance, and song. As Afro-Hispanist critics have pointed out, in his poetry, and also in his prose, Guillén was more committed to developing a social and racial consciousness among Cuban blacks.[9] Particularly noteworthy in this respect was his critique of the ideology that undermined the aesthetic value of physical characteristics traditionally associated with the black physique, as evident in his poems "Mulata" and "Negro bembón."[10] As Fernando

Ortiz already demonstrated in a 1936 essay, Guillén's poetry was particularly successful at incorporating Afro-Cuban musical forms into the formal texture of his poetry (1973c). This accomplishment explains why Guillén's poetry is seen as questioning the divisions between the popular and the erudite, and also as radically altering or "transculturating" the Western literary tradition (Miller 2003, 246; Pérez Firmat 1999). Guillén's poetry is also of particular interest because it reflects the desire for an absolute unification or fusion of the black and the white more directly than the work of any other afrocubanista poet. This can be seen in poems such as "Balada de los dos abuelos" and "La canción del bongó."[11]

The above characteristics show that Guillén's work richly deserves extensive critical attention. Nevertheless, the exclusive focus on his poetry to the detriment of a wider study of poetic afrocubanismo means that many important aspects of this movement have not yet been analyzed in depth. In this book the analysis of the afrocubanista poetic movement as a whole not only sheds new light on the movement, it also opens the way for a reevaluation of assumptions about Guillén that are central to Afro-Hispanist criticism.

This book considers the Afro-Hispanist thematic approach to afrocubanista poetry in light of the questioning within recent Latin American cultural criticism of the appropriateness of mechanically transposing and applying interpretative paradigms to Latin American literary and cultural production. Such procedures overlook the fact that these paradigms tend to be elaborated in other contexts and in relation to literatures whose development may differ radically from Latin American writing (D'Allemand 2000, 51). As D'Allemand explains, it has been further objected that such paradigms may obscure the particularities of Latin American literary production by ignoring the social and cultural specificities of Latin American regions and societies. Above all, the links of these literatures with the region's non-Western cultural traditions are glossed over. An image that is closely related to this problem is that of Latin American culture as an "imperfect" copy of European cultural trends. This conception, D'Allemand argues, ignores the way in which European discourses are re-elaborated and reinterpreted in Latin American contexts. This intertextual dynamic "constitutes a new product with characteristics distinct from the 'original,' with a new function and new meanings conferred upon it by its own socio-cultural environment" (D'Allemand 2000, 8–9).

As made clear earlier, in Afro-Hispanism the literary production of poetic afrocubanismo is analyzed with the preestablished assumption that "authentic black literature" is marked by a series of concrete themes and concepts. As Lewis's definition shows, these themes and concepts (confrontation, dualism, identity, and liberation) have been established on the basis of literatures connected to the ideology of *Négritude* and U.S. black literature. Arguably, then, from the Afro-Hispanist thematic approach, interpretations of Cuban negrista poetry stem from the social and cultural characteristics of societies where non-Cuban literatures developed. This perspective clearly suggests an essentialist conception of black culture as something that manifests itself in similar ways everywhere. Particularly telling in this respect is the uncritical acceptance of the notion of "authenticity," a romantic and mythical category closely linked to the idea of a primordial, natural, and immutable essence containing the "true nature" of peoples or nations.[12] The notion that there is a clearly definable universal black essence encourages critics to approach black literature with a preestablished idea of what it should be like. This approach discourages detailed analyses of how the characteristics of the literature are related to the specific sociocultural circumstances from which it emerges.[13] Not surprisingly, then, much Afro-Hispanist criticism of afrocubanista poetry has failed to explore the poetry's links to the specificities of Cuban society. This is patent in the tendency to view afrocubanismo as a corollary to or result of European primitivism, which undermines the full significance of the Cuban political, social, and cultural concerns behind the rise of the movement (Jackson 1984, 5; Coulthard 1962, 94). A similar criticism applies to the assumption that negrista poets were not able to represent Afro-Cuban culture accurately because they did not write "from within" or because they were insufficiently knowledgeable about it.[14] This interpretation is not based on a thorough evaluation of the poets' interactions with the specific black Cuban sectors and cultures they sought to represent. Nor does it include an analysis based on ethnographic and anthropological studies of Afro-Cuban culture of the poetry's connections to Afro-Cuban cultural elements. The lack of consideration for Cuba's social and cultural particularities is also noticeable in the scant attention paid to afrocubanista intellectuals' writings on national culture and identity. Most of the studies outlined above do not analyze the notions about blacks and Afro-Cuban culture put forward in afrocubanista essays and the way in which they relate to afrocubanista representations.[15]

On the other hand, within the feminist tendency to approach the poetry as predominantly an expression of white male fantasies, the question of whether it bears any relation to images of black women present in

Afro-Cuban culture is not even considered. A case in point is Kutzinski's deconstruction of afrocubanista poetry as, essentially, objectifying, eroticizing, and commodifying black women, a view that does not take into account the extent to which afrocubanista representations may stem from the Afro-Cuban cultural practices they portray (1993, 183–88). And yet this inquiry seems essential if, in line with Kutzinski's approach, one is to assess fully the "race-sex-gender dynamics" of afrocubanismo (1993, 15). Indeed, if it transpires that the poetry reflects images of women that were also found in the represented practices, it would be necessary to explore various other factors: above all, the sociocultural history of these Afro-Cuban images and their meanings for the practitioners of Afro-Cuban culture. These are particularly important considerations if one is to avoid uncritically imposing criteria originating from Western feminist criticism onto afrocubanista representations.

Outside Afro-Hispanism, the perspective adopted by Gastón Baquero—that Cuban black culture had no African components—also overlooks the specific features of 1920s and 1930s Cuba. He does not back his claim with relevant research on the sociocultural composition of the black population at this time. Inevitably, the interpretations put forward in all these approaches create an image of afrocubanista poetry by whites as disconnected from Cuban sociocultural reality.

In this book I engage primarily with the Afro-Hispanist approaches outlined above because it is within this body of criticism that the vast majority of criticism on afrocubanista poetry has been written in the last twenty years. The intention, thus, is to carry out a thorough assessment of the latest critical tendencies. Nonetheless, this study also redresses a wider lack of in-depth attention to poetic afrocubanismo on the part of most specialists in Cuban and Latin American literature. Studies of Cuban, Caribbean, or Latin American black literature give the movement as a whole only a short and superficial treatment.[16] Thus, although Afro-Hispanists have been the most condemning critics of afrocubanista poetry written by white authors, they have also been the only ones who have granted it some degree of critical attention. In addition, their questioning of the ideas of racial harmony that underpin the above-outlined interpretations is one of the most important contributions to the study of the afrocubanista poetic movement. My book incorporates this perspective and thoroughly questions afrocubanista intellectuals' use of *mestizaje* as a symbol of Cuban racial harmony. However, another objective is to maintain a more balanced approach to the afrocubanista discourse on black and white fusion than that adopted by most Afro-Hispanists, who do not pay sufficient attention to its productive elements. This study reveals the ways in which the afrocubanista desire for racial and cultural harmony also led these intellectuals to transcend problematic ideas about races as permanent, separable types of human beings and about the "authenticity" or "purity" of cultures. Thus, what is made evident throughout is a tension in afrocubanista discourse between problematic and productive conceptions of race and culture.

By bringing together contributions from the study of Andean and, in particular, indigenista literature and Afro-Hispanist perspectives, this book shows how these two critical tendencies can complement each other. Whereas recent work on indigenista and indigenous literatures within Latin American cultural criticism has privileged the study of the representation of indigenous culture, there has been less emphasis on the representation of race.[17] The opposite tendency is evident in Afro-Hispanism, where the main intent is the deconstruction of racist representations. It is interesting to note that this divide neatly mirrors the split with which the study of blacks and Indians was introduced into social science. According to anthropologist Peter Wade, "The assumption has been that the study of blacks is one of racism and race relations, while the study of Indians is that of ethnicity and ethnic groups," which places more emphasis on the analysis of Indian cultural features. This difference responds to the belief that, whereas Indian identity relies predominantly on cultural signifiers and is thus malleable, "black" is often seen as a category that is determined by fixed phenotypical markers (Wade 1997, 37). The tendencies in Afro-Hispanism and indigenista studies outlined above reproduce the same problematic notions that Wade attributes to the divide in the study of blacks and Indians in social science. The first is that the category "Indian" historically developed as a racial category and still retains elements from that history. The second is that black or mulatto racial categories can often rely also on cultural and social criteria, which means that these identifications are also malleable (Wade 1997, 37–38). Chapter 2 of this study makes clear the benefits of paying greater attention to the characteristics of Cuban black culture in the 1920s and 1930s. Chapters 5, 6, and 7 offer the first detailed analysis of the representation of Afro-Cuban culture in afrocubanista poetry to date.

In terms of overall organization, the book is divided into seven chapters. My aim in the first chapter is to contextualize the rise of poetic afrocubanismo. In this chapter I outline the social conditions experienced by Cuban blacks in the first two decades of the Cuban republic, the period immediately preceding the movement's emergence. I give attention to the repressive and intolerant attitudes toward black Cubans and Afro-Cuban culture on the part of successive governments and leading Cuban intellectuals. The discussion then moves on to an analysis of the social, cultural, and political developments and concerns to which the rise of the afrocubanista poetic movement responded.

My aim in the second chapter is to establish whether afrocubanista poetry can be understood as a literature that stemmed from the culture of contemporaneous black sectors. Through a detailed analysis of the sociocultural composition of the black population in Cuba, I evaluate the claim that there were no African elements in the culture of Cuban blacks and then examine the relationship between afrocubanista poets and the black sectors they sought to represent. I use the intraracial differences of Cuban blacks to question the Afro-Hispanist division between Guillén and white afrocubanista poets.

The third chapter focuses on Fernando Ortiz's writings on Cuban culture, Cuban identity, and afrocubanista poetry. In this chapter I examine the notions about culture and race in Ortiz's thought on the national that underpinned the afrocubanista project, then move into a discussion of the role that Ortiz assigned to Afro-Cuban culture in his conception of afrocubanista poetry, afrocubanista music, and national identity.

My main aim in the fourth chapter is to analyze the afrocubanista utilization of the idea of "folklore." I outline the way in which the intellectuals of the Sociedad del Folklore Cubano (Society of Cuban Folklore) first appropriated the notion in the early Cuban republican period. I then assess the role the notion plays in Ramón Guirao's anthology *Órbita de la poesía afrocubana, 1928–1937,* foregrounding ideas central to poetic afrocubanismo and comparing them with those that characterized the project of the Sociedad and other folklore projects elsewhere.

The fifth chapter deals with the representation of the black female rumba dancer in afrocubanista poetry. My main objective in this chapter is to evaluate interpretations of the representation of black women in afrocubanista poetry as being rooted in the sexist male fantasies of the poets. I also assess afrocubanista representations of black women in relation to the choreographic features of African and Afro-Cuban dances. I analyze other tendencies in feminist criticism of afrocubanista poetry on the basis of the particularities of Afro-Cuban music and dance.

In the sixth chapter I examine afrocubanistas' conception of Afro-Cuban culture as oral and performative, and I evaluate the poetry's formal incorporations of nonwritten Afro-Cuban cultural forms, assessing these incorporations in relation to other representations of blacks and

Afro-Cuban culture in Cuban literature. I then discuss the poetry's formal assimilations of Afro-Cuban culture in relation to the afrocubanista belief in a process of black and white social and cultural unification.

My main concern in chapter 7 is to evaluate the notion put forward by some critics that afrocubanista poets utilized Afro-Cuban culture to promote their ideological objectives. Through an analysis of the role of Afro-Cuban dance as a means of cultural resistance, I explore the religious and feminist meanings that afrocubanistas introduced into their poetry by representing rumba. I then appraise the compatibility of these meanings with notions central to afrocubanista discourse.

In the conclusion I offer an assessment of the afrocubanista poetic movement based on the most important findings of the book. I also make suggestions for the direction of future research on afrocubanista poetry and Latin American literature about blacks in general.

1 Redefining the Mulatto Nation
The Rise of Afrocubanismo

THE REVALORIZATION of Afro-Cuban cultural traditions in the 1920s and 1930s came after a period of profound disenchantment for Cuban blacks. Despite their major role in the Second Cuban War of Independence against Spain (1895–98), the U.S. occupation government that supervised Cuba's transition to an independent republic from 1898 to 1902 introduced a series of policies that destroyed blacks' hopes for equality. Among such policies were the dismantling of the Liberation Army, in which blacks were overrepresented, and the approval by U.S. authorities in March 1900 of an electoral law that limited voting rights for blacks. Spain had granted Cuba universal male suffrage along with self-government in January 1898. However, this new law ruled that voters would have to be male, literate, and at least twenty-one years old; own a minimum of $250 worth of property; or have served in the Liberation Army prior to 18 July 1898 (Helg 1995, 89, 94; De La Fuente 2001, 57). The military governor of Cuba at the time, General Leonard Wood, acknowledged in private that the new law was intended to exclude black voters (De La Fuente 2001, 57). It certainly served its purpose. According to Aline Helg, only 19 percent of the voters in the 1900 municipal elections were black when, in fact, up to 37 percent of the Cuban male population was of African descent. Most of these black voters had qualified because of their service in the Liberation Army (Helg 1995, 89, 94). The requirements for entry into the new military and police forces, which were set up by the U.S. administration to guard U.S. rural property, also discriminated against Cuban blacks. Candidates for these forces were expected to be literate and own all the necessary equipment, such as uniforms and horses. Blacks were also discriminated against by the penal code. Introduced under Spanish rule, it increased liability when a black committed a criminal act against a white, but the U.S. administration did nothing to modify it (Helg 1995, 97). Furthermore, the U.S. government tacitly supported U.S. citizens who maintained a color bar in their public establishments (Helg 1995, 96–97). In fact, the only U.S. reform that would perceptibly benefit Cuba's black population was the integration of public education. During the republican period, it would contribute to a substantial increase in literacy among blacks.[1]

Discriminatory attitudes toward black Cubans were by no means exclusive to the U.S. administration. Although the first republican constitution of 1901 stipulated equal opportunities for all Cubans, the first independent Cuban government, led by president Tomás Estrada Palma (1902–6), continued most of these discriminatory policies. Furthermore, it attempted to whiten the population through new laws that were aimed at increasing Spanish immigration. As a result, between 1902 and 1907 approximately 128,000 Spaniards migrated to Cuba. Around sixty thousand of them planned to settle on the island on a permanent basis, a substantial number considering that the total population of Cuba was only around two million at the time. Without active antidiscriminatory policies in place, the increased immigration of unskilled laborers made the market of blue-collar employment even more difficult to penetrate for black Cubans (Helg 1995, 99; Moore 1997, 28; Brock 1998, 16).

Because of the blatant failure of these governments to address the inequalities affecting blacks, by the time of the second U.S. occupation (1906–9) Cuban society continued to be largely divided along racial lines. As in colonial times, white society resisted interracial marriage vehemently. Although public education was integrated, private schools still excluded black students, thus limiting their access to universities. Blacks were not allowed to attend certain Methodist and Presbyterian schools that were attended by many twentieth-century political leaders and intellectuals (Dodson 1998, 93). Highly prestigious American schools such as the Ruston Academy and Cathedral School (which was Episcopal) took in only white students. The Colegio Champagnat (Marist) and the Colegio Belén (Jesuit) were also discriminatory (De La Fuente 2001, 145).

Segregation persisted in the area of entertainment as well. Recreational associations such as the Havana Yacht Club, the Miramar Yacht Club, the Asociación de Dependientes (Employees Association), the Casino Español (Spanish Casino), the Club Americano (American Club), and the Club Ateneo (Athenian Club), among others, did not accept black members. Several restaurants did not serve black customers. Segregation was enforced in parks and social clubs, and even working-class locales that allowed black participation often divided the dance floor into white and black sections by means of a rope, a practice also maintained in public baths (Helg 1995, 97–99; Dodson 1998, 93; Moore 1997, 38). Openly favored by the Creole elite, all these policies were particularly effective because they drew on patterns of race differentiation that were firmly rooted among the Cuban population (Helg 1995, 97). Racial discrimination was also strong in the employment sector. In his analysis of the situation of the Cuban labor market in the first three decades of the twentieth century, De La Fuente includes many examples of the discrimination that blacks faced in various sectors of the economy (2001, 98–137).

In response to these and other examples of overt discrimination, many blacks began to protest. The first violent manifestation of their discontent was the August Revolution of 1906, after the fraudulent reelection of Estrada Palma. The president's administration put an end to the revolution by murdering its leading figure, General Quintín Banderas, in his sleep (Helg 1995, 120). Much fiercer was the repression of the black armed revolt of 1912, which was staged in response to the ban of the PIC, the Partido Independiente de Color (Independent Party of Colored People). In 1910 the Partido Liberal (Liberal Party) managed to introduce an amendment to electoral law prohibiting political parties that, like the PIC, were organized along racial lines. After exhausting all legal means to combat the amendment, the PIC organized armed uprisings in the region of Oriente (Cárdenas and McGarrity 1995, 89). The United States warned President José Miguel Gómez that unless the Cuban government could guarantee the well-being of U.S. citizens in Cuba, U.S. forces would be sent in. In the run-up to the 1912 elections, this would have been a devastating blow to President Gómez, who had made political capital out of his patriotic anti-Americanism. The president concluded that the only way to convince the Americans that the situation was under control was to openly confront the Independientes. An army led by General José de Jesús "Chucho" Monteagudo was sent to Oriente to suppress the rebellion (De La Fuente 2001, 75). Thousands of Cuban whites voluntarily formed local self-defense militias and joined in the fight against the rebels. In response to the Cuban army's increasingly violent behavior, black protesters committed acts of sabotage and burned some buildings. This provoked the escalation of antiblack violence throughout the island, resulting in various massacres over the next two months. Particularly horrific was the bloodshed of 31 May in La Maya. In this small town in Oriente, 150 peaceful black peasants, including women and children, were wounded by soldiers who were demonstrating to journalists the efficiency of new machine guns acquired by the Cuban army (Helg 1995,

194, 210–11). After two months of armed conflicts between the rebels and the white armed groups and soldiers, the uprising was crushed. Estimates of the total number of black casualties oscillate between 2,000 and 6,000 (Helg 1995, 224–25).[2]

As Helg explains, the 1912 massacre effectively put across the message that blacks could not openly challenge the established order. After this date, they adopted more discreet strategies of struggle. From the 1920s on they limited themselves to participating in new workers' unions and leftist political parties and to continuing their cultural traditions of African origins (Helg 1995, 246). Nevertheless, according to De La Fuente, the events of 1912 did not mark the end of black participation in Cuban politics. The fact that the Constitutional Convention of 1901 had sanctioned universal male suffrage meant that Cuban race relations had to be at the top of the agenda of the dominant political parties and that they had to compete for the support of black voters. One of the ways in which they sought to gain black support was to open up positions for black candidates. For instance, the participation of black Cubans in the national government increased in the first decade of the republic, although not enough to match the percentage of blacks in the voting population. The importance of the black vote also allowed some black leaders to obtain a number of concessions from the state (De La Fuente 2001, 55–56, 64).

Throughout the early republic, racism toward Cuban blacks manifested itself in the growing repression of cultural traditions of African origins. The strength of these traditions can be traced back to the nineteenth century, when there was a substantial increase in slave shipments from Africa in order to cope with the labor demands occasioned by the collapse of Saint Domingue and the resulting international demand for Cuban sugar. The increase in slave shipments was such that by 1841 blacks comprised more than 50 percent of the total population of the island (Paquette 1988, 298). At this time and up to the early 1950s, the white population in Cuba was actually in the minority, although it did exceed 40 percent of the population (Knight 1977, 261). Nevertheless, the mere demographic prominence of African-born blacks cannot be the sole explanation for the spread of African culture in the Cuban colonial context. Benítez Rojo points out that during the nineteenth century all the islands of the Caribbean had much larger African populations, and yet the strength of African influences in Cuba is unparalleled in any of them, with the exception of Haiti.[3] A factor that may explain the pervasiveness of African culture in Cuba is the relative tolerance on the part of Cuban colonial slave owners toward the cultural practices of their slaves. Slaves in rural areas, who tended to be African-born, were allowed time for recreation (Moreno Fraginals 1977b, 30; Paquette 1988, 38). As Fernando Ortiz indicates, a circular dictated by the captain-general of Cuba in 1839 established that rural slaves should be permitted to dance in the customary fashion of their places of origin. They could do this during the evenings of national holidays in gatherings known as *tambores* without the participation of slaves from other plantations (Ortiz 1988, 213–16). The determination on the part of the dominant class to discourage contact between slaves from different plantations is also patent in the 1789 Carolino Código Negro (Carrera Damas 1977, 38). In urban areas black slaves were allowed a certain amount of freedom to practice their traditions in the *cabildos de nación,* associations of mutual aid that, in theory, were supposed to gather urban African-born slaves of the same ethnic origin. Ortiz reproduces various eighteenth- and nineteenth-century edicts that dictated that these associations were allowed to hold their celebrations on days of national holiday and at particular times (1992, 9). This type of legislation allowed the members of the cabildos de nación to salvage oral cultural traditions (myths, legends, stories, prayers), religious rituals, and visual and musical practices of African origins.[4] It is worth noting that traditions of African origins were not practiced only under the auspices of the cabildos de nación. For example, devotees of the Afro-Cuban religion Regla de Ocha, often known as Santería, frequently visited their priest in what were called *casas de santo* (saints' houses), without being part of any legal association (León 1984, 37). African religious notions were preserved and transmitted in the family context as well, as is evident in the testimony of Lydia Cabrera's informants (Cabrera 1975a, 42).

Under slavery, the Creole elite and government officials viewed the associations as a necessary release valve. While they provided a means of self-expression, they had the added advantage of isolating Africans from the rest of society (Scott 1985, 266–67). The cabildos de nación were also expected to have a divisive effect by separating Africans along ethnic lines (Castellanos and Castellanos 1988, 113). But, as Scott demonstrates, tolerance began to turn into growing suspicion from about the 1880s onward. As the abolition of slavery approached, the Creole elite and government officials began to regard these organizations as potentially dangerous. Because of their ownership of property and their internal political structures, the governing elite feared that the cabildos de nación could become powerful independent political institutions representing the social and cultural interests of lower-class blacks. Furthermore, it was widely felt that cultures of African origin had to be exterminated if freed slaves were to become worthy members of society (Scott 1985, 266). As a result, in 1884 cabildo members were banned from marching in the celebrations of the Día de Reyes, and in 1888 the government finally ruled that the cabildos de nación were no longer allowed to have their own systems of government (Ortiz 1992, 11).[5] Partly because of this prohibition, but also in compliance with the petitions of some cabildos, the associations were gradually replaced by *sociedades de color* (Societies for Colored People), such as El Adelanto (Improvement), which was exclusively for mulattos, La Armonía (Harmony), La Unión (Unity), El Progreso (Progress), and El Porvenir (The Future). As many of these names suggest, these new organizations sought mostly to encourage blacks' integration by promoting education. In fact, some of their requests to become *sociedades de color* also show that their members (or, at least, their leaders) often assimilated the dominant discourse on culture of African origin. For instance, the request of the Cabildo de Nación Gangá Purísima Concepción claimed that "as they lived in a society of culture and progress they wanted to learn the most elementary notions of human knowledge in order to deserve the consideration of the more educated social classes and not to remain in the state of ignorance and backwardness in which they were born under the sun of the African coast" (as translated in Helg 1995, 30). Paradoxically, while the *sociedades de color* generally advocated unity between "pure" blacks and mulattos, many of them were select clubs with high membership fees that only admitted black Cubans with a regular income and a formal education (Helg 1995, 30–31).

The final abolition of slavery in 1886 contributed to promoting further misgivings among the elite. The migration of many rural ex-slaves into urban areas brought Afro-Cuban practices closer to the attention of urban whites.[6] As Moore explains, these migrants, lacking the cultural skills to prosper in urban society and unable to compete with Spanish workers, usually ended up becoming part of the large urban underclass that had developed during the economic depression of the mid-1880s. As they attempted to integrate into society, their African traditions suddenly became visible and more threatening to Cuban whites,[7] a situation that resulted in a much more pronounced antagonism toward cultures of African origins in the dominant discourse (Moore 1997, 30). This antagonism continued in the early republic as the white elite sought to attribute the subordinate position of blacks to their cultural backwardness (Leal 1982, 234). The strict official regulation of Afro-Cuban cultural practices during this period is undoubtedly linked to these developments. An ordinance by Havana mayor Estrada Mora prohibiting the use of African drums in public gatherings and outlawing Afro-Cuban street musical groups was published on 6 April 1900 in *Gaceta de La Habana: Periódico Oficial del Gobierno* (The Havana Gazette: Official Government Newspaper) (Moore 1997, 229). The government of Estrada Palma maintained a similar approach in launching a campaign against Afro-Cuban cultural practices (Helg 1995, 107). Prohibitive laws continued under the subsequent government of José Miguel Gómez. It officially banned the secret societies of the ethnic group of African origins known as Abakuá or Ñáñigos in 1903, although, according to Helg, Abakuá associations had already been outlawed under Spanish rule back in 1876 (Kutzinski 1993, 5; Helg 1995, 108). The policies of these governments were dutifully implemented during the first decade of the twentieth century through police raids of private homes, registered associations, and ceremonies. On 21 May 1902, for example, fifty-seven blacks and two whites were arrested in a private Havana household on suspicion of carrying out an Abakuá initiation ceremony. More alleged Abakuá suspects were arrested in September of that year, and another sixty blacks were apprehended in 1903 while worshipping a saint in Pinar del Río (Helg 1995, 107).

Persecution of Afro-Cuban practices escalated due to growing fear of *brujería* (sorcery). This concept was often applied to all traditions of African origin, which were believed to include human sacrifice and cannibalism. For example, shortly after the disappearance of a twenty-month-old baby called Zoila on 11 November 1904, members of the Cabildo Congo Real in the village of Gabriel were rumored to have sacrificed her in order to use her heart and blood for specific cures. About two months after Zoila's disappearance, fourteen illiterate blacks, all acquainted with each other and linked to this cabildo, were arrested and charged with her murder on the basis of weak and circumstantial evidence. Sensationalist journalism, which often associated cannibalism and murder with cultural practices of African origins, was greatly responsible for the public hysteria that led to such examples of overt injustice. Newspapers, particularly *El Mundo*, attributed the disappearance of white children to black *brujos* and continuously demanded stricter official sanctions against Afro-Cuban cultural practices (Helg 1995, 111–13). In general, during the earlier part of the republic, the police often targeted houses of Afro-Cuban worship by arresting, imprisoning, or fining their members (Moore 1997, 30–32).

Social intolerance and active persecution of Afro-Cuban practices continued into the 1920s. In 1922 the administration of Alfredo Zayas decided to prohibit Lucumí Afro-Cuban dances throughout the republic, especially the one known as "Bembé." The reason for this prohibition was, according to the edict, that these dances were not safe for the public and that they undermined the moral values, good manners, and civilization of the Cuban people. They were also described as symbols of barbarism and as jeopardizing the social order (Moore 1997, 230). As late as 1925, the president of the republic, Gerardo Machado, reinforced these policies through a decree published in the *Gaceta Oficial de la República de Cuba* prohibiting "any sort of activity in public streets employing 'drums or analogous musical instruments of African nature' or involving 'bodily contortions that offend morality'" (Moore 1997, 232). According to Cárdenas and McGarrity, while Afro-Cuban religious cultural practices were repressed in this period, Catholicism, which was not very popular in Cuba, was openly supported by the ruling elites. This was so despite the fact that the mostly Spanish hierarchy of the Catholic church in Cuba had supported colonialism and slavery (1995, 88).

Anthropological studies of Afro-Cuban culture by prominent Cuban intellectuals in the first two decades of the republic served to justify the repression of Afro-Cuban culture. According to Moore, the work of Israel Castellanos was influenced by the criminology of Cesare Lambroso, and it concentrated on drawing links between the "moral degeneracy" and physical imperfections of incarcerated blacks in Havana in the early 1900s. The main solution to Cuba's backwardness, according to Castellanos, was to "elevate the moral and cultural level, and educate the unrefined mental processes of those who continue holding fast to the barbarous foundations of their race." He also believed that it was important to "subdue those organisms who were incapable of adjusting to the legal framework of civilized nations." Castellanos examined Afro-Cuban dances and argued that their rhythms and sexually suggestive body movements evinced the inferiority of blacks. He considered the *íreme* or *diablito* (little devil) dances of the Abakuá, which had been a favorite motif of nineteenth-century Cuban *costumbrista* painters, "a vulgar tradition representing pre-modern civilization." For Castellanos, some black Cubans had improved in the twentieth century thanks to the influence of Western culture, but their parents and grandparents did nothing but jerk irrationally to the irregular beating of drums in the barracks. "The miserable slaves," he wrote, "danced with savage movements the African dances of the slave barracks, like barbarians. Their dances are better described as the leaping of irrational beings" (Moore 1997, 32–34).

Although in the 1930s Fernando Ortiz would take part in the afrocubanista valorization of Afro-Cuban culture, in his 1906 *Los negros brujos* (The Black Sorcerers) his approach was quite similar to Castellanos's in that he set out to study Afro-Cuban "witchcraft" with the intention of facilitating its elimination. As Luis Duno Gottberg explains, Ortiz at this point of his intellectual trajectory was guided by a modernizing and positivist desire to attain the stability of the newly founded republic, and he believed that this could be achieved through the direct repression of Afro-Cuban cultural practices (2003b, 122). This assumption stemmed from the scholar's belief that basic attributes of Cuban blacks, such as superstition and lust, were, at least in part, a consequence of the more "primitive" stage of their civilization (Mullen 1987, 117). This is why throughout the book Ortiz emphasized the idea that cultural backwardness was what held blacks from moving out of the lowest social spheres (1973a, 20). In order to combat the harmful effect that cultural traditions of African origins had on blacks and whites in Cuba, Ortiz recommended strict persecution of all *toques de tambores* (drumming events), *danzas rituales* (ritual dances), and *fiestas de santo* (celebrations for the saints). Another solution he offered, as did Israel Castellanos, was an increase in education (1973a, 249).[8]

Although Ortiz thought that education would help Cuban blacks to leave behind such practices of African origins as *brujería,* he did not completely discard the notion that to some extent they were biologically attached to these practices (1973a, 230). The tension between biological and cultural explanations of behavior that characterized Ortiz's and Castellanos's writings would become a central feature of afrocubanista discourse, as will be illustrated in chapters 3 and 4. It is interesting to note that a similar tension characterized other Latin American intellectual discourses in the postindependence context. As Graham and Wade point out, in Latin American countries with substantial numbers of *mestizos,* blacks, and Indians, accepting the idea that non-Caucasians and the racially mixed were intrinsically inferior was tantamount to accepting perpetual backwardness. Consequently, many Latin American intellectuals of the newly formed Latin American polities adopted European scientific racism (social Darwinism) while elaborating theories that contradicted biological determinist ideologies (Graham 1996, 1–5; Wade 1997, 30–35). An illustrative example of this approach is *La raza cósmica* (The Cosmic Race) by the Mexican José Vasconcelos. In this book, which was first published in 1925, Vasconcelos asserted that racial mixture could produce positive results if accompanied by a "spiritual factor." He also argued that "in a few centuries Christianity made Indians progress from being cannibals to being relatively civilized" (1958, 906).

The writings of Ortiz and Castellanos did not exactly awaken the interest of Cuban artists and writers in the aesthetic potential of Afro-Cuban culture. López Segrera explains that the first republican period (1902–23) was characterized by an obsession with "universal culture" and an endeavor to dilute typically Cuban elements. In erudite painting and music in particular, artists deliberately tried to avoid any influence from vernacular Cuban culture (López Segrera 1989, 105, 124–26, 137). Clearly, this tendency applies equally to the first generation of republican intellectuals. Ann Wright describes the intellectuals of 1913–23 as being profoundly elitist and consciously rejecting all forms of vernacular and popular culture. She argues that the members of the intellectual elite saw themselves as "a vanguard leading the masses to enlightenment, not as partners in a patriotic enterprise." Furthermore, their journal, *Cuba Contemporánea* (Contemporary Cuba), was a "high-culture magazine" whose learned content and austere format made no concession to popular taste (Wright 1988, 113). This elitism is evident in the formal concerns guiding the literature of this period. In poetry, the works of Regino Boti (1878–1958) and José Manuel Poveda (1888–1926) are characterized by a *modernista* obsession with literary form and technique (De Armas 1997, 237). Similarly, the novels of Jesús Castellanos, Miguel del Carrión, and Carlos Loveira used modes of narration derived from the French naturalist and realist novels (López Segrera 1989, 119). On the rare occasions that these writers turned their attention to the popular sectors, it was actually the rural white peasants or *guajiros* who appeared as representative of Cuban national identity. Significantly, these had been used in nineteenth-century Cuban *siboneísta* literature to argue for the fundamental whiteness of Cuban culture (Pérez Firmat 1999, 103–4). Jesús Castellanos's 1906 book of short stories, *De tierra adentro,* reflects a similar intent, as Cuban critic Ambrosio Fornet points out (1967, 25–26). Even as late as the 1920s, some Cuban writers continued to emphasize the Spanish origins of Cuban culture. A case in point is Carlos Loveira's 1927 novel entitled *Juan Criollo*. This work is consciously based on Spanish picaresque novels such as *Lazarillo de Tormes* and *Guzmán de Alfarache,* although, as Pérez Firmat demonstrates, Loveira actually converses with and transforms these literary models (1999, 119–32).

Nevertheless, by this time a younger generation of Cuban artists and intellectuals was also beginning to reassess the value of Afro-Cuban culture. Their newly found interest was related to developments that had been taking place in foreign artistic and intellectual movements. As is well known, during the first two decades of the twentieth century, the writings of European scholars such as Leo Frobenius, Guillaume Apollinaire, and, in particular, Oswald Spengler brought attention to the artistic potential of African and other "primitive" cultures. In this period European modernist artists engaged in a revalorization of African aesthetics, as is evident in the paintings, music, and poetry of Picasso, Juan Gris, Stravinsky, and Cendrars, among others (Kutzinski 1993, 150; González Echevarría 1977, 52).[9] This primitivist European vogue contributed to the emergence in the 1920s and 1930s of culturally nationalist movements in several parts of Latin America, where, as Duany points out, the search for national identity was a major concern for intellectuals (2000, 20). In Mexico and the Andean countries these movements drew upon the figure of the Indian, while in the Caribbean they drew upon the black (Brookshaw 1986, 87).

Richard L. Jackson points out that many critics view poetic afrocubanismo as "simply an echo of this *moda europea*" (1984, 5). Jackson himself claims that the movement "generated a dilettante image because of its close similarity to European negrophilia or the scholarly and artistic interest shown in the Black by Leo Frobenius, Pablo Picasso, André Gide, Blaise Cendrars, Igor Stravinski and others fascinated, for example, with jazz, black art and with the literature of the Harlem Renaissance" (1984, 5). G. R. Coulthard has argued that "Afro-Cubanism was a conscious attempt to be primitive" and that, despite its Cuban or Caribbean "setting," the movement was "a reflection of the European fashion of the 1920s for the primitive" (1962, 94).

Nevertheless, the rise of European primitivism and other non-Cuban black movements, such as the Harlem Renaissance in the United States and *Négritude* in the French Caribbean, is not enough to explain such a radical shift in Cuban erudite culture from an emphasis on the Hispanic elements of the nation to a revalorization of its African ones. In order to understand fully the emergence of poetic afrocubanismo, it is essential to consider specific aspects of the Cuban context from which foreign discourses on African culture were being interpreted and reformulated.

An important consideration is the U.S. economic and political domination of the island, an issue that had become increasingly worrisome for many Cuban intellectuals in the 1920s. Although the U.S. occupation had ended in 1902 with the inauguration of the first independent Cuban republic, the United States had forced the Cuban government to sign the Platt Amendment. Essentially, the amendment authorized U.S.

troops to invade the island at any time to protect U.S. property. Because it also restricted Cuba's freedom to engage in relations with other countries, as well as its right to accrue foreign debt, U.S. businesses were free from international competition (Helg 1995, 98; Roig de Leuchsenring 1935, 211). The fact that by 1927 American sugar mills were responsible for about 82 percent of Cuba's sugar production provides an idea of the extent to which U.S. businesses were able to invest in this context (Kutzinski 1993, 136).

This state of affairs did not cause widespread discontent in Cuba in the first two decades of the twentieth century. The literature of the period—with a few exceptions, such as the poetry of Bonifacio Byrne—similarly did not express frustration with Cuba's lack of autonomy (Gómez García 1998, 214–15). This was partly due to the fact that the economy enjoyed relative prosperity in the 1910s as international demand for Cuban products such as sugar rose consistently. Schwartz points out that during the first two decades of the Cuban republic, Cuban sugar production rose from 2.7 percent of the world's output to 21.1 percent, and that each year yielded more sugar than the preceding year (1977, 21). Resentment toward U.S. economic dominance began to build in Cuba in the 1920s owing to the economic hardship that resulted from falling demand for sugar. After rising to an incredible 23 cents a pound in May 1920, the price had fallen from 22.5 to 5.51 cents per pound by the end of the year. This decline affected the living standards of all Cubans. The situation worsened throughout the rest of the decade, with unemployment, hunger, and poverty increasing rapidly (Schwartz 1977, 21–22; Gómez García 1998, 215).

As Gómez García points out, in this context of economic depression it became increasingly obvious that a foreign elite minority was growing richer as the majority of Cubans grew poorer (1998, 215). Pérez points out that in the 1920s Cuban public opinion was completely united against the Platt Amendment (1988, 244–45). The literature of this decade saw the emergence of the anti-imperialist and social-protest poetry of Rubén Martínez Villena, Francisco Javier Pichardo, Felipe Pichardo Moya, Agustín Acosta, and Regino Pedroso (Gómez García 1998, 214–23). Resentment toward U.S. interventionism increased in the early thirties, after the collapse of the U.S. stock market in 1929 had devastated what was left of the Cuban economy. Opposition to Machado also escalated. The president had been elected in 1924 and had soon after illegally extended his mandate for another six years. In the context of widespread discontent created by the Great Depression, Machado's move provoked civil unrest, and there were violent confrontations between the government and the opposition. In 1930 the University of Havana, the high schools, and the normal schools had to be closed. In August 1933 a general strike paralyzed Havana, and Machado fled the country (Luis 2001, 9; Pérez 1988, 252–64). After the very short presidency of Carlos Manuel de Céspedes, who had taken over with U.S. support, a coup d'état in 1933 resulted in a new government led by a revolutionary junta, at first, and then by President Grau San Martín until 1934. This was the first government of the republic that was formed without the support of the United States, and it organized its program along "the lines of democracy . . . and the pure principles of national sovereignty." It abolished the Platt Amendment and introduced a series of reforms aimed at benefiting working-class Cubans. Because the new government jeopardized U.S. interests, Ambassador Jefferson Caffery threatened intervention and facilitated a new coup by Batista. Batista transferred the government to Colonel Carlos Mendieta in 1934, who then ruled with the support of the United States. A general strike similar to the one that brought down Machado was carried out on 11 March 1935 in protest against the repressive measures of the Mendieta government. The strike was violently suppressed by Batista, the leader of the armed forces, who from 1935 to 1944 became the real political leader of the country, installing and overthrowing different presidents at will (Pérez 1988, 266–84; Luis 2001, 9–10). Thanks to a 1934 reciprocal trade agreement with the United States signed under the Mendieta government, throughout the 1930s "Cuba was again closely linked to the United States, thereby returning the island to the patterns of pre-depression dependency" (Pérez 1988, 280). As De La Fuente also points out, "US interference in domestic politics diminished under the Second Republic (1933–1958), but North American interests and concerns continued to shape internal affairs in important ways" (2001, 10).

During this period of economic, social, and political turmoil, prominent Cuban intellectual and political figures began to stress the importance of a distinct Cuban national culture for the Cuban struggle against U.S. dominance. For example, in a 1934 publication Fernando Ortiz put forward the need for Cubans to know themselves and to maintain Cuban "essences" uncontaminated by U.S. influences. Ortiz's description of vernacular music as "one of the most vigorous expressions of a nation" shows that he looked upon popular Cuban music as the potential source of an authentically Cuban culture (as quoted in Madrigal 1990, 61).[10]

A comment by Emilio Roig de Leuchsenring in 1927 further illustrates that the belief of Cuban intellectuals in a distinctive Creole art was a response to the threats posed by, in the words of José Martí, Cuba's "vecino formidable" (1985c, 90–92): "For some time, and in many ways, there has been a call among us for a unique form of Cuban Creole art. If as a result of well-known geographic, economic, and political circumstances we must in order not to perish as a sovereign state and even as a people, maintain our own language, land, and economy, we also must have our own artistic forms. These will contribute, along with other factors, to national vitalization and greatness" (as translated in Moore 1997, 261). These pronouncements were partly motivated by a widespread concern about U.S. cultural influences in Cuba (De la Fuente 2001, 180–82). In this intellectual climate, Afro-Cuban culture began to appear as the perfect raw material for the production of a distinctive Cuban art, because it was assumed not to have been affected by U.S. culture. As Alejo Carpentier put it in his afrocubanista novel *Écue-yamba-ó*, Afro-Cuban deities had nothing to do with such things as "Yankee hotdogs." Thus, the Afro-Cuban drum *bongó* of the "tradición antillana" preserved by Cuban blacks could be used as an instrument of resistance against U.S. economic imperialism: "Only the blacks fervently preserved an Antillean character and tradition. The *bongó* drum, antidote to Wall Street! The Holy Spirit venerated by the Cué family did not allow Yankee sausages between pieces of its votive bread! No hot dogs for the saints of Mayeya!" (as translated in Kutzinski 1993, 141).

Naturally, Afro-Cuban culture also offered the possibility of distancing Cuba from its old colonial occupier. The need to turn away from the cultural models posited by Spain was expressed by Alejo Carpentier in his 1927 "Carta abierta a Manuel Aznar sobre el meridiano intelectual de nuestra América" (Open Letter to Manuel Aznar Regarding the Intellectual Meridian of Our America). In this article the young afrocubanista writer objected to the suggestion by the Spanish intellectual Manuel Aznar that Madrid should be considered the "intellectual meridian" of all Latin American writers.[11] He argued that Latin America had to find meridians within itself. In fact, he added, the considerable differences that existed between Latin American nations meant that it was best for the continent's intellectuals to avoid having any meridians at all (1974, 149). Salvadorian journalist and poet Gilberto González Contreras would express a similar view in an article he wrote in 1936 during his stay in Cuba (González Contreras 1973, 111–12).

In his introduction to his anthology of afrocubanista poetry entitled *Órbita de la poesía afrocubana, 1928–37*, Ramón Guirao linked the rise of afrocubanista poetry to the Cuban history of struggle for political liberation from the colonial metropolis. According to Guirao, in the nineteenth century the desire for emancipation from Spain had led the Cuban Creole to attempt to produce an authentic and distinctive Cuban poetry. This project had failed, he argued, because, generally speaking, Spanish-style poetry had remained predominant. He added that with the advent of poetic afrocubanismo, Cuban writers had finally found "the most genuine manifestation of their insular sensitivity" (1938, xii). Further on in the introduction, Guirao established a comparison between *indigenismo* and *afrocubanismo* that also reflects how afrocubanista poetry stemmed from a desire to establish a distance from Spanish cultural influences. Guirao argued that, in the same way as other Latin American countries had turned to the spirit and forms of pre-Hispanic cultures to find their originary form of expression and thus escape their European heritage, Cubans had found their own poetic style through afrocubanista poetry (1938, xxv). Guirao's comparison shows that, unlike in these other Latin American countries, Cuba's singular spirit was not to be found in the cultures of the island's indigenous inhabitants, which had almost entirely disappeared, but in the mixture of the African and the Spanish.[12] Thus, afrocubanista poetry would serve to signify that Cuba was a unique composite resulting from this mixture.

The idea that the African/Spanish hybridity of the poetry would highlight Cuba's distinctiveness vis-à-vis Spain is also illustrated by the conception of the national that guided Guillén's work. The poet argued that Cuba was not Spanish, but rather "el concierto histórico y psicológico de la esencias africanas y españolas, de modo que entre ambas reunidas dan lo que somos, y sobre todo darán lo que seremos, como las dos corrientes humanas de mayor volumen en nuestra hidrografía social. . . . Ambas a dos, juntas y revueltas, dan la cubanía, un precipitado nuevo, ni español ni africano, o mejor dicho, africano y español, en una síntesis profundamente nacional" (the historical and psychological coming together of African and Spanish essences, which have merged to produce what we are, and, as the two most important currents in our social hydrography, will continue to produce what we will be. Both, together and mixed with each other, produce the Cuban identity, a new precipitate, which is neither Spanish nor African, or rather, it is both African and Spanish) (as quoted in Castellanos and Castellanos 1994, 13–14). Significantly, 1930s Cuban intellectuals such as Alberto Lamar Schweyer and Regino Boti used Guillén's poetry to illustrate the distinctiveness of Cuban literature with respect to Spanish literature (Lamar Schweyer 1931, 255; Boti 1932, 90).

This endeavor to fuse the African and the Spanish, which gave rise to afrocubanista poetry, was equally related to the desire of Cuban intellectuals for the disappearance of racial conflicts and divisions in Cuba. This desire has a long history in Cuban culture. Benítez Rojo argues that an early manifestation of what he terms "Creoles' integrationist desire" is the foundational legend of the cult of the Virgen de la Caridad del Cobre, which he traces back to the seventeenth century. In this legend the Virgin saves the lives of a black, a white, and an Indian, named Juan Esclavo, Juan Criollo, and Juan Indio, respectively. Benítez Rojo offers his interpretation of the story:

> In this way, the Virgen de la Caridad represented a magical or transcendental space to which the European, African and American Indian origins of the region's people were connected. The fact that the three men carried the name Juan—they are known as the Three Juans—that they were together in the same boat, and that all were saved by the Virgen conveys mythologically the desire to reach a sphere of effective equality where the racial, social, and cultural difference that conquest, civilization and slavery created would coexist without violence. (1992, 52)

A more immediate antecedent of this integrationist desire for the afrocubanista movement were the writings of Cuban intellectual José Martí, a leading figure in nineteenth-century Cuban nationalism. Martí's intention was to convince Cubans of all colors to fight together for independence from Spain. Through the notion of "nuestra América mestiza" (our half-cast America), he sought to counteract the Cuban whites' fear that in an independent Cuba blacks would rise up and take over the island (Martí 1985a, 69; 1985b; 1985c, 89). Although Martí used the phrase to promote an image of Cuban racial unity, he did not specifically refer to the phenomenon of miscegenation in Cuba or to the hybridity of Cuban culture. He tended simply to deny the fact that there was any antagonism between Cuban blacks and whites, who had fought side by side in the Cuban wars for independence (Martí 1985b, 52–53).[13] Cuban intellectuals of the 1920s and 1930s reelaborated Martí's construct into the more specific idea that Cuba was undergoing a process of racial and cultural mixture that would culminate with a single Cuban mulatto race, culture, and identity. In order to bring attention to this process, they felt it was necessary to foreground Cuban "mulatto" cultural forms, that is, cultural forms made up of both African and Spanish elements. This belief is reflected in the objectives of the Sociedad de Estudios Afrocubanos (Society of Afro-Cuban Studies), which was founded in 1936 and whose members included afrocubanista intellectuals Fernando Ortiz, Emilio Ballagas, Ramón Guirao, Nicolás Guillén, and Marcelino Arozarena (Sociedad de Estudios Afrocubanos 1937c). Members of the Sociedad assumed that racial divisions in Cuba could be solved by bringing to the fore cultural forms that had resulted from the coexistence of blacks and whites throughout Cuban history. "Los estatutos de la Sociedad de Estudios Afrocubanos" (The Statutes of the Society of Afro-Cuban Studies) established that the society's objective was to study the phenomena that had resulted in Cuba from the interactions of different racial groups, particularly blacks and whites. The society expected that this study would help to create a greater degree of mutual understanding and sympathy among the various elements that made up the Cuban nation and thus contribute to the fulfillment of their common historical destinies. The statutes also show that the Sociedad was conceived as an instrument for making blacks and whites understand that they were equally responsible elements in this historical force (Sociedad de Estudios Afrocubanos 1937b, 5, 7). An associate of the society, Nicolás Guillén regarded afrocubanista poetry as one of the phenomena that had resulted from the contact between blacks and whites and would serve to facilitate their unification. In the introduction to his 1931 collection of afrocubanista poems, *Sóngoro cosongo,* the poet explained that his poetry contained the same elements that made up Cuban ethnicity, which resulted from the process by which "the two races that rise up to the surface of the water on this island throw an underwater hook to each other." He added that he intended his poems to advance the day in which there would be only one race in Cuba (as cited in Madrigal 1990, 75).

The belief that the solution to the nation's problems could be found in autochthonous culture must be seen in the context of U.S. racial conceptions of Cubans that relegated them to perpetual backwardness. De La Fuente makes clear that on the basis of the "one-drop rule," upon which the U.S. construction of race was based, and the belief that race mixture produced an inferior racial type, all Cubans could be classified as belonging to a lesser race of people. At the time, several U.S. observers attributed Cubans' inability to achieve social and political stability to their racial degeneracy. After the obvious failure of the whitening policies of various governments, nationalist Cuban intellectuals had to acknowledge that Cuba could never be racially white. One way to challenge the determinist vision of an inferior Cuban race was to uphold the notion that Cuba had to be understood in terms of cultural factors rather than biological ones. The celebration of a mulatto autochthonous culture also sent out the message that racial mixing could be a positive phenomenon, a message that gave Cubans hope that their nation could progress out of the deterministic cul de sac to which U.S. racial discourse had relegated it (De La Fuente 2001, 177–78).

The desire to produce mulatto cultural forms that symbolized the coming together of the black and the white is also related to the endeavor to protect Cuba from another U.S. occupation. Many Cuban intellectuals of the 1920s and 1930s feared that the political mobilization of blacks would provide an excuse for the United States to take political control of the island again (Kutzinski 1993, 140, 143).[14] This fear partly explains the popularity of Martí's ideals at this time—in particular, his view of Cuba as a *mestizo* nation.[15] One of the advantages of this construct is that it could discourage black separatism by making blacks feel part of the same oppressed Cuban people as are whites. The tendency to identify the repression of blacks with that of the entire nation under imperialism was certainly widespread in this period (Fernández Robaina 1990, 138).

At another level, it is important to bear in mind that, as De La Fuente argues, the influence of the black electorate was partly responsible for the centrality of Martí's vision of a racially harmonious Cuba in Cuban political and nationalist discourse in the 1930s. Since 1901, the need to gain the black vote had meant that Cuban political parties had to fight over who could realize Martí's ideals of racial equality, which had contributed to the overwhelming participation of blacks in the Second Cuban War of Independence (De La Fuente 2001, 54–55). One of the objectives of the Cuban communist party, for example, was to "mobilize the oppressed black masses, which constitute a third of the Cuban population, and incorporate this enormous revolutionary army to the struggle for the anti-imperialist agrarian revolution" (as quoted in Fernández Robaina 1990, 137). Other Cuban political parties competing for the support of blacks also subscribed to the anti-imperialist belief in nationalizing the land (Raby 1975, 12–14; Fernández Robaina 1990, 116–18, 146; Marinello 1998). It is interesting to note that the black speaker of Ramón Guirao's poem "Ni guapo ni matone" expresses his support for an agrarian revolution (Guirao 1934).[16]

Since the power of the black electorate was an important reason for the prominence of Martí's ideals of racial equality in mainstream discourse, and this in turn contributed to the rise of afrocubanismo, it can be argued that the Cuban black did play some active role in the emergence of this movement. As Luis Duno Gottberg notes, this is one of the peculiarities of afrocubanismo that is concealed by the tendency to explain its origins as a mere reflection of European primitivism (Duno Gottberg 2003a, 147–48).

More specifically, afrocubanistas may have also hoped that their literature would convince blacks to stand alongside whites against U.S. dominance, a hope suggested in Ramón Guirao's description of *afronegrista* poetry as being designed to encourage blacks to behave responsibly: "Hoy, al amparo de una comprensión más cabal de los tratos y contratos desfavorables que gravitan en nuestra economía y dificultan la afirmación de nuestra naciente nacionalidad, se intenta propagar, movido de la necesidad de que la población negra participe responsablemente de este momento crítico, que la poesía afronegrista, esto es, de tema negro, es la más genuina manifestación de nuestra sensibilidad insular" ("Today, with the benefit of a more accurate understanding of the unfavorable bargains and contracts that burden our economy and make difficult the affirmation of our nascent national identity, one wants to propose, motivated by the necessity that the black and mixed population participate responsibly in this critical moment, that *afronegrista* poetry, that is, poetry about black themes, is the most genuine manifestation of our insular sensibility") (Guirao 1938, xii, as translated in Kutzinski 1993, 144). In the specific context of late 1920s and early 1930s Cuban politics, for afrocubanistas such as Guirao, making blacks "behave responsibly" may have included dissuading them from supporting Machado. As De La Fuente points out, it was widely believed at the time that Machado had the support of the majority of Cuban blacks. The president had certainly tried to gain that support through a number of ways. He had appointed several blacks to prominent posts in the public administration, and he had designated the date of the death of black Cuban independence hero Antonio Maceo as a national holiday. His government also ordered the dissolution of the Ku Klux Klan in 1928. In this same year, Cuba's most prominent black societies organized a homage to Machado as a demonstration of gratitude on behalf of all Cuban blacks (De La Fuente 2001, 92–93). Machado had also sponsored Abakuá societies and had augmented the rural army or *ejército permanente* (permanent army) and the police, forces in which blacks found opportunities for social advancement (Thomas 1971, 606, 683; Raby 1975, 10). It is interesting to note in this context that in Ramón Guirao's afrocubanista poem "Quiero se permanente" (I Want to Be a Permanent) the black speaker appears solely interested in keeping his stomach full and in not having to work very hard, aspirations that he expects to achieve by joining the *ejército permanente* (Guirao 1934). Through this satirical representation, Guirao was obviously trying to discourage this kind of attitude among blacks, which he may have viewed as a sign of their inability to see beyond the immediate gratifications afforded to them by Machado's policies. It is important to remember that even if the work of Guirao and other afrocubanistas was guided by the belief that all blacks were behind Machado, this notion was actually a myth. De La Fuente notes that important black political movements at the time strongly opposed the president and were very critical of the close collaboration of black societies with him (De La Fuente 2001, 200–201).

To return to the issue of the influence of foreign artistic and intellectual movements on the emergence of afrocubanismo, it must be stressed that the desire for, and celebration of, racial and cultural synthesis that arose in the Cuban context were very different from notions central to the European revalorization of non-Western cultures. For example, Spengler, whose *The Decline of the West* is cited as an important influence on the afrocubanista project by such critics as González Echevarría (1977, 55–56), Coronil (1995, xviii–xix), and Kutzinski (1993, 150), did not approve of combining African and European art. As Guirao explained, Spengler was a racist who thought that, because of its penchant for all things African, France had betrayed European culture. According to Guirao, for Spengler this nation had turned to the African continent because of its own artistic impotence and in doing so had allowed a perverse miscegenation that had poisoned the blood of Europe. Guirao also pointed out that Jacques Lipchitz acknowledged the African elements in his sculptures, but denied that this meant that his art had become mulatto. In a similar manner Picasso had questioned the idea of a half-cast aesthetics in the plastic arts (1938, xviii, xvii).

The fact that these perceptions clash so drastically with the afrocubanista desire for a harmonious synthesis of the black and the white illustrates the importance of avoiding interpretations of afrocubanista poetry that reduce it to European "influences." Afrocubanistas reelaborated some aspects of the European revalorization of African culture into a discourse that celebrated racial mixture rather than difference. It is not a question of denying that Spengler's *The Decline of the West* had an impact on the cultural debate in Cuba, as it certainly did in other parts of Latin America. The problem lies in the tendency to approach the role of this text in afrocubanismo through readings of "influences" that fail to account fully for the functions that it served in the Cuban context, as well as the ways in which it was reelaborated in relation to specific Cuban concerns. Alberto Flores Galindo's description of the use that Latin

American intellectuals made of *The Decline of the West* reflects the kind of approach that could yield more productive results in the context of afrocubanismo. The book, argues Flores Galindo, became a best-seller in Latin America at a time when few suspected that Spengler would become one of the main ideologues of Nazism. Nevertheless, this reactionary text had unforeseen revolutionary consequences in Latin America, whose intellectual elite used it as an instrument with which to build a critique of European culture and revalorize autochthonous Latin American cultural forms (as cited in D'Allemand 2000, 27).

To sum up, this chapter has brought to light the precarious social conditions experienced by Cuban blacks during the first three decades of the Cuban republic. The movement to revalorize Afro-Cuban traditions at this time emerged in response to a series of economic and political developments as well as nationalist concerns. In particular, afrocubanista poetry responded to the desire to promote an image of an ideal future Cuba without racial divisions. This desire for black and white unity is one of the elements of afrocubanismo that most clearly distances this Cuban movement from the European revalorization of non-Western cultures.

2 "Rumbas, guarachas y solares"
Afrocubanista Poetry and the Afro-Cuban Sectors

A RECURRING notion in the criticism on poetic afrocubanismo is that its literary production is disconnected from the reality of 1920s and 1930s Cuban blacks. This is certainly the impression conveyed by Gastón Baquero in his 1969 essay "Sobre la falsa poesía negra: Tres notas polémicas" (On False Black Poetry: Three Controversial Points). For this black Cuban poet, afrocubanista poetry was "false black poetry" because it presented an image of Cuban blacks as African when, in reality, the culture of Latin American blacks did not have any African characteristics. This misrepresentation demonstrated that the aim of afrocubanistas was not to represent blacks accurately but to Africanize them perpetually in order to exclude them from Cuban nationhood. Baquero extends this criticism to the anthropological studies of blacks by Fernando Ortiz, which presented blacks as having a "rich musical folklore," "a highly developed religious fantasy," and "a great capacity for dance." He argues that these characterizations were based on the Latin American black of the fifteenth and sixteenth centuries, and he even denies the actuality of the instruments and religions of African origins featured in Fernando Ortiz's studies. Baquero accuses Ortiz of not paying any attention to the many examples of blacks who had mastered forms of European culture in Cuba. He mentions various Cuban blacks, such as Brindis de Salas, who had become prominent classical musicians and who had nothing to do with Afro-Cuban drums (1969, 212, 213–14).[1]

In his 1976 study *The Black Image in Latin American Literature*, Afro-Hispanist Richard L. Jackson uses Baquero's characterization to support his interpretation of afrocubanista poetry by white authors, or "negrista poetry," as "false." He argues that afrocubanista images of blacks in performance of African cultural practices resulted from the intention identified by Baquero (the *africanización perpetua* of blacks). He concurs with the Cuban critic in arguing that these images did not convey a reliable vision of the modern-day black. Jackson reinforces this characterization with the argument that "the white practitioners of poetic Negrism overlooked essential parts of black life in Latin America" because "these white poets did not see the black *por dentro,* or from the inside, as the expression goes" (1976, 40–44).

Marvin Lewis makes use of similar arguments to question the connection between negrista poetry and Cuban blacks. Applying the term "Afro-Hispanic" to the poetic works of Latin American black writers that he analyzes in his 1983 study, he defines negrista literature in the following manner: "*Negrista,* just as *indigenista* (superficial interpretation of Indian culture), creates a problem because it refers to works written about Afro-Hispanic and Indian peoples by authors who do not belong to these ethnic groups and who do not possess the necessary cultural sensitivity to interpret accurately the experiences portrayed."[2] Thus, he establishes a difference between literature about blacks written by whites and that written by blacks, asserting that "Afro-Hispanic poets interpret their experiences from within rather than by merely describing a set of circumstances with which they are familiar" (1983, 2, 3).

Other critics reinforce the notion that afrocubanista poetry was disconnected from the human groups and culture it sought to represent by referring to afrocubanistas' lack of knowledge of Afro-Cuban culture (Mullen 1998, 155; Moore 1997, 200; Kubayanda 1982, 23). This notion seriously undermines the afrocubanista poetic movement. For afrocubanistas and contemporaneous advocates of their project, it was precisely the poetry's connections with the living black reality of Cuba that made it a distinctively Cuban literature, one that was also superior to the black poetry produced by foreign movements. Ramón Guirao made this point clear in the introduction to his 1938 anthology *Órbita de la poesía afrocubana, 1928–1937.* The poet argued that the links of the poetry to "nuestra realidad negra" (our black reality) distinguished it from European primitivism and made it the most accomplished product of "la modalidad afroantillana" (the Afro-Antillean modality) (1938, xviii–xix). The notion that the presence of blacks and black culture in Cuba offered its intellectuals the possibility of making more profound and sophisticated black art than in other parts of the world was also expressed by Juan Marinello in 1933 (1933, 141–42). Along similar lines, in 1936 Salvadorian journalist and poet Gilberto González Contreras differentiated the afrocubanista poetic movement from European primitivism on the basis of the living presence of black culture in Cuba (1973, 111–12).

The main aim of this chapter is to establish whether afrocubanista poetry can be understood as a literature that drew upon the culture of existing sectors of the 1930s Cuban black population. The first section examines Baquero's argument that the poetry's representations of African-derived practices do not correspond to the reality of blacks in the period when the afrocubanista movement was active. The second section evaluates the argument that afrocubanista poetry was disconnected from 1930s Cuban blacks due to the exteriority of afrocubanista poets and to their lack of knowledge about the culture they sought to represent.

The Afro-Cuban Sectors

The notion in Baquero's above-outlined characterization of afrocubanista poetry—that Cuban black culture was not African-derived—can be traced back to Cuban black middle-class discourses from the 1930s. In his 1939 *El negro en Cuba* (Blacks in Cuba), black Cuban intellectual Alberto Arredondo objected in a similar fashion to the afrocubanista compositions of Gilberto Valdés, which featured black singers and percussionists from African-derived religious traditions.[3] He argued that these compositions did not represent the preferences of contemporary blacks but, rather, the "cultural regression" of black slaves. The Cuban music and culture of blacks, he added, had evolved, leaving behind any African vestiges, so blacks should not be represented as if they still spoke the *bozal* Spanish of slaves and sang primitive war chants (Arredondo, as cited in Moore 1997, 212–13). Juan Antonio Martín also maintained in 1937 that vestigial customs of African origins had disappeared as blacks had gradually improved themselves (as cited in Moore 1997, 211).

These claims certainly seem to reflect the cultural reality of some sectors of Cuba's black population. Already in the nineteenth century many blacks did not have a culture of African origin. They were Creoles with long-standing status and residence, descended from literate artisans and semiprofessionals (Helg 1995, 28–29). Moreno Fraginals describes this sector of free blacks as a small but significant black bourgeoisie, whose members had assimilated the culture of the dominant white class and had distanced themselves from the rest of the black population (1996, 179). The notion that these blacks tended to follow the norms of the dominant culture is also reflected in an observation made by the aristocrat José del Castillo in relation to the 1840s. Del Castillo recalled many blacks and mulattos who were very rich and who dressed, talked, and behaved like old-fashioned Cuban white gentlemen. Many of them, he added, even read learned books and wrote poetry (as quoted in Deschamps Chapeaux

1971, 24). Helg explains that this sector was decimated in the repression of *La Escalera* (The Ladder) Conspiracy. In 1844 the government of Leopoldo O'Donnell was under the impression that this black middle-class sector of Havana was involved in a conspiracy to raise the island's slaves. As a result, the "confessed" ringleaders were rounded up, tortured, and executed. The authorities, purporting to have discovered the existence of a wider conspiracy, also accused the Creole intellectuals Domingo del Monte and José de la Luz y Caballero and executed the black poet Gabriel de la Concepción Valdés, also known as Plácido. By the end of 1844, thousands of black people had died or disappeared. The conspiracy was named *La Escalera* because slaves were tied to a ladder and whipped while they were interrogated (Paquette 1988, 3–4; Kutzinski 1993, 81–100). Nevertheless, according to Helg, this urban black sector had regained its economic position by the 1880s. As throughout most of the nineteenth century, "several of its members actively followed the modes of the dominant Spanish culture in literature, journalism, philosophy, music, and religion. Some mulattos among them also assimilated prevailing racial prejudices and distanced themselves from blacks, former slaves, or Africans" (Helg 1995, 29).

The republican period saw an increase in the tendency among blacks to distance themselves from other blacks by assimilating dominant cultural norms. The reason for this was the emergence of a more culturally based construction of race, by which social differentiation and status came to rely more on literacy, education, and Western culture (Helg 1995, 13).[4] This new construction partly facilitated the social advancement of a small proportion of blacks during the first two decades of the republic. Helg cites data from the 1919 "Census of the Republic of Cuba," which was carried out at a time when blacks constituted 28 percent of a total population of 2,889,004. The census shows that out of 1,578 lawyers, 38 were black, and out of a total of 1,771 medical doctors, 85 were black. In addition, some black Cubans were registered as bankers and brokers. In total, according to the census, blacks made up to 4.4 percent of the upper middle class. The census also registered more blacks as lower middle class than in 1907. The proportion of Cuban blacks in public service had also increased substantially during the early part of the republic, now constituting, according to the census, 10 percent of the 11,004 government officials and employees (Helg 1995, 243).

Since at this time culture of African origin was considered evidence of backwardness and inferiority, many of these blacks must have felt increasing social pressure to avoid "Africanisms" as they entered a dominant social matrix. Alejo Carpentier wrote that "le nègre qui sort de l'Université feint d'ignorer absolument l'existence des *ñáñigos*" (blacks who come out of universities pretend not to know that *ñáñigos* exist) (1929, 103).

The Club Atenas (Athenas Club), an association founded by black professionals, generally kept cultural forms considered African out of its public activities:

> Neither *Motivos de son* nor *Yambambó* would have been agreeable names for our "good society," which has outlawed the *son* (along with its *bongó,* its *maracas,* and its singing) in its meeting rooms. On principle, our "good society" hates its monstrous son, the *son*. The "sophisticated" black wanting to forget his sorrows with a good dance can only find Afro-Cuban music in the infamous lowest social spheres. If he does not dare to go that far, he will bring a *son* sextet to his house or will see it at a friend's house. However, he will never be able to see it at the *Club Atenas* or at the *Unión Fraternal* (Fraternal Unity) or at any other of our best societies. (Gustavo Urrutia, as cited in Feijoó 1986, 303)

In 1930 Guillén pointed out that this attitude toward black African-influenced culture was common among many Cuban blacks at the time: "One of the ways in which the Cuban black restricts our thought is by ignoring his own beauty. If someone is listening he repudiates the *son,* which is very black, he denigrates the *rumba,* whose warm rhythm contains the yawn of the African midday, and he closes his eyes, as if to hide any signs of understanding, when summoned by the *bongó* with its deep grandfather voice. It seems that there is a fear of being black" (as quoted in Williams 1995, 52–53, and Augier 1965, 114). In fact, throughout the republican period middle-class blacks did not merely avoid taking part in any African-derived cultural practices; they actively sought to eradicate those practices. Already in 1899, when the island was under the government of the United States, the highest representatives of various prestigious black associations had demanded the prohibition of the *comparsas,* marching bands through which blacks represented their cabildos de nación during the Día de Reyes (Day of Kings) celebrations on the sixth of January (Moreno Fraginals 1996, 298; Ortiz 1992). In 1902 a group of university-educated black professionals appealed to the government of Estrada Palma to ban these and other "embarrassing" African-derived manifestations (Kutzinski 1993, 140; Carrera Damas 1977, 51).

Nevertheless, Baquero's and Arredondo's comments do not apply to all blacks of Cuban republican society. In contrast to the black sectors described above, and as explained in chapter 1, many blacks, particularly in urban areas, had preserved their traditions of African origin in the cabildos de nación and other contexts. In Cuban slave society these blacks tended to be dark-skinned or "pure" blacks rather than mulatto. Rebecca J. Scott argues, for example, that ties of kinship connected slaves and free dark-skinned blacks, who tended to be members of the cabildos de nación. She points out that, by contrast, "mulatto free persons had often sought to distance themselves from blacks in an effort to avoid the 'stain' of shared slave ancestry and to assert the importance of differences in social status and gradations of color" (1985, 9). Walterio Carbonell expresses a similar view in a short essay on the nineteenth-century black Cuban poet Plácido, arguing that in the nineteenth century mulatto blacks had moved closer to white culture, were often skilled workers, owned property, and held social gatherings away from "pure" blacks (as cited in Paquette 1988, 19–20). Paquette confirms this view when he argues that "the lighter and more Hispanicized people of color tended to stay away from the *cabildos*, preferring their own dances and celebrations" (1988, 127). Jorge and Isabel Castellanos write,

> In general terms, the level of education of mulattos was higher than that of pure blacks, and the latter kept on growing in number as more African slaves arrived who did not assimilate the language and the culture of the country for a long time. Saying mulatto was like saying Creole, an adjective that indicates that one is, at the very least, a second-generation Cuban. In addition, the whitening of the skin tended to improve economic and social relations with the dominant white class. Mulattos tried to whiten as much as possible by procreating with whiter partners and, also, by trying to be more like whites in all aspects of social life. (1990, 377–78)

These social tendencies throughout the nineteenth century may be partly the reason why there appeared to be a correlation between blacks' social extraction and their attachment to African/European culture in the early period of the Cuban Republic. At this time, it was lower-class blacks, a racial minority without wealth or power, who continued to engage in practices of African origins, which partly explains why all presumed *brujos* arrested during the *brujería* scare in the first decade of the twentieth century had little or no formal education (Helg 1995, 246, 114–15). As opposed to members of middle-class black associations, which had periodical publications such as *La Antorcha* (The Torch), lower-class blacks had no means of expressing their perspectives and worldviews in dominant society. It was this situation that made many of them turn to Afro-Cuban cultural traditions. As Helg argues, "To them, attachment to a reconstructed African culture was not only a symbolic retreat against a racist society but also a dissident sub-culture that permitted collective self-affirmation. It reflected lower-class Afro-Cubans' stubborn resistance to the ideology and social order of the Western white elite" (1995, 244–47).

It would seem appropriate to employ the category "Afro-Cuban" to refer specifically to the black lower-class sectors that followed cultural traditions of African origins in the republican context. This would serve to distinguish them from the black middle-class sectors that identified with the dominant culture of Spanish origins. It is worth recalling, nevertheless, that Salvador Bueno has questioned the very validity of this category. He has argued that the prefix "Afro" places excessive emphasis on the African components of Afro-Cuban culture, thus undermining its heterogeneity. According to Bueno, the term "Afro-Cuban" is a redundancy precisely because Cuban identity and culture are the fusion of the Hispanic and the African. Cuban cultural manifestations, he adds, are made up of a variety of elements from divergent origins (1976, 98–99). It has to be acknowledged that Bueno's comment accurately reflects the Spanish/African heterogeneity that has always characterized Cuban African-derived cultures. This heterogeneity can be illustrated with several examples. Writing with reference to the Cuban colonial context, Jorge and Isabel Castellanos mention the use of prayers against illnesses and everyday disasters as well as the use of holy water, both practices being characteristic of popular Catholicism in Cuban African-derived religion (1992, 12–13). They also reproduce a song or *mambo* from the Bantu-derived religion known as Regla de Palo that is mostly written in the Castilian spoken by Africans in Cuba (*bozal*) and that blesses the initiates (*nganguleros*) in the same way that a Catholic priest blesses devotees in mass (1992, 172). According to Argeliers León, in the altars found in the headquarters of the cabildos de nación in the colonial period, there were images of Catholic saints (1984, 38). Similar images were used in the *comparsas* of the cabildos de nación (Ortiz 1992, 8).

The secular dance and music forms of black lower-class sectors of Cuban republican society were also hybrid or heterogeneous. Rumba drumming, for instance, displayed "African polyrhythmic concepts and European timbre placement by using the highest voice as the major improviser" (León 1984, 155).[5] Furthermore, rumba lyrics are in Spanish and follow Spanish verse patterns (León 1984, 158). Natalio Galán specifically detects Andalusian influences in the melodic aspects of rumba (1983, 336). *Son* also synthesizes African and European elements, as evident in the fact that its lyrics combine concepts from African oral literatures and the poetry of the Spanish *romance* tradition (Manuel 1985, 259; Alén Rodríguez 1994a, 31). These examples confirm Stephan Palmié's argument that Melville Herskovits's notion of African survivals is insufficient in the Cuban context. Palmié explains that Herskovits's research was concerned with finding African cultures in the Americas to measure deviations from an "African cultural baseline." He argues against this, stating that there cannot be "an unbroken continuity of Afro-Cuban religious culture from the onset of the transatlantic slave trade down to our present day" (1993, 337).

Nevertheless, the problem with Bueno's claim is that it relies exclusively on what is known in anthropology as an etic approach, in which identities are assigned to groups of people on the basis of the morphological characteristics of their culture. As Barth argues, this approach does not take into account how members of such groups perceive and define their ethnic identities.[6] He posits instead that "ethnic groups are categories of ascription and identification by the actors themselves" (1969, 10–12). Since Barth made this point, it has become a widely accepted principle in social anthropology that definitions of what are perceived as distinct groups of people should take into account the perspectives of their members. In anthropology this way of delineating ethnic groups is known as an emic approach (Eriksen 1993, 11; Wade 1995, 123; Jenkins 1986, 176; Verma 1984, 2). The etic/emic dichotomy is similar to what Richard Adams refers to as internally and externally defined ethnicities. The former is a native group's definition of self-identity. The latter is their identity as defined by outsiders (as quoted in Behague 1994b, v).

The term "Afro-Cuban" may not reflect the African/Spanish heterogeneity of Afro-Cuban culture sufficiently, but from an emic point of view it does convey the perspectives of its practitioners. In a society in which overtly African-influenced cultural practices were often violently persecuted on the basis of their Africanness, blacks who continued to practice them did not conceive of them as "syncretic" or "mulatto" but rather as black or African oppositional forms. The regulations of the Cabildo Arará Magino y sus Descendientes, founded in 1909, illustrate this notion. They stipulated that the objective of the association was to "perpetuar lo que fue nación arará en La Habana" (perpetuate in Havana what the Arará people used to be). They also established that on the first of every January the cabildo would hold a traditional celebration in the style of its members' country of origin (Ortiz 1992, 14). The term "Afro-Cuban" also reflects the fact that, despite their African/Spanish heterogeneity, Afro-Cuban religions have always played an important role in the maintenance of African ethnic boundaries among Cuban blacks.[7] For instance, the Afro-Cuban ethnicity Lucumí was based on the worship of Lucumí deities (orisha) in Cuban slave society (Brandon 1993, 56, 74–78). In addition, Ortiz and León point out that, for members of the cabildos de nación, Catholic images in their rituals actually represented African deities (León 1984, 38; Ortiz 1992, 8).[8]

Furthermore, Bueno overlooks certain features of Afro-Cuban culture that support the adequacy of the term "Afro-Cuban" even from an etic perspective. Brandon makes the point that the heterogeneity of the constitutive elements of Afro-Cuban culture may not be as important as the patterns and structures that organize them; relying on this perspective, he makes the case for a degree of continuity of Yoruba cultural traditions in Cuba. The centrality of collective cultural practices is an organizational principle of Afro-Cuban culture that has African origins. For example, Brandon points out that "the image of the African past held and recited in *Santería*'s mythology is conveyed, sustained and reinforced in its ritual performances" (1993, 126–57, 148). The following description by Michael Huet and Claude Savary highlights the importance of collective cultural practices in Africa: "Ritual activities still form an integral part of African culture. . . . Admittedly, there are different categories of rites, according to regions, peoples, religious systems and their mythological foundations, and also their aims. In fact, it is nearly always a question of a collective activity, something that goes beyond the individual and concerns his extended family as well as his neighbors, members of his age group or the association to which he belongs" (1995, 14).[9]

Another cultural feature of these black sectors that suggests continuities with African culture is the importance of dance and music genres, such as rumba and *son*. John Mason describes music in Yoruba culture as being "all-pervasive," adding that "without it people cannot create poetry, record history, educate children, celebrate at festivals, praise or abuse, entertain, marry or die" (1992, 8). The oral nature of Afro-Cuban culture as described by Ortiz is equally significant in view of the oral character of African traditional verbal art (Ortiz 1938, 314; 1973b, 156–57; Julien 1992, 7).[10]

It is worth clarifying at this point that the argument that 1920s and 1930s Cuban black culture had no African elements stemmed from the desire of middle-class blacks to be seen as fully integrated members of hegemonic society (Moore 1997, 210–14). By denying the actuality of Afro-Cuban culture, 1930s black middle-class commentators aimed to undermine dominant representations of blacks as African. It is important to remind ourselves that such representations served the ruling elite only too well to justify the subalternity of blacks in the Cuban republican context, which exemplifies the way in which "ethnic groups sometimes have identities imposed on them to restrict their mobility and to facilitate their exploitation and oppression" (Rex 1986, 71). The ruling elite's use of representations of blacks as African to this end is illustrated in Helg's comments that the press of the early republican period "was the most outspoken and far-reaching voice of racial prejudice. Mainstream Cuban newspapers continued the Spanish colonial effort to present Afro-Cubans as inferior and uncivilized in order to justify their lower position in society. . . . Almost all of the daily newspaper journalists were white and wrote as spokesmen of 'civilization' against 'barbarism.'" Helg explains that the images conveyed in the press, along with the repression of Afro-Cuban cultural practices that accompanied them, "cast a negative shadow on the image of heroes that Afro-Cubans had acquired during the War for Independence. It hurt their new pride and helped to justify their lower position in society on educational grounds" (1995, 106, 115). Nevertheless, by denying that Afro-Cuban culture was a part of the black community instead of questioning the evolutionist notions that guided such representations, these middle-class intellectuals actually excluded the Afro-Cuban sectors from their definitions of Cuban blackness. The commentaries regarding the inaccuracy of afrocubanista representations on the part of Baquero and Arredondo can be seen as resulting from this black middle-class desire to "erase," as it were, the "less evolved" sectors of the black population. The elitist attitude of the black middle classes toward "less civilized" blacks is evident in the following extract from the 1918 manifesto of the Club Atenas: "And this is the aim of the Club Atenas within the black race: to classify us in classes. De facto, we, the responsible blacks with established families, with culture, fully capable of practising our duties and rights as citizens, we are different from those who have an imperfect idea or no idea at all of these social rights and duties" (as translated in Helg 1995, 244). According to Reynaldo Peñalver Moral, the Club Atenas was only one of many exclusive and segregated black societies of which, even as late as the 1950s, "a black newspaper vendor could not be a member" (2000, 45–46). The urge to emphasize class differences on the part of many middle-class blacks is made clear by Gustavo Urrutia in an article entitled "Burguesía negra" (Black Bourgeoisie), published in *Diario de la Marina* in 1932. Urrutia wrote that a black Cuban had invited him to cofound a tennis club that would consist "de personas de vida independiente, que no practiquen el servicio doméstico ni otros subordinados" (of people with independent lives who do not work in domestic service or other such lowly occupations). His criteria were the following: "Blacks who reach the level of a small bureaucracy, through study, business, bureaucracy, politics or other means, must form a separate class and exclude from their circles all those who are looked down upon by the bourgeoisie, such as domestic servants, laborers, shoeshiners, porters, etc." (as quoted in Habibe 1985, 13).[11]

Baquero and Arredondo's arguments, then, derive more from an extreme black middle-class reaction to a dominant white discourse on blacks than from an objective analysis of Cuban republican society. It is interesting to note that in this same period the black middle classes in the United States adopted a similarly Eurocentric and elitist approach in defending their race against dominant racist discourses (Brock 1998, 18). At the same time, the heterogeneous composition of the black population that has been brought to light here reveals that afrocubanista poetic representations do not provide a complete image of the culture of all Cuban blacks. A more pluralistic representation might have included black middle-class characters and their perspectives, as well as the specific types of discrimination affecting their lives. Nevertheless, the restricted focus upon African-derived cultures in all afrocubanista arts does not stem solely from a reductionist conception of black culture as African, like the one that Baquero attributed to Ortiz's work in his earlier-cited argument about Brindis de Salas. It also stems from a conscious intent to work specifically with the culture of the Afro-Cuban sectors. This intent was made clear by poet, novelist, and musicologist Alejo Carpentier, who situated the referent of afrocubanista musical compositions in Regla, a lower-class neighborhood across the bay from the white and middle-class areas of Havana. As Carpentier argued, "Those who already knew the music of 'The Rite of Spring' were beginning to realize that in the neighborhood of Regla, across the bay, one could find rhythms that were as complex and interesting as the ones that Stravinski had invented to recreate the primitive games of pagan Russia. Everyone's eyes and ears turned towards that which was living and nearby" (1961, 171). The notion that afrocubanista poetry took its subject matter directly from the black lower-class neighborhoods of Havana is implicit in a 1932 article by Víctor de la Serna in which he characterized the neighborhood of Jesús María as being more interesting and subtle than Harlem.[12] He also referred to Nicolás Guillén, a young black Cuban poet who had written a book entitled *Sóngoro cosongo* (Carpentier, as quoted in Augier 1965, 187).

53   "*Rumbas, guarachas y solares*"

These associations of the black lower-class neighborhoods of Havana with Afro-Cuban culture cannot be dismissed as false, white dominant stereotypes. On the contrary, they accurately reflect the spatial distribution of Afro-Cuban culture in 1920s and 1930s Havana. The evidence suggests that by the nineteenth century lower-class blacks were already concentrated in peripheral neighborhoods such as Jesús María, a pattern that was reinforced by the arrival of many rural blacks into the city centers after the abolition of slavery in 1886.[13] At a time when Afro-Cuban culture was persecuted by the authorities, such marginal neighborhoods offered the only spaces where these migrants could continue to practice their traditions (Moore 1997, 40). The fact that afrocubanista poets conceived of their poetry as focusing specifically upon black lower-class sectors is reflected in Emilio Ballagas's essay "Poesía afrocubana," in which the poet pointed out that "la poesía afrocubana" (afrocubanista poetry) specifically incorporated the speech modes of lower-class urban and rural blacks. These sectors, he argued, had remained more isolated from the white population and had preserved the musical and religious traditions of their ancestors (1973b, 80).

There are textual factors that further sustain the notion that afrocubanistas based their representations on the lowest strata of the black population. For example, many afrocubanista poems attempt to reproduce the speech of uneducated, and thus lower-class, blacks. Representative examples are all the poems in Nicolás Guillén's *Motivos de son* (1990, 65–73), the poems "Para dormir a un negrito" (Poem for Getting a Little Black Boy to Sleep) and "Lavandera con negrito" (Washerwoman with a Little Black Boy) in Emilio Ballagas's *Cuaderno de poesía negra* (Black Poetry Notebook) (1984, 83–85), and the entire collection *Bongó: Poemas negros* (*Bongó*: Black Poems) by Ramón Guirao (1934). Furthermore, most afrocubanista poems present blacks in settings of poverty. The speaker in Guillén's "Hay que tener voluntá," for example, asks his woman to pawn their iron and to look for a *real*. Similar problems concern the speaker of Guillén's "Búcate plata," who declares that he is so weak from lack of food that he cannot even walk (1990, 69–71). In Ramón Guirao's "Macucho con tu rumba," the black speaker describes the black he addresses as being blind with hunger (1934).[14]

There are also numerous references in afrocubanista poetry to the lower-class occupations of the black characters. Guillén's "Organillo" (The Hurdy-Gurdy), for instance, represents an impoverished man trying to make some money playing a hurdy-gurdy, while enticing his black woman (whom he refers to as "mi conga") to keep dancing along to it (1990, 83). His poem "Chévere" deals with the popular type of the truculent black pimp or well-dressed black street man. The main character is described as a "chévere del navajazo" who cuts up several things, including the moon (a clear homage to Lorca) and his "negra" (1990, 80).[15] In "Sabás," in *West Indies, Ltd.*, the main character is a beggar (1969, 79). Similarly, Emilio Ballagas's "Elegía de María Belén Chacón" (María Belén Chacón's Elegy) is dedicated to a black washerwoman, as suggested by the fact that an iron causes her death: "¡La plancha, de madrugada, fue quien te quemó el pulmón!" (It was the iron that burned your lung in the small hours!) (Guirao 1938, 107). Other poems that feature a black washerwoman are "Rumba de la negra Pancha" (The Rumba of Pancha the Black) by José Antonio Portuondo and Ballagas's "Lavandera con negrito" (Guirao 1938, 135–37, 111–12).

Perhaps the reason why afrocubanistas' specific interest in the Afro-Cuban sectors has not been acknowledged in most criticism is that their own use of racially based terms, such as Guirao's "poética negra" (black poetry writing) or Ballagas's "verso de inspiración negra" (black-inspired poetry), promotes the erroneous impression that they conceived of their poetry as an all-inclusive representation of the Cuban black population (Guirao 1938, xix; Ballagas 1973b, 78).[16] This imprecision results from the poor referential value of racial epithets. Adjectives such as "black" or "Indian" do not have a clear referent even from a strictly phenotypical point of view, since, as Peter Wade explains, "the apparently natural fact of phenotypical variation is itself socially constructed" (1997, 15). The term "black" has even less referential value when applied to culture. It certainly did not have a single referent in early Cuban republican society, where, as shown, some blacks followed Afro-Cuban cultural traditions and others favored dominant cultural norms.

The Exteriority of Afrocubanista Poets

There is no denying that, with the exception of the poet Marcelino Arozarena, most afrocubanistas would not have been able to put forward an interior vision of the Afro-Cuban sectors.[17] Like the majority of the second generation of republican intellectuals, most of these poets belonged to the white middle classes and were highly educated within the parameters of the dominant culture.[18] Emilio Ballagas, for example, came from a white middle-class family in Camagüey. He had received a university education and held a teaching position in the Escuela Normal de Santa Clara (Normal School of Santa Clara) during the period when he was involved in the afrocubanista poetic movement (Moore 1997,

199; Pryor Rice 1966, 17). The poets José Z. Tallet and Alejo Carpentier, both white, were educated in the United States and France, respectively, and both were part of the *minoristas,* a political group with artistic interests whose members came from relatively wealthy backgrounds (Guirao 1938, 64, 76; Moore 1997, 191–202). It can be safely argued that afrocubanista poetry focuses upon cultural practices that were not part of the cultures of the social sectors to which these intellectuals belonged. In this sense, the category "negrista" as employed by Afro-Hispanists has the advantage of conveying the notion that the poets did not belong to the human groups and culture that they sought to represent. It is the suffix *ista* that reflects the exteriority of the authors. Accordingly, *literatura negra* is literature written by blacks and *literatura negrista* is literature written by whites about blacks. Like the category "negrista," the category "afrocubanista" reflects the exteriority of these poets, but it also captures the idea that their intended referent was the Afro-Cuban sectors.[19]

The characteristics of these sectors that were outlined earlier suggest that it is inappropriate to separate Nicolás Guillén from white afrocubanistas on the basis of his interior perspective. Jackson argues that Nicolás Guillén's afrocubanista poetry is "authentic" and written "from within": "Accusations of inauthenticity . . . can hardly be levelled at the literature of Candelario Obeso, Nicolás Guillén, Adalberto Ortiz, and Juan Pablo Sojo, four representative black authors whose expressions of literary Americanism grow out of their own lived experiences" (1988b, 51). He also asserts that "Nicolás Guillén felt the tragedy of the Cuban black from below and from within and while negrista authors came to see in the Black a source for a new beginning, the early black literature of Nicolás Guillén provides the most authentic insight into the social, historical and racial events that formed the backdrop of that moment in the literary history of Latin America" (1984, 8). And yet the poet did not come from a lower-class background. His father was a journalist and a prestigious politician who had served as a senator from 1909 to 1912 under the liberal government of José Miguel Gómez (Augier 1965, 13, 15). There is no indication in Angel Augier's biography of the poet that Afro-Cuban traditions were practiced in Guillén's family home. What is specified, by contrast, is his father and grandfather's erudition in the literature of the dominant culture, which clearly fueled his literary interests from an early age. Guillén traces his passion for poetry to his paternal grandfather, a professional carpenter who wrote *décimas* (Augier 1965, 17). Guillén described his father as a learned, studious man who was deeply familiar with the literature of his time. His numerous books of European and international literature were also responsible for Guillén's artistic interests (Morejón 1974b, 32). Classics of Spanish literature could always be found in the library of the Guillén family (Augier 1965, 17).

Considering Guillén's background, it would prove hard to demonstrate that his "lived experiences," to borrow Jackson's words, were exactly the same as those of the lower-class blacks featured in the poems of *Motivos de son* and *Sóngoro cosongo*.[20] He certainly would not have experienced the same degree of marginalization as them, although he did of course experience the kind of discrimination that many middle-class blacks encountered at the time, as Fernández Robaina notes (2003, 128). All the evidence suggests, furthermore, that before his afrocubanista period the middle-class existence he had enjoyed had kept him in ignorance of the peculiarities of black lower-class culture. Dahl has even suggested that the poet's escapist *modernista* phase, which preceded his Afro-Cuban-inspired poetry, must be understood in the context of his "distance from the socio-economic situation of Cuban blacks, the lack of awareness of their speech rhythms and folkways, and the lack of an identification with his African roots" (1995, 14).

Guillén's own comments regarding his composition of the poems in *Motivos de son* attest to his exteriority with respect to the black sectors on which his poetry was based. In a letter published in *El Diario de la Marina* in 1930, for example, his distance from the type of black that his poetry represented is patent in his description of the poems as "unos versos primarios escritos en la forma en que todavía hablan—piensan—muchos de nuestros negros (y no pocos blancos también) y en los que se retratan tipos que a diario vemos moverse a nuestro lado" (basic poems that are written the way in which many of our blacks [and quite a few whites too] think and talk, and which portray human types that we encounter in our everyday life) (as quoted in Augier 1965, 134). Equally relevant in this respect is the following extract from his 1974 interview with Nancy Morejón: "Me pareció el negro camagüeyano más integrado en la familia, menos externo y aún más ingenuo. El de La Habana me dio la impresión de ser más violento, más 'bachetero,' rítmico y popular. Yo no hubiera podido escribir los *Motivos de son* en Camagüey" (Blacks from Camagüey seemed more integrated in their families. They seemed less external and even more ingenious. Those from Havana seemed more violent, more rhythmical and more popular. I would not have been able to write *Motivos de son* in Camagüey) (Morejón 1974b, 40). The fact that Guillén was experimenting with a series of cultural forms that were not his own (like most afrocubanistas) is noticeable in a letter he wrote to

Ramón Vasconcelos wherein he acknowledged that the poems of Motivos de son "me costaron muchísimo trabajo, porque pretendí comunicarles una ingenuidad de técnica que nunca he tenido" (took me a lot of work because I tried to infuse them with a technical simplicity that I have never had) (as quoted in Augier 1965, 134). This is not to deny that Guillén's blackness and the discrimination that he suffered as a result of it allowed him to feel a deeper identification with other Cuban blacks. Nevertheless, as has been made clear, the referent of afrocubanista poetry was a very specific sociocultural sector within the Cuban black population, and Guillén did not belong to it. Therefore, to continue describing his poetry as the most authentic representation undermines the sociocultural specificity of these sectors and obscures Guillén's cultural and social distance from his object of representation. It could be argued that the idea that Guillén wrote about the represented sectors "from within" elides the problematic nature of his eye.[21]

Paradoxically, according to Jackson's approach, Guillén's exteriority would automatically undermine the validity of his representations, since, like white negrista poets, he was not actually writing "from within." Thus, it is worth stressing that, as Cornejo Polar shows in relation to indigenismo, the exteriority of a group of writers with respect to the human groups they write about does not by itself justify dismissing their literature as a superficial or inaccurate representation (1978, 1980). This dismissive tendency in Afro-Hispanism reflects the influence of the notion that only blacks can write "authentic black literature" (Jackson 1978, 43), a view that is sharply illustrated by Jackson's writings. Jackson comments that most white Latin American writers' work on the "ethnic peoples in America" was merely "the literary expression of 'concerned' white humanists who, despite their advocacy, remain on the outside looking in." He adds that "inauthenticity was one of the major criticisms levelled against the 'old masters': while their focus was American ethnic reality, they still were writing about other peoples' lived experiences" (1988b, 37). Marvin Lewis's decision to restrict his 1983 study of Afro-Hispanic poetry to works of literature written by blacks responds to his view of literature written by whites about non-whites as "superficial" and "inaccurate" (1983, 2).[22] Thus, like Jackson, Lewis assumes that whites are incapable of producing literary representations of blacks of any significance. This aprioristic assumption carries with it ideas about an essential authenticity that only blacks can imprint on their work. It is thus hardly surprising that these critics should have shied away from confronting the issue of Guillén's sociocultural distance from the represented sectors. As

Gilroy argues in relation to certain tendencies in black criticism, intraracial differences make easy essentialism simply untenable (1993, 36).

A more important factor than the poets' racial makeup in determining their poetry's connection to the represented sectors is the extent of their familiarity with Afro-Cuban culture. A widespread assumption in criticism is that afrocubanistas did not even have any personal contact with Afro-Cuban cultural practices. For instance, Edward Mullen comments that "much like that of Fernando Ortiz, Emilio Ballagas's knowledge of Afro-Cuban culture was more a product of reading than of lived experience" (1998, 155). Robin Dale Moore makes a similar comment in relation to afrocubanista arts in general: "As in the United States and Europe, a majority of elite white artists in 1920s Havana who embraced afrocubanismo had little personal understanding of Afro-Cuban culture." In writing about afrocubanista visual art at the time, he asserts that it was predominantly confined to the "white Hispanic middle classes who had little first-hand exposure to black street culture" (1997, 194, 200). Another critic who questions the poets' knowledge of Afro-Cuban culture is J. Bekunuru Kubayanda, who argues that "most *negristas* were themselves insufficiently immersed in the African cultures to be able to cultivate ideophones with imaginative originality" (1982, 23).[23]

On the one hand, it has to be acknowledged that witnessing more secretive Afro-Cuban practices such as rumba and those that were part of Afro-Cuban religious groups did pose difficulties for afrocubanistas. Writing about afrocubanista musical compositions at the time, Carpentier explained that, unless one had intelligent and loyal informants, it was impossible to know when and where an Afro-Cuban religious ceremony or a profane drumming and dancing event was going to take place. He also added that genuine members of the Abakuá society were strongly opposed to outsiders transcribing or recording their music, for they viewed this as a desecration of their secrets (1961, 165). Furthermore, attending Afro-Cuban rituals was a daunting prospect for middle-class artists and intellectuals, as exemplified by the following comments by afrocubanista painter Eduardo Abela:

> I don't want to hide from you that since that time I have been left with the unpleasant sensation that by abandoning afrocubanista painting, I lost my artistic touch. Even now just talking about it—and it was more than thirty years ago!—I feel ill at ease and bitter. If I had gone to see *santeros babalaos, bembés, fiestas de negros* and all that stuff that Alejo used to talk to me about in Paris, I might have found my inspiration. But, leaving aside the lack of time, how could I experience all these things by myself when I did not know how to

behave in the places where they took place? And I say alone because there was not a single person amongst my acquaintances at that time who had professed an interest in learning about such things from the inside. There was also a fear of blacks, fear of their customs, which, perhaps due to ignorance, were seen as vulgar. I have to also mention that there were people—more than you, who didn't live the epoch, might think—who thought that all blacks were criminals, or at least potential criminals. (As quoted in Moore 1997, 270)

On the other hand, available photographic evidence shows that, despite the difficulties, white middle-class intellectuals at the time did attend live Afro-Cuban cultural practices in black working-class suburbs of Havana, such as Regla and Jesús María. In his 1969 anthology of José Z. Tallet's poetry, Helio Orovio includes a picture taken sometime in the 1930s that shows the Argentinean reciter Berta Singerman in a *solar* in the neighborhood of Jesús María accompanied by a group of Cuban journalists. Orovio points out that the photograph portrays Singerman in search of "a live stimulus" for her performance of Tallet's afrocubanista poem "La rumba."[24] Like her, Alejo Carpentier himself attended Afro-Cuban religious ceremonies in order to find inspiration for his work. He explained in an article published in 1928 that during the previous week he had attended an Abakuá celebration, along with Cuban composer Amadeo Roldán and the Mexican folklorist Tata Nacho. They had stayed there for nine hours, taking notes, writing down rhythms, and "studying popular art from the most authentic source" (as cited in Habibe 1985, 19). This experience guided his own description of an Abakuá ritual in his 1927 novel *Écue-yamba-ó*: "The passage about the *ñáñigo* initiation is based on what I noted down in ceremonies that I attended with Amadeo Roldán when we were working on the text and music for the ballets 'La rebambaramba' and 'El milagro de anaquillé' (The Miracle of Anaquillé). Since then these issues have been studied in more depth, but considering that this was not a rigorously scientific approach, my description is a rather accurate representation" (1982, 20–21). Carpentier must have based his afrocubanista poem "Liturgia," which was published in 1930 in the last issue of *Revista de Avance*,[25] on these or other similar experiences. This kind of ethnographic methodology was certainly common at a time when most Cuban writers believed in the importance of fieldwork. As Carpentier explains, their approach consisted in "choosing a specific environment; researching it, observing it, experiencing it for a while, and then starting to work on the basis of the material that had been gathered" (1964, 10–11).[26] Amy Fass Emery argues that Carpentier's urge to work with firsthand documentary evidence fits in with what James Clifford describes as "the predominant mode of modern fieldwork authority . . . 'you are there . . . because I was there'" (1996, 33).

If all afrocubanistas were as eager as Carpentier to come into direct contact with their raw material, in 1920s and 1930s Havana they would have found it easy to gain firsthand exposure to some forms of Afro-Cuban culture that had become popular. A case in point is *son* music, a theme that features in many afrocubanista poems such as, for example, Ballagas's "Nombres negros en el son" (Black Names in *Son*), Hernández Catá's "Son," and Gómez Kemp's "Fuego con fuego" (Fire with Fire) and "Son con punta" (Pointed Son) (Guirao 1938, 112–14, 129–31, 157–59). By the 1920s, *son* had achieved widespread popularity among all sectors of Cuban society, thus becoming the first Afro-Cuban musical genre in Cuban history to attain national acceptance without stylistic modifications. In the latter half of the decade, following the first public *son* festival, the government of Gerardo Machado announced that *son* music and dance, as long as it was not "scandalous" or "immoral," would henceforth be permitted in hotels, cabarets, and restaurants (Moore 1997, 89, 104). Thanks to the growing availability of records and record players and the beginning of Cuban radio broadcasting, *son* became so fashionable in the 1920s that at one point there were over four dozen *son* bands or *conjuntos* playing regularly in Havana (Robbins 1990, 186; Benítez Rojo 1998, 46; Moore 1997, 97).

Naturally, afrocubanista poets also relied on available descriptions of Afro-Cuban cultural practices that could be found in erudite and popular culture. Chief among such secondary sources were the ethnographic studies of Afro-Cuban culture by Fernando Ortiz. The respect that afrocubanistas felt toward the scholarship of Ortiz's research is reflected in the following extract from Emilio Ballagas's introduction to his 1935 *Antología de la poesía negra hispanoamericana*:

> The first person to study the Afro-Cuban psique with a serious intention and a scientific approach was the anthropologist Dr. Fernando Ortiz. Before he came, everything to do with blacks was misunderstood in the same sociological chaos. Dr. Fernando Ortiz studied the blacks that had come to Cuba during the slavery period and analyzed the characteristics of blacks from different African regions. He showed us the complexity of the Afro-Cuban social psychology, clarifying in detail many of its characteristics in pages that have become a classic in the literature on this subject. Dr. Fernando Ortiz, who continues to work with growing enthusiasm and improving results, is at present the highest authority amongst those who study the psychology, the music, the customs and the language of blacks. (1935, 17–18)

As Nicolás Guillén pointed out, lyrics of the musical genre known as *guaracha* were an important source of representations in popular culture (Morejón 1974b, 41–42). Several nineteenth-century compilations of guaracha lyrics were available to afrocubanista poets, but the one most authors refer to is A. O. Hallorans's 1882 *Guarachas cubanas, curiosa recopilación desde las más antiguas hasta las más modernas* (Cuban Guarachas, Curious Compilation from the Oldest to the Most Recent).[27] As Roberto Fernández Retamar indicates, the following verses from Hallorans's compilation are reminiscent of José Z. Tallet's "La rumba":

> Si el compañero no es hombre listo
> Y se descuida y pierde el compás,
> Ella lo llama, y le dice "¡Entra!"
> Y él, poco a poco, bailando va.
>
> Ella lo llama y lo vuelve loco;
> Ella lo mata con su bailar;
> Él, que no es bobo, deja matarse,
> Porque al morirse gozando va.
>   (As cited in Fernández Retamar 1954, 47)
>
> If her dancing partner is not a clever man
> And he loses his concentration and the rhythm,
> She calls him and says to him, "Come in!"
> And he goes over slowly, dancing.
>
> She calls him and drives him crazy;
> She is killing him with her dancing;
> He is not stupid and lets himself be killed
> Because as he dies, he enjoys great pleasure.

Fernández Retamar adds that the poetry of Nicolás Guillén and Emilio Ballagas was also based on the following guaracha lyrics:

> Mulata santa,
> Ponte una bata,
> Y asómate a la ventana
> A escuchar mi serenata.
> ¡Adiós, nené!
> ¡Qué lindo pie!
> Zapatos de punta dura
> Mulata, te compraré.
>   (1954, 47)

> Saintly mulatto woman,
> Put a robe on,
> And lean out of the window
> To listen to my serenade.
> Bye, babe!
> Such a beautiful foot!
> Hard-pointed shoes
> I will buy you, mulatto woman.

Fernández Retamar refers to these guaracha lyrics as "las canciones populares en que el negro, socialmente preterido, e impedido por regla general de utilizar las vías de la poesía culta, había manifestado durante años su peculiar espíritu. Esas canciones mostraban su visión alegre, fuerte—a veces misteriosa" (popular songs in which for many years blacks, who had been socially excluded and generally not allowed to use the medium of erudite poetry, had expressed their peculiar spirit. These songs displayed their strong, optimistic, and sometimes mysterious perspective) (1954, 47). It would be unwise to conclude that all guarachas were written by whites. However, to assume that they were musical forms by blacks, as Fernández Retamar does, is equally inadvisable, because, as Feijóo has argued, it is impossible to establish with any certainty the black or white origins of most popular *cuartetas*, the poetic forms used in the guaracha (1987, 40–41). Nevertheless, as will be explained in chapter 4, this musical genre was characteristic of *teatro bufo* plays, which were written by white authors and performed by white actors in front of white audiences. Naturally, therefore, guaracha lyrics very often reflect white racism toward blacks.

It seems logical to assume in view of the above explanations that all afrocubanista poets based their representations on a mixture of empirical observations of Afro-Cuban cultural practices and available representations of these in popular and erudite culture. Carpentier's description below specifically illustrates that attending Afro-Cuban rituals (in this case the initiation ceremonies of the Abakuá) and reading Fernando Ortiz's studies were activities that guided the composition of afrocubanista poems simultaneously: "Despite the age difference, Fernando Ortiz mixed with the younger guys. Everyone read his books and folkloric values were exalted. Suddenly, the black became the centre of attention. Also because it was a way of outraging the old-school intellectuals, we all religiously attended initiation ceremonies of the *ñáñigos* and we paid tribute to the dance of the *diablito*. This is how the *afrocubanista* tendency arose, and for more than 10 years it would influence poetry, novels, and sociological and folklore studies" (1961, 172).

There is no denying that because of their partial reliance on secondary sources, afrocubanista poets sometimes did represent obsolete Afro-Cuban cultural practices. An illustrative example is Nicolás Guillén's poem "Sensemayá," which, as the poet explains in the following extract, was partly inspired by Ortiz's writings:

> I remember the day on which I wrote it without really intending to, without ever having thought about doing it: It was January 6, 1932, the "Día de Reyes." I was in bed sick, in a Havana hotel on San Rafael Street where I was staying. Perhaps the enforced idleness gave wings to my thoughts and took me back to my childhood. Ever since I have been a child, in my native Camagüey, a Negro song kept resounding in my mind, a popular song, composed for killing snakes: "Sámbala, culembe; sámbala, culembe; sámbala, xulembe[.] . . ." How, why did this come to my mind then? Perhaps because I had been reading parts of Fernando Ortiz's work on black sorcerers; perhaps because of the prestige of that day, the "Día de Reyes," evoking events from colonial Cuba. (As translated in Kutzinski 1987, 139)

In his 1906 study *Los negros brujos,* the renowned Cuban scholar included a description of a Día de Reyes dance for killing a snake. The lyrics sung in the dance are very similar to the ones cited by Guillén, which suggests that Ortiz's book may have been a stronger influence than the poet suggested: "There may have been a connection between Vudu and the old *Dance of the Snake,* which blacks used to dance on the Day of Kings around an artificial boa. After taking the snake around Havana they deposited it on the palace courtyard and danced around it to a song that was half Spanish and half African, as the last part of the chorus said: The snake has died. / *Sángala muleque*" (Ortiz 1973a, 48).[28] Ortiz's description came from an 1887 treatise by Antonio Bachiller y Morales, and the dance in question had ceased to be practiced in the nineteenth century.[29] This was not the only occasion on which Guillén employed elements that were not a part of contemporaneous Afro-Cuban culture. His poem "Canto negro" (Black Song), which for Lemuel Johnson betrays "a dilettante's familiarity with the exotic names in Ñañiguismo," clearly borrowed elements from a 1677 poem by Mexican writer Sor Juana Inés de La Cruz (Johnson 1971, 143; Feijóo 1986, 79–80).

But not all afrocubanista poems based on secondary sources produced representations of Afro-Cuban cultural practices that were no longer a part of the culture of 1920s and 1930s blacks. Indeed, many of Ortiz's studies on Afro-Cuban culture focused on cultural traditions that continued to be practiced in Cuba at the time, thus providing afrocubanistas with ethnographic descriptions of contemporaneous black culture. This was certainly the case with his 1937 speech "La música sagrada de los negros yorubas en Cuba" (The Sacred Music of Yoruba Blacks in Cuba), with which he introduced and described the performance of an Afro-Cuban religious ritual by Cuban Lucumí blacks in the Havana theater Campoamor (Ortiz 1991c). Throughout his works published in the 1950s, which probably relied to some extent on research carried out in the 1930s, Ortiz repeatedly referred to aspects of Afro-Cuban culture that he had observed in contemporaneous Afro-Cuban practices.[30]

Moreover, there is no reason to doubt that available forms of popular culture such as guaracha lyrics also contained representations of contemporaneous Afro-Cuban cultural practices that afrocubanistas could use to represent 1930s black culture accurately. The verses from Hallorans's compilation quoted earlier are a case in point, since they accurately describe the dancing that characterizes the rumba episode known as *vacunao*, which will be described in detail in chapter 5. Other representations of contemporaneous Afro-Cuban cultural practices in white popular culture of the time include those found in vernacular theater. The actor Pepe Serna, for instance, brought choreographic configurations from Afro-Cuban cultural traditions to *teatro bufo* plays of this period. As Moore explains, this white Ñáñigo or Abakuá from Matanzas was one of the few theatrical dancers who were respected by black *rumberos*, and he was "one of the first to bring the virtuosic and physically taxing movements of traditional male solo *rumba* to the theatre" (1997, 58). Another incorporation of an Afro-Cuban cultural form in *teatro bufo* of the time is the rhythmic pattern known as *tango-congo*, which bears a strong similarity to Santería drumming patterns used in the dances to the deity Yemayá (Moore 1997, 53–60, 254).

To sum up, afrocubanista poetry focused upon Afro-Cuban cultural traditions that were practiced among specific sectors of the Cuban black population. Although most afrocubanista poets did not belong to these sectors, their representations cannot be dismissed as completely disconnected from the cultures they sought to represent. Drawing from a combination of direct research, ethnographic studies, and secondary sources, afrocubanista poets were able to include in their poems elements from the cultures of the Afro-Cuban sectors. The various ways in which they incorporated such elements will be analyzed in further chapters of this book.

3 Transculturation and the Cuban Stew

Fernando Ortiz's Discourse on Cuban National Identity and Afrocubanista Poetry

FERNANDO ORTIZ'S first book on Afro-Cuban culture was published in Madrid in 1906 under the title *Hampa afrocubana: Los negros brujos (Apuntes para un estudio de etnología criminal)* (The Afro-Cuban Criminal Underworld: The Black Sorcerers [Notes for a Criminal Ethnology Study]). As I explained in chapter 1, with this book Ortiz intended to facilitate the elimination of Afro-Cuban traditions. However, in the mid-1930s the scholar shifted toward a greater appreciation of Afro-Cuban culture, moved by the same ideological motivations that guided the afrocubanista movement (Moore 1994, 33; Duno Gottberg 2003b, 140; Lienhard 1996, 27). From this period on, Ortiz began to promote the study of Afro-Cuban culture through publications and active participation in groups such as the Sociedad de Estudios Afrocubanos. His writings on Afro-Cuban culture, which continued up to the mid-1950s, are widely recognized today as having been central to the formation of Afro-Cuban studies (Kutzinski 1993, 145; Moore 1994, 32–33; Ortiz Herrera 1996, xii–xiii).

Throughout the first three decades of the twentieth century, Ortiz's work played a vital part in poetic afrocubanismo. As shown in the previous chapter, his studies offered afrocubanista poets a source of ethnographic research on Afro-Cuban culture. Equally significant was his role as a critic of their literary production. In the introduction to his anthology *Órbita de la poesía afrocubana, 1928–1937*, Ramón Guirao remarked upon Ortiz's role as a critic of afrocubanista poetry, arguing that "the Afrologist and researcher Fernando Ortiz, whose adherence to the positivist school of thought has naturally led him to the issue of the black problem, and Juan Marinello, with the fine sensitivity and sharp intuition of a poet in recess, are the two most insistent critics of this dark poetry" (1938, xii–xiii). The various essays on afrocubanista poetry written by Ortiz in the 1930s constitute the most extensive analysis of poetic afrocubanismo by one of its participants. It is therefore crucial to analyze them in order to understand the movement fully.

Another vital contribution was Ortiz's thought on Cuban national identity. From about 1928 until 1940, a considerable proportion of the intellectual's critical output was concerned with elaborating definitions of the nation as culturally hybrid, thereby providing a philosophy of the national that sustained the production of all afrocubanista arts. It is thus also imperative to analyze this aspect of Ortiz's work in order to grasp the notions about Cuban culture and identity that guided the production of afrocubanista poetry. Nevertheless, afrocubanista poets were not merely passive recipients of Ortiz's influence. Because the proliferation of afrocubanista poetry from the late 1920s predates his shift toward a more positive discourse on Afro-Cuban culture, it is very likely that afrocubanista poems played a part in awakening Ortiz's interest in the potential of Afro-Cuban cultural forms. The African/Spanish cultural forms produced by afrocubanistas certainly helped the scholar to develop his definitions of Cuban identity. It was in the process of writing about afrocubanista poetry and music that Ortiz began to formulate the ideas that underpinned the ultimate expressions of his afrocubanista discourse on the national: his description of Cuba as an *ajiaco* (a traditional Cuban stew) and his definition of the term "transculturation." Being the main theoretical offshoots of afrocubanismo, these concepts contain some of the most important characteristics of the redefinition of the national intended by the movement. Examining them in relation to Ortiz's writings on afrocubanista music and poetry will shed light on some of their imagery.

Criticism on the work of Fernando Ortiz can be divided into two main perspectives. A number of scholars tend to focus on productive elements of the scholar's writings that can still be used to further our understanding of Cuban identity, culture, and history. For Antonio Benítez Rojo, Ortiz's *Contrapunteo cubano del tabaco y el azúcar* contains a characteristically Caribbean response to the question of postmodernity based on notions drawn from Afro-Cuban traditions (1988, 1992). Enrico Mario Santí sees this same book as one of the most innovative essays of the Hispanic world in the twentieth century and as an indispensable tool for the study of Cuban and American history in general (2002, 17). Gustavo Pérez Firmat exalts the way in which Ortiz appropriated or "transculturated" foreign cultural elements in order to create a distinctive Cuban discourse (1989, 1999). Firmat also praises the antiessentialism of Ortiz's concept of transculturation. He argues that it captures the "mutability," "uprootedness," and "fluidity" of Cuban culture, which reflects Ortiz's belief that "the essence of Cuba lies in not having one" (1989, 16–66, 26). For Adriana Méndez Rodenas, Ortiz's definition of transculturation prefigures contemporary definitions of the phenomenon of diaspora (2002, 217). Catherine Davies outlines the ways in which "transculturation" avoids contemporary interpretative strategies through which Latin American culture continues to be objectified (2000, 156–61).

This tendency is counterbalanced by a growing number of critics who are beginning to emphasize the presence of several problematic notions in Ortiz's discourse on Afro-Cuban culture. Robin Dale Moore argues that Ortiz did not view the Afro-Cuban cultural forms of Cuban blacks as ultimately national. According to Moore, the author was influenced by cultural evolutionist notions that led him to consider African and Afro-Cuban cultures inferior or not fully developed, even when he appreciated some of their valuable elements. Moore concludes that, in the end, "it is only the 'reinvented' or reinterpreted Afro-Cuban music heard in the compositions of conservatory elites, as opposed to that of the *solar* or urban slum, which gains Ortiz's unequivocal support" (1994, 45–46, 49). Fernando Coronil explains Ortiz's position in terms of Spengler's influence: the German philosopher did awaken Ortiz to the potential of non-Western cultures, but he also led him to accept an evolutionary framework (1995, xix). More recently, Luis Duno Gottberg has identified Ortiz's bias toward Spanish or European cultural models in several descriptions of Spanish, African, and indigenous cultures in Ortiz's definition of "transculturation" and in his *ajiaco* metaphor (2003, 117–55). Similarly, Jorge Duany points out that in Ortiz's telluric imagery in his *ajiaco* metaphor, the European ingredients appear as the most important and, as a result, "the African contribution to national identity is underestimated and subordinated" (200, 24).[1]

The assessment of Ortiz's work in this chapter draws upon these two perspectives in exploring both the problematic and the productive notions of the scholar's writings. The analysis is based on the connections between Ortiz's thought and the afrocubanista poetic project, connections that, despite the recent flourishing of criticism on Ortiz, have not yet been analyzed in detail.

As explained in the first chapter of this book, afrocubanista poets and other 1930s Cuban intellectuals believed that the unification of the nation beyond racial conflicts could be achieved by bringing to the fore Cuban cultural forms containing a mixture of elements from the cultures of black and white Cubans. Ortiz's thought on national identity brings to light two theoretical notions that underpinned this approach. The first of these is a rejection of race as a valid component of Cuban identity. In his 1939 speech "Los factores humanos de la cubanidad" (The Human Factors in Cuban Identity), the scholar claimed that Cuban identity could not be understood as a racial concept, because "race" is merely an arbitrary construct: "After all, race is just a civil status, signed by the anthropological authorities; but this racial condition tends to be so conventional and arbitrary, and often so changeable, just like the civil status that is given to men of this or that nationality" (1991b, 13). Ortiz had already argued that culture was much more important than race in the search for definitions of Latin American national identities. In a speech he gave in Madrid back in 1929, he stated, "Race is a static concept, culture is a dynamic one" (as cited in Jarnés 1929, 9). Ortiz's professed low regard for the concept of race at this time flew in the face of racist notions that were still dominant in the Cuban sciences of the late 1920s. According to De La Fuente, various Cuban speakers at the Pan American Conference on Eugenics and Homiculture, held in Havana in 1927, openly declared their belief that the superiority and inferiority of different races were determinant factors in the evolution of human societies. De La Fuente also points out that the notion of race itself was not widely scrutinized by Cuban intellectuals until the Second World War and that "in the early 1930s nationalist intellectuals referred to the new *cubanidad* as a 'Cuban race'" (2001, 43, 178).

Ortiz's rejection of the validity of "race" as an objective, and thus scientific, concept drew upon the writings of José Martí. In his 1891 essay "Nuestra América" (Our America), Martí argued that the idea of race was an intellectual construct devised by small-minded scholars intent on disproving what he saw as the irrefutable existence in nature of a universal human identity: "No hay odios de razas, porque no hay razas. Los pensadores canijos, enhebran y recalientan las razas de librería, que el viajero justo y el observador cordial buscan en vano en la justicia de la Naturaleza, donde resalta, en el amor victorioso y el apetito turbulento, la identidad universal del hombre. El alma emana, igual y eterna, de los cuerpos diversos en forma y en color" (There is no hatred between different races because there are no races. Small-minded thinkers thread and reheat the races that exist in books, but the impartial traveler and the cordial observer look for them in vain in the justice of nature, where all that stands out, in the victorious love and turbulent appetite, is the universal identity of mankind. The same eternal soul emanates from all the bodies, regardless of their form and color) (1985a, 92). The notion that Martí's position influenced Ortiz's approach to the idea of race is supported by the fact that in his 1946 study *El engaño de las razas* (The Deception of the Races), Ortiz begins his prologue by quoting Martí's description of the concept (1974, 29). It is important to remember that, in challenging the concept of race, Ortiz was also able to draw upon the efforts of some Cuban physicians, hygienists, and scientists who during the first three decades of the twentieth century were using environmentalist explanations to refute the notion of Cuban blacks' biological inferiority (De La Fuente 2001, 178–80). As Ortiz makes clear, various Latin American and North American anthropologists were also questioning the concept of race in the 1930s (1974, 32–33, 369–402).

In "Los factores humanos de la cubanidad," Ortiz also undermined the idea of a pure race with the argument that all human groups were a mixture of races, a fact he illustrated with reference to the history of intense miscegenation, or *mestizaje,* in Cuba:

> The four main common races have embraced each other and crossbred time and time again on our land producing new generations. Cuba is one of the most mixed nations, a half cast from many different progenitors. And by the time they arrived in Cuba, each of the so-called big races was already the complex product of the unions between different ancestors.... And the slave shipments brought Africans that descended from various different melanoid races, so much so that, paradoxically, many of the blacks that inhabited Cuba, like the Congolese or the Bantu, nowadays cannot be considered black, because the science of anthropology forbids it; and on the other hand, there are many ethnologists who maintain that in Africa there is not a single human group left that has remained untouched by the white race. (1991b, 18)

Since race was not a valid concept, he argued that Cuban identity had to be defined as a "cultural condition." Ortiz's idea that culture was a more consequential component of Cuban identity than race was obviously linked to the afrocubanista belief that racial divisions could be solved through a cultural approach.

The second theoretical notion behind the afrocubanista project brought to light by Ortiz's thought on the national is an antiessentialist vision of Cuban culture and identity. Following his rejection of the concept of "race" in "Los factores humanos de la cubanidad," Ortiz proposed that Cuban identity had to be found specifically in "las culturas que se han ido fundiendo en Cuba" (the cultures that have gradually fused in Cuba), thus moving away from the idea of an "original," "pure" national culture

(1991b, 13–14, 19). He used the image of a traditional Cuban stew known as *ajiaco* to conceptualize ultimate Cuban identity as the mixture of different cultures resulting from the intense interactions of different human groups throughout Cuban history:

> At every moment our community has had, like the *ajiaco,* new and raw elements that have recently been put in the stew; a heterogeneous conglomerate of various races and cultures, and of many meats and vegetables, which rustle, mingle and disintegrate in the same social stew. And there, at the bottom of the pan, a new already-settled mass, produced by the elements that, having disintegrated in this stew throughout history, have gradually deposited their most tenacious essences into a richly garnished mixture that is already distinctive. Miscegenation of cuisines, races, and cultures. . . . One could assume that one could only find Cubanness in this gravy of new and synthetic succulence formed through the fusion of the lineages dissolved in Cuba. But no, Cubanness is not only in the result but also in its complex process of formation, . . . in the substantial elements involved in it, in the environment in which it takes place and in the events that occur during it. (1991b, 16)

By presenting *cubanidad* as a process, Ortiz preempted the postmodernist understanding of identity. As Wade explains, in postmodernist thought "identity is seen as constructed through complex processes of relationality and representation; it is a process, not a thing" (1997, 80–81).[2] An equally fluid conceptualization of culture can be found in other parts of "Los factores humanos de la cubanidad." Ortiz claimed at one point that all cultures in Cuba were dynamic, not only in the form in which they had been transplanted to the island but also in the local transformations they experienced there. Thus, he concluded that Cuban culture was generative, dynamic, and social and that it should be understood as a vital concept of constant fluidity. It was not a known, ready-formed synthetic reality, he argued, but the experience of the numerous human beings who had arrived in the island and were still arriving, becoming part of the Cuban people and influencing their culture (1991b, 14).

Ortiz's antiessentialist emphasis on the interactions between cultures of different origins is equally central to his definition of the term "transculturation" in his 1940 *Contrapunteo cubano del tabaco y el azúcar* (Cuban Counterpoint: Tobacco and Sugar). In a chapter entitled "Del fenómeno social de la 'transculturación' y de su importancia en Cuba" (On the Social Phenomenon of "Transculturation" and Its Importance in Cuba), the scholar argued that this term should replace "acculturation," a term used by leading anthropologists at the time to designate cultural phenomena resulting from the contact of different cultures. Ortiz was obviously referring to the 1936 definition by anthropologists Robert Redfield, Ralph Linton, and Melville H. Herskovits, who established that "acculturation comprehends those phenomena which result when groups of individuals having different cultures come into continuous first-hand contact, with subsequent changes in the original cultural patterns of either or both groups" (as quoted in Coronil 1995, li). Through his contribution Ortiz wanted to stress that in situations where two cultures came into contact, neither one managed to eliminate the other. He argued that the school of functionalism founded by the anthropologist Bronislaw Malinowski, who wrote the introduction to *Contrapunteo cubano del tabaco y el azúcar*, had demonstrated that what resulted from these situations was always a third product that contained elements from both but was distinctive in its own right. The term "transculturation" captured this and all the other phenomena that occurred in the process of cultural change better than "acculturation," which, he pointed out, suggested merely the adoption of a new culture:[3]

> I am of the opinion that the word "transculturation" better expresses the different phases of the process of transition from one culture to another because this does not consist merely in acquiring another culture, which is what the English word "acculturation" really implies, but the process also necessarily involves the loss or uprooting of a previous culture, which could be defined as a deculturation. In addition it carries the idea of the consequent creation of new cultural phenomena, which would be called neoculturation. In the end, as the followers of Malinowski's school maintain, the result of every union of cultures is similar to that of the reproductive process between individuals: the offspring always has something of both parents but is always different from both of them. (As translated in Ortiz 1995, 102–3)

Ortiz was already applying his questioning of the idea of race and his antiessentialist vision of culture to his analyses of afrocubanista poetry in the 1930s. In "Los últimos versos mulatos" (The Latest Mulatto Poems), he brought attention to the movement of cultural forms across racial groups when he argued that Cubans at various points in history had been able to write black or white poetry, irrespective of their racial background. He cited the example of the nineteenth-century Cuban mulatto poet Plácido, who was "a master of white poetry." "At this high poetic level," claimed Ortiz, "the genius of the Afro-Cuban managed to create poetry like that of the white poet; white because of its subject matter, its form and its feeling" (1973b, 157–58). In the same way as this black nineteenth-century poet had been able to write white poetry, in the republican period white afrocubanistas had produced a new type of Afro-Cuban poetry: "The generation born after the incorporation of Afro-Cubans to the political system of the Republic has been able to enjoy the advantages of tranquility and of the education of the bourgeoisie. This generation has developed in the bureaucracy and on its margins, with a more developed culture, a greater awareness of contemporary spiritual dimensions, a finer introspection of its own values and more self-confidence. And from this generation has emerged another Afro-Cuban poetic expression that has already yielded good fruits" (1973b, 158). His belief in the ability of white afrocubanistas to produce an "Afro-Cuban poetic expression" relied on a rejection of the concept of race. In one particular passage in "Los últimos versos mulatos," he questioned Gustavo Sánchez Galarraga's comment that the secret of writing "Afro-Cuban poetry" was all "in the blood." He argued that, like all "black" or "white" culture, "mulatto" poetry did not have a biological origin. As evinced by the case of afrocubanista poet Emilio Ballagas, who had managed to "penetrate the black ethos," the secret of writing afrocubanista poetry did not have to do with the author's racial makeup but with his accurate representation of Afro-Cuban cultural characteristics, such as the phonetic peculiarities of black speech (1973c, 177–78). Since, as explained in the previous chapter of this study, most afrocubanista poets were actually white, it is clear that this idea constituted an important theoretical justification for their poetic project. Ortiz's conviction that whites could write black poetry certainly underpinned Emilio Ballagas's understanding of afrocubanista poetry. In a 1946 essay entitled "Situación de la poesía afro-americana" (The State of Afro-American Poetry), the poet presented this notion as one of the defining factors of Latin American black poetry: "Blacks and mulattos from their own intuitive lyric center, can accurately offer this expression of the sensibility of the person of color; and whites can do the same thing, but as a reflected phenomenon, at times very diaphanous, which supposes not only a fortunate identification but, beyond that, a throwing off of the historicist and sociological burden that leads again to the identity of humanity and the Christian idea of its shared origin" (as translated in Kutzinski 1993, 156).

On the one hand, it cannot be denied that this emphasis on the ability of whites to write black literature glosses over the drastic sociocultural differences between afrocubanista poets and the black sectors on which they based their poetry, differences that were illustrated in chapter 2 of this study. It was the afrocubanistas' desire for the disappearance of black and white differences in Cuba, which was explained in the first chapter, that often led them to gloss over existing black and white differences. Kutzinski brings attention to this problem in relation to Ballagas's above statement, which she describes as betraying a dehistoricizing approach that avoids racial divisions in order to uphold national unity (1993, 156–57). Other Afro-Hispanists have identified the assimilationist aspect of this afrocubanista notion. Lewis criticizes afrocubanistas for failing to distinguish between the poetry of white and black poets, thereby not allowing for their different perspectives (1983, 1). For Mullen, Ballagas's rejection of race as an inherent property of texts in his article "Poesía negra liberada" (Freed Black Poetry) is a "rejection of Afro-Cuban cultural distinctiveness" (1998, 158).

On the other hand, these critics fail to pay sufficient attention to the fact that, as Ortiz's writings demonstrate, the afrocubanista belief in whites' ability to write black literature also stemmed from highly productive ideas. For instance, it is necessary to acknowledge that this belief was derived from a questioning of the very idea of race. Similarly, reducing this aspect of afrocubanista discourse to an attempt to assimilate blacks culturally overlooks the fact that it emerged from an antiessentialist conception of culture.

Furthermore, it is equally important to consider that Ortiz upheld the validity of black poetry written by whites without undermining the distinctiveness of black culture. Although he believed that whites could write mulatto poetry by imitating Afro-Cuban cultural traits, he did not suggest that this was an easy feat. He was aware of the particularities of Afro-Cuban culture and constantly warned afrocubanistas of the need to learn its complex codes. For instance, he explained that in Afro-Cuban religious rituals every deity had specific dances, as well as songs and rhythms, that Afro-Cubans learned from childhood. To write mulatto poetry it was necessary not only to learn the complex symbolism of the rhythms and dances of Afro-Cuban rituals but also to understand the emotional effect that these cultural forms had on Afro-Cubans (1973c, 182). Ortiz would continue to bring to light the multiple meanings conveyed through Afro-Cuban cultural forms in his 1950s publications. In *La africanía de la música folklórica de Cuba* (The Africanness of Cuban Folkloric Music), he refuted the notion put forward by R. B. Marett that African words in religious rituals had no function other than providing rhythmic support. He argued that the metaphoric or referential quality of many African phonemes was the reason why to the noninitiated they may have seemed to lack any semantic meanings. In this same work he termed this aspect of African languages *holófrasis*, "short words, like expletive interjections, that encapsulate the expression of a whole sentence, . . . evoke the entire cycle of an action, with pronouns, adjectives, verbs, adverbs and attributes." In both *La africanía de la música folklórica de Cuba* and *El teatro y los bailes de los negros en el folklore de Cuba* (Black Theatre and Dances in Cuban Folklore), Ortiz displayed a profound awareness of the semantic dimension of nonverbal expressions, such as rhythmic cells played on the Afro-Cuban *batá* drums and dancing movements employed in Regla de Ocha or Santería practices (1965, 187, 189, 192, 221, 259–63; 1981, 229).

Aware of the complex multiplicity of oral, choreographic, and musical forms in Afro-Cuban culture, Ortiz explained how afrocubanista poets had to find ways of incorporating into their poetry cultural forms based on a variety of modes of expression. He argued that the secret of writing "poesía completamente negroide" ("completely negroid poetry") with its characteristic rhythmic complexity was in the ability to capture visual and musical Afro-Cuban elements (1973c, 183–84). It was not only a question of superficially incorporating these cultural forms into the poetry from a thematic point of view. He illustrated this notion with a humorous comparison: "A poem can have a negroid theme and be full of words and verbal expressions that are typical of the brown masses in Cuba, and yet not be substantially mulatto. At the most, it will be white poetry with negroid incrustations, like the torso of a Nordic sailor covered with tattoos characteristic of people from the torrid regions" (1973c, 178–79). In relation to the language of the poetry, he argued that it was necessary to do more than simply insert the occasional Afro-Cuban term, because the poetry achieved through this kind of approach would not be *negroide* (1973c, 179). The type of incorporation Ortiz was advocating becomes clear in his analysis of Nicolás Guillén's poetry, in which he outlined the combination of characteristics that made a poetic composition typically mulatto. He argued that this poet's "La canción del bongó" (The Song of the Bongo Drum) was mulatto because of the author, the theme, and the thought, but not because of the language or rhythm, which were authentically Castilian. Guillén's poem "Rumba" was mulatto because of the author, the subject matter, "la idea y las variaciones del ritmo" (the idea and the rhythmic variations). Nevertheless, added Ortiz, "there is no mulattoness in the language, but in terms of prosody and syntaxis it adapts Castilian expressions to the popular rhythm of a Cuban *son*." The metric patterns at the end of this poem, explained Ortiz, were a faithful reproduction of the musical features of rumba, translated into verbal expression (1973c, 184–86). As prototypical examples of mulatto poems, Ortiz put forward Guillén's "Canto negro" and "Sóngoro cosongo." These poems were mulatto because their author was a mulatto, they dealt with mulatto themes, and they were written from a mulatto perspective. In addition, they incorporated the rhythms of the drum and of black speech (1973c, 186). Of course, it cannot be denied that, despite his rejection of the idea of race, by taking into account Guillén's racial makeup Ortiz failed to completely leave behind the biological determinist perspective that was often evident in his writings on Afro-Cuban culture (1973a, 230; 1973c, 177). Nevertheless, for Ortiz an equally important consideration in determining the *mulatez* of an afrocubanista poem was its assimilation of Afro-Cuban themes, modes of thought or concepts, language, and rhythm. As illustrated by his references to the reproduction of rumba rhythm in the metric patterns of Guillén's "Rumba," Ortiz thought that afrocubanistas were producing a formally mulatto literature by incorporating Afro-Cuban forms into their poems.

Ortiz's writings on afrocubanista poetry show that the poets' adoption of this approach was also linked to their desire to produce an image of harmonious unification between Cuban blacks and whites. This connection becomes clear in Ortiz's 1934 "La poesía mulata: Presentación de Eusebia Cosme, la recitadora" (Mulatto Poetry: Introducing the Reciter Eusebia Cosme). In this essay Ortiz used the emergence of a formally distinctive mulatto art to promote a distorted image of increasing social equality between blacks and whites. As will be shown later, this integratory conception of Cuban identity also restricted the plurality of his definitions of the national. Ortiz then argued that in this context of greater social equality it had been possible for the afrocubanista poets Emilio Ballagas and Nicolás Guillén to penetrate the "mulatto soul" and write mulatto poetry "from within" (1934, 207, 209–10). Ortiz's subsequent description of their poetry as the "mulatto daughter who resulted from the inextricable embrace between Africa and Castile" reinforced the idea of afrocubanista poetry as resulting from a process of increasing harmony between Cuban blacks and whites (Ortiz 1934, 210). The image of a loving embrace between two cultures specifically brings to mind the definition of the term "transculturation," in which, as shown earlier, the scholar described the contact between cultures as an embrace (1978, 96). Significantly, Ortiz would use the term "transculturation" to refer to a Cuban process of increasing black and white harmony in his 1945 "Por la integración cubana de blancos y negros" (For the Cuban Integration of Blacks and Whites). This article outlined the five phases of Cuba's transculturative process. The first had been a hostile phase, in which the white man had enslaved the black. The second had been a tolerant phase, in which relations between blacks and whites had improved as they adjusted to their new environment. In the third phase, which Ortiz termed "adaptive," blacks had tried to "improve themselves" by imitating the white and rejecting their color and their African heritage. Cuba was now in the fourth phase, he argued, which was one of affirmation. In this phase the black was gradually recovering his dignity and racial and cultural pride in a context of greater cooperation between the two races, even if racial prejudice had not yet completely disappeared. Ortiz then added that Cuba still had to reach a fifth phase, which was one of integration. In this final phase of tomorrow, he argued, all the cultures will have fused into a new culture and a perfectly integrated community will have resulted, one in which all racial conflicts and divisions will have disappeared (as cited in Iznaga 1989, 58–62).

This description brings to mind another afrocubanista notion that is also linked to the idea of formally mulatto poetry in Ortiz's writings. The references to a third entity and to a new community reflect the afrocubanista endeavor to redefine Cuban culture and identity as a new distinctive African/Spanish hybrid, which was illustrated in the first chapter. Ortiz made clear the connection between this notion and the idea of formally mulatto poetry in the 1934 article mentioned earlier, "La poesía mulata: Presentación de Eusebia Cosme, la recitadora." Having described formally mulatto poetry as resulting from increasing equality between the black and the white, the language he used in his description of Guillén's and Ballagas's poems demonstrates that he also viewed this type of poetry as a symbol of a distinctive hybrid Cuban identity: "Emilio Ballagas and Nicolás Guillén penetrate the mystery of the unexpressed soul, they take its own voice to say intimate things, and reveal the hot fragrances of a new poetry, born of a mixture of singular values that has produced a new one that is valuable in its own right, just like it happens with the most heterogeneous and contradictory religions, which gradually syncretize their dogmas and liturgies until one day there emerges a new anthem in a new language, for a new faith that is already aware of its own existence" (1934, 209–10). The presence of this perception of Cuban identity in Ortiz's writings on afrocubanista poetry again illustrates the connection between his thought on poetic afrocubanismo and his definition of the term "transculturation." The definition upheld this afrocubanista vision of Cuban culture and identity by stressing that all cultural contact resulted in a new product that contained elements from both predecessors but was different from them. In this way "transculturation" provided the theoretical framework required for the study of Cuba: "These questions of sociological nomenclature are not to be disregarded, in the interests of a better understanding of social phenomena, especially in Cuba, whose history, more than that of any other country of America, is an intense, complex, unbroken process of transculturation of human groups, all in a state of transition. The concept of transculturation is fundamental and indispensable for an understanding of the history of Cuba" (as translated in Ortiz 1995, 103). The significance of Ortiz's intent has to be seen in relation to a widespread approach in contemporaneous Western anthropology to situations in which a dominant and a dominated culture came into contact. Many anthropologists at this time concentrated predominantly on studying the changes undergone by dominated cultures, a tendency that betrayed the assumption that those changes undergone by dominant ones were not significant enough to merit attention. This tendency was revealed by Melville Herskovits in a 1935 essay entitled "What Has Africa Given America?" in which the anthropologist explained that the influence of African culture on U.S. whites was a largely unexplored field (1966, 169). A specific example of an anthropological study that explored only the effects of a dominant culture upon a dominated one is Bronislaw Malinowski's 1945 *The Dynamics of Culture Change: An Inquiry into Race Relations in Africa*. Ralph Beals explains that this work was solely concerned with the study of acculturative processes as they arose in connection with the impact of European culture upon native culture. This is highly ironic in view of the fact that, in his introduction to *Contrapunteo* in 1940, Malinowski strongly agreed with Ortiz about the ethnocentric semantic implications of the term "acculturation" and promised to use "transculturation" instead (1978, 3–4).[4] Beals provides other examples to demonstrate that, at the time, most British discussions and definitions of "culture contact" were wholly concerned with the impact of European cultures upon native ones (1962, 380–82). Martín Lienhard has characterized the practical applications of the theory of acculturation by anthropologists such as Robert Redfield, Ralph Linton, and Melville Herskovits as "a discourse of assimilation of folk sectors to 'modern' urban culture" (1997, 190).

The use of the term "acculturation" to refer to cultural contact was a manifestation of this widespread approach in anthropology. The letter *a* at the beginning of the word was an abbreviation of the Latin preposition *ad*, which means "toward" and thus suggests the idea of a one-directional process of cultural change. Applying this term to the phenomenon of contact between cultures suggested that members of the weaker or dominated culture were necessarily assimilated by the dominant one (Ortiz 1978, 96; Malinowski 1978, 4).[5] This perspective was inadequate for the study of Cuba, where the influence of Spanish culture had not effected the disappearance of African traditions. These had resisted the imposition of the dominant culture, interacting with it to form a new and distinctively Cuban composite, a process that brings to mind Oswald de Andrade's conception of Brazilian identity in his 1928 "Manifesto Antropófago" as a cannibalization of European culture. By highlighting the dynamic role of Afro-Cuban culture in his endeavor to provide a suitable theoretical framework for Cuba, Ortiz also redressed the failure of anthropologists to fully explore the counterhegemonic potential of dominated cultures. After *Contrapunteo* he would often use the concept of "transculturation" to bring attention to ways in which black cultures in Cuba had transformed the culture of the dominant classes.[6]

It was the potential of "transculturation" to highlight the counterhegemonic capacity of dominated cultures that led Ángel Rama to appropriate the concept in his influential 1982 study of Latin American literature, *Transculturación narrativa en América Latina* (Narrative Transculturation in Latin America). The Uruguayan critic was interested in Ortiz's notion because he saw in it a refusal to accept that, in the contact between two cultures, the dominated culture suffered all the losses and was incapable of inducing alterations in the dominant culture (1882, 38–39). One of the ways in which Rama develops the theoretical productivity of Ortiz's concept is by stressing the persistence of Latin American regional cultures in the face of advancing modernization. He also stresses the counterhegemonic potential of literary works articulated to these cultures, in particular those by José María Arguedas, Gabriel García Márquez, Juan Rulfo, and Augusto Roa Bastos (D'Allemand 2000, 53).[7]

The work of afrocubanista poets helped Ortiz to develop the awareness of the counterhegemonic capacity of dominated cultures that sustained his vision of Cuban culture. It was precisely when he started to analyze afrocubanista poetry in the 1930s that the scholar began to highlight the ways in which the cultures of blacks had deeply transformed dominant white culture in Cuba. In "Los últimos versos mulatos," he explained that in the nineteenth century the African elements in the dance and music form known as *danzón* were generally unacknowledged or attributed to indigenous culture. The *danzón* and other musical forms popular among lower- and upper-class whites (Ortiz mentions the *habanera*, the *tango*, and the *cucuyé*) were examples of how "the rhythmic art of blacks deeply penetrated Cuban society through its music and then through its dance" (1973b, 156–57). In "La poesía mulata: Presentación de Eusebia Cosme, la recitadora," he brought attention to the influence of the languages spoken by black slaves upon the Spanish spoken by Cuban whites (1934, 207–8). The notion that dominated cultures resist dominant ones was equally central to his descriptions of formally mulatto poetry. It must be remembered that afrocubanista poetry was erudite literature in Spanish, a genre originating from Spanish tradition. Consequently, by drawing attention to afrocubanistas' formal incorporation of Afro-Cuban forms, Ortiz brought out the counterhegemonic role that Afro-Cuban culture was playing in their poetry by radically transforming formal principles of the dominant literature. His awareness and celebration of this phenomenon further undermines the tendency in Afro-Hispanism to characterize the afrocubanista poetic project as an attempt to assimilate blacks into the dominant culture.

The notions that have been outlined above suggest that Ortiz desired an eventual mulatto Cuban culture and identity that would be strongly based on Afro-Cuban cultural principles. Nevertheless, there is a clear tension in the scholar's discourse between this idea and his often disparaging descriptions of Afro-Cuban cultural forms. One such description may be found in *Glosario de afronegrismos,* where he characterizes the Afro-Cuban rumba as "an Afro-Cuban dance that is disgustingly lascivious from the beginning" (1924a, 406–10). His treatment of African religions was similarly virulent. Ortiz viewed these as repositories of primitive African attitudes and worldviews that were incompatible with Cuba's modernization. In "La religión en la poesía mulata" (Religion in Mulatto Poetry), he described African religion as the product of a paralogic mentality that killed the intellectual curiosity of African blacks, making them stagnant and hostile to radical innovation (1991e, 146–47). In "Los factores humanos de la cubanidad," he further argued that religious syncretism allowed blacks to adopt "higher and freer forms of conceiving and treating the supernatural." As examples of these forms he mentioned agnosticism, Presbyterianism, Methodism, and Baptist Protestantism (1991b, 25).

Following the line of thought opened by critics such as Moore, Coronil, Duno Gottberg, and Duany, one cannot help but notice that, in his 1930s writings on afrocubanista poetry, Ortiz did not often describe Afro-Cuban forms as being ultimately national in their own right. For example, although he advocated the introduction of Afro-Cuban liturgies into popular and public spheres, he also pointed out that they would have to be "stylized." It was these reelaborated versions and not the Afro-Cuban liturgies themselves that Ortiz praised as "a powerful, inimitable and very Cuban artistic attraction, made with native elements that are waiting to be liberated" (1991e, 175). As is the case with his discourse on musical forms, Ortiz openly favored afrocubanista poetry over Afro-Cuban oral literature. He described the work of afrocubanista poets as "a creative insistence in national art," and he also referred to it as "the new Cuban poetry with negroid motifs" (1973b, 156; 1973c, 175). By contrast, he never applied the adjectives "Cuban" or "national" to the secular song forms of blacks, and he described them as having developed "at a lower intellectual level." His cultural evolutionist perspective is patent in the way he situated afrocubanista poetry with respect to other types of "poesía afrocubana." In contrast to his enthusiastic description of afrocubanista poetry as having yielded "good fruits," and contradicting his own references to the sophistication of Afro-Cuban culture, Ortiz described Afro-Cuban oral forms as "a genre of song characteristic of societies whose means of expression are not very developed." He then referred to the oral forms employed in Afro-Cuban religions—such as prayers, spells, and liturgical choruses—as being "part of a rhythmic complex of music, dance and chanting, like all primitive poetry" (1973b, 157).

Ortiz's approach to afrocubanista music and poetry strongly suggests that he conceived of afrocubanista poets as responsible for the construction of a distinctive Cuban national literature that was erudite but that also formally incorporated some valuable Afro-Cuban elements. Arguably, then, for Ortiz, afrocubanista poetry was an instrument through which to introduce these elements into truly national erudite literature without granting national status to inferior Afro-Cuban oral forms.

The influence of the idea of purifying or stylizing Afro-Cuban cultural elements in afrocubanista poetry is certainly palpable in the writings of many intellectuals of the 1920s and 1930s. For instance, Jorge Mañach argued that Nicolás Guillén's *Motivos de son* stylized and purified black folklore, turning it into artistic material (1931, 253). The notion that afrocubanista poetry had to filter Afro-Cuban culture was reiterated by Gilberto González Contreras, who, like Ortiz, clearly regarded it as a kind of raw material: "It could be assumed that it is possible to capture black beauty by simply reaching it with one's hand. But it is not like that. It is necessary to classify it, submitting it to a process of filtering. This is achieved in the melting pot of the poem. Those who achieve it are Guillén, Ballagas, Tallet, Guirao, Gómez Kemp. All of them operate with the crust, with the resin, with the black sap" (1973, 112). Luis Amado

Blanco argued that afrocubanista poetry was a way of improving black culture by mixing it with white cultural elements. In an essay entitled "Poesía mayor de edad" (Adult Poetry), he wrote that the significance of Guillén's work rested on cultural fusion, because Afro-Cuban culture could only realize its full potential by coming into contact with white culture (as cited in Mullen 1998, 10–11). These descriptions reveal a widespread view of afrocubanista poets as converting inferior Afro-Cuban cultural elements into acceptable literary forms by combining them with Spanish elements.

Ortiz's writings on afrocubanista music reveal that an elitist and evolutionist perspective also affected his conception of the process by which a mulatto Cuban culture was consolidating. For Ortiz, afrocubanista music symbolized a process of evolution toward a superior form of national culture that was erudite, even if it was strongly based on Afro-Cuban cultural principles. This idea is particularly well reflected in *La africanía de la música folklórica de Cuba*:

> We have to take our national music to its supreme victory. Our music has to be freed from the excessive complacency and the degenerative infections of vulgarity and disdain. We must preserve it, make it stronger and elevate it to the highest levels of art. In this, like in everything else, Cuba needs to be "technified." Cuba's characteristic music changed from being African and European to being Creole, from black and white to mulatto, from being folkloric it then changes to being popular; and now, without any pigments over which to discriminate ("Cuban and nothing more than Cuban"), it will also become classical through the marriage, motivated as much by calculation as by love, of the beautiful and rich heiress of the multiethnic primitiveness and the young and powerful artistic techniques that are opening up our future. This will be a new and definitive step upwards through hypergamy. (1965, 140–41)

Ortiz considered that Amadeo Roldán and Alejandro García Caturla were examples of afrocubanista composers who had taken Afro-Cuban music to a "higher level" (1965, 141). It is evident, then, that in the final upward stage of this evolutionary process, mulatto popular music would evolve into afrocubanista music, thus becoming an erudite form. Ortiz's elitist and evolutionist perspective is particularly well reflected in his description of this process as one that would "elevate" Cuban music to "the highest levels of art," as well as in his depiction of the last stage as "a step upwards." That he also viewed this final transformation as a further step forward in the formation of Cuban national identity becomes evident in the following page, where he describes it as necessary for "strengthening of our national identity" and as having to be effected by "musicians with patriotic fervor" (1965, 142). By presenting afrocubanista music as the culmination of this process of evolution, Ortiz again excluded Afro-Cuban cultural forms from his definition of the ultimate national identity.

The restrictive slant in Ortiz's conception of this process is also reflected in his theorizing on Cuban identity, particularly in his tendency to describe it as culminating in a single culture.[8] The idea of Cuban identity as one culture is at the heart of his endeavor to define Cuban identity as cultural, rather than racial, from the beginning. This can be seen in a 1929 publication in which he argued that the one thing that could unite all Cubans and eliminate all the divisions created by the damaging concept of race (which was false) was to have one single common culture (Iznaga 1989, 62–63). The idea of Cuban identity as a single unit affects both the *ajiaco* metaphor and the definition of the concept of "transculturation." Although in the former Ortiz described *cubanidad* as a complex process of interaction between ingredients, he also ended up attributing the more developed sense of Cuban identity or *cubanía* to the single common juice that had consolidated at the bottom of the pan:[9] "But if Cuban identity has received emanations from all these cultures, which of these cultures did the ultimate Cuban identity infiltrate the most? Like in the *ajiaco,* the synthetic and new parts are at the bottom, in the already rotten, precipitated, mixed and molten substances that have assimilated into a common juice, a broth and mixture of peoples, cultures and races" (1991b, 29). In a similar manner, in his definition of "transculturation," Ortiz compared the contact of cultures to individuals whose copulation results in the birth of a single creature (1978, 96–97).

The idea of unity present in Ortiz's understanding of transculturation processes has marked later uses of the concept. For instance, Nancy Morejón starts her 1982 *Nación y mestizaje en Nicolás Guillén* (Nation and Miscegenation in Nicolás Guillén) with a chapter entitled "Transculturación y mestizaje," in which she uses both these concepts to explain the process by which "the different formative elements of the Cuban nation merge into a common substance, one which is looking for an identity in the most legitimate national independence." "What characterizes Cubans," she continues, "is that they have set themselves the mission of gestating a nation that is homogeneous in its heterogeneity, moved by a political objective that leaves behind senseless cultural or racial controversies. Hence the adequacy of the term 'transculturación' to describe our cultural history" (1982, 28–29).[10] The idea of unity is equally present in

Jorge and Isabel Castellanos's use of the concept of "transculturation" to describe the emergence of Afro-Cuban culture as the result of the cultural struggles between masters and slaves during Cuba's slavery period. In this description these authors describe slaves and masters as initially having their own cultures. However, they do not describe the result of cultural interaction between the two groups as resulting in changes to the cultures of each group, but as the emergence of a new, single, fused entity (1988, 110).

By portraying Cuban identity as a single unit made of a mixture of the black and the white, these images exclude the nonmulatto cultures and identities of Cuba. It is significant in this respect that Ortiz did not often describe Afro-Cuban cultural forms as hybrid, but as pure African survivals. For instance, he described rumba as having been preserved in Cuba as it was first imported from Africa (1924a, 406–10). According to him, religious Afro-Cuban cultural forms had also survived in the island uncontaminated by other cultural influences (1991e, 146). Since, in Ortiz's mind, these cultural forms were entirely African, they could not be a part of the single mulatto identity that is described in the definition of "transculturation" and the *ajiaco* metaphor. It is particularly significant that, in the latter, Ortiz acknowledged the presence of pure ingredients in the nation but did not grant ultimately national status or *cubanía* to them. As explained earlier, Ortiz attributed this condition solely to the mass or substance that was consolidating through the disintegration of raw elements in the cooking process. The implication of this image is that those raw ingredients that had not yet disintegrated were not as national as those that had. The metaphor also conveys the idea of a process of "stewing" through which the pure ingredients would eventually disintegrate and become part of the single amalgamated substance at the bottom. This image clashes with Ortiz's antiessentialist descriptions of culture and identity, which were outlined at the beginning of this chapter. The substance at the bottom of the pan is a consolidated entity composed of "tenacious essences." Furthermore, whereas the key notion of a postmodernist approach is that identities should be understood as ever-dynamic, ever-changing processes, in Ortiz's image *cubanía* appears as the culmination of a process of stewing rather than as the process itself.[11]

In his writings on afrocubanista poetry, Ortiz often expressed his belief in the gradual disappearance of Afro-Cuban forms. In "Los últimos versos mulatos," he argued that some "Afro-Cuban forms of verbal rhythmic art have disappeared," and he dismissed many of the ones that survived as having "merely a folkloric or historic value" (1973b, 158). For Ortiz, afrocubanista poetry symbolized the gradual disappearance of Afro-Cuban cultural forms like these. In "La religión en la poesía mulata," he used afrocubanista poetry as a sign of the desirable disintegration of African religions in Cuba. He explained that afrocubanista poets were not adherents of African religions and that this was the reason why their poetry did not deal with any African religious themes in depth. This was not to be lamented from a social point of view, he argued, because it meant that the religious emotions of blacks were gradually being replaced by more purified impulses that had a more stimulating human meaning (1991e, 169). He went on to argue that the absence of African religiosity in afrocubanista poetry mirrored the process of evolution that African religion had undergone at the social level. "The three phases of religious evolution," he claimed, "are reflected in Afro-Cuban poetry: the gods are born, the gods triumph, the gods perish: Manna, myth and science" (1991e, 173).

It is evident, thus, that Ortiz used afrocubanista poetry as a discursive instrument by which to uphold his belief in a mulatto Cuban identity that implied the disappearance of pure African cultural forms. The influence of this aspect of his conception of Cuban identity upon the afrocubanista poetic project is reflected in Nicolás Guillén's use of the concept of "transculturation" to invalidate the possibility that there could ever be such a thing as an Afro-Cuban poetry or art that was distinct from the national African/Spanish hybrid culture (Feijóo 1986, 285). For Guillén, the term "Afro-Cuban" erroneously suggested the presence of an African-derived ethnic identity among Cuba's blacks (Castellanos and Castellanos 1994, 13). As Duno Gottberg explains, Guillén reiterated his rejection of the term "Afro-Cuban" on the basis of this same argument in a 1951 article published in the Venezuelan newspaper *El Nacional* (2003a, 158). The second chapter of this study made clear, with reference to Salvador Bueno's dismissal of the term "Afro-Cuban," that this kind of approach undermines the perspectives of those blacks who maintained African identities in Cuba. Clearly, they were among those constitutive elements of the Cuban nation that, as Lezama Lima argued, would resist the imposition of the afrocubanista definition of Cuban identity as *mestizo*.[12]

To conclude, Ortiz's writings shed light on the afrocubanista ambivalence toward Afro-Cuban culture. While afrocubanistas celebrated a future Cuban national culture that was firmly based on some Afro-Cuban cultural principles, their evolutionist and elitist perspective stopped them from simply accepting the Afro-Cuban cultural forms of Cuban blacks as forms of ultimately national culture. Afrocubanista poetry was the perfect expression of this ambivalence. From the perspective of afrocubanistas, the poetry remained erudite literature and was superior to Afro-Cuban oral forms, even if it incorporated Afro-Cuban culture at the level of form. For them, it also pointed to a forthcoming mulatto culture and identity that implied the extinction of pure Afro-Cuban cultural forms and contestatory Afro-Cuban identities.

4   Folklore and Afrocubanista Poetry in Ramón Guirao's *Órbita de la poesía afrocubana, 1928–1937*

ESSAYIST AND POET Ramón Guirao (1908–49) was one of the leading participants of poetic afrocubanismo. The publication of his poem "Bailadora de rumba" in 1928 marked the beginning of the movement. After this date, Guirao wrote a substantial number of afrocubanista poems, most of which were published in his 1934 collection *Bongó: Poemas negros*. He also played a vital role as an anthologist and critic. His 1938 *Órbita de la poesía afrocubana, 1928–1937* is the only anthology that is dedicated exclusively to the poetry of afrocubanismo. Its introduction contains the longest and most sophisticated analysis of the movement of all the introductions to anthologies of Latin American "black" poetry ever published.[1] Because the anthology appeared at a time when afrocubanismo had just come to an end, this essay is also an invaluable retrospective analysis of the movement by one of its most important figures. In addition, *Órbita* includes the most thorough compilation of afrocubanista and Cuban black poetry ever published. It starts with a selection of eighteenth- and nineteenth-century texts belonging to Afro-Cuban and other Cuban popular traditions, then is followed by poems by the nineteenth-century black poet Juan Francisco Manzano and by representative works of twelve different afrocubanista poets. These are not only well-known authors, such as Nicolás Guillén, Emilio Ballagas, José Zacarías Tallet, and Alejo Carpentier, but also lesser-known ones, such as Rafael Esténger, José Rodríguez Méndez, and Teófilo Radillo, whose work may have otherwise remained unpublished. The combination of all the above characteristics makes Guirao's anthology one of his most important contributions to the study of the afrocubanista poetic movement.

This chapter examines Guirao's use of the concept of "folklore" in the anthology in order to illustrate the afrocubanista utilization of the idea.

87 Folklore and Poetry in Órbita de la poesía afrocubana

Particular attention is paid to the ways in which afrocubanistas elaborated upon the notion of Cuban folklore developed by the first generation of Cuban republican intellectuals.

In the introduction to his anthology, it becomes apparent that Guirao viewed afrocubanista poetry as a means of defining the nation's "original" or "authentic" spirit. This can be perceived in his comparison between afrocubanismo and indigenismo, which was cited in the first chapter of this book. As explained there, he compared the afrocubanista poetic movement to those movements in other Latin American nations that were trying to find their originary form of expression in the spirit and forms of pre-Hispanic cultures, in order to escape the influence of their European heritage. His ensuing description of afrocubanista poetry is also significant, for he argued that, to create a distinctive Cuban poetic accent, it was necessary to establish that afrocubanista poetry contained the most authentically national essence (1938, xxv). In order to reinforce the idea of afrocubanista poetry as authentically national, Guirao was able to draw upon a previous Cuban folklorist project that had already redefined Afro-Cuban and other popular Cuban cultural traditions as repositories of the nation's original spirit. Ortiz had become interested in Cuban folkloric traditions after visiting European museums of folklore. He wrote in a 1913 article entitled "Folklore cubano" that such museums were indispensable for those who enjoyed studying "the deepest folds of the soul of a people." As opposed to the attention paid to folklore in European countries such as Belgium and Germany, he complained that in Cuba nothing had been done, even when there was a great deal of folklore in the island. Because of this, he argued further that "although it would be difficult for us to set up an art museum that impressed foreign visitors, we could, with everyone's collaboration, form a rich museum of folklore that would help foreigners who come to Cuba understand us better. It would also help us to understand ourselves better, because it has to be said that we do not know ourselves very well" (1986b, 85). In 1923 Ortiz's enthusiasm for Cuban folklore led him to cofound and preside over the Sociedad del Folklore Cubano, among whose members were important Cuban intellectual figures such as Lydia Cabrera, Ramiro Guerra, Israel Castellanos, and Emilio Roig de Leuchsenring (Sociedad del Folklore Cubano 1924a, 82). The objectives of the Sociedad are described in the "Actas de la Sociedad del Folklore Cubano" (Minutes of the Society of Cuban Folklore), which were published in the first issue of the society's magazine, *Archivos del Folklore Cubano* (Archives of Cuban Folklore). The society was designed to compile, classify, and compare traditional popular objects, such as oral stories, proverbs, and legends, that had been preserved in the popular oral tradition, and this was intended as a project of national reconstruction (Sociedad del Folklore Cubano 1924a, 77–78). The society's intention to strengthen national identity through the study of popular culture is particularly in evidence in the description of *Archivos del Folklore Cubano* put forward in the article "Esta revista cubana" (This Cuban Journal), which was written by the editors of the magazine. According to them, *Archivos del Folklore Cubano* was designed to function as "a means of collaboration and a forum for the exchange of ideas between Cubans who like to savor the fruits of popular wisdom and peer into the most distinctive and traditional parts of the soul of our people" (Sociedad del Folklore Cubano 1924b, 5). This emphasis on patriotic sentiment is equally noticeable in "Cuestionario de literatura popular cubana" (Cuban Popular Literature Questionnaire). In this piece José María Chacón y Calvo established that "contributions to our folklore can come from anyone who feels our national life, its most traditional aspects, its most solemn forms, and its most modest, everyday manifestations: love for our national life, which amounts to a deep and generous understanding of our life. This is the only prerequisite for being a Cuban folklorist" (1924, 10).

One of the most important functions that this conception of popular culture played in the anthologist's discourse was to distance afrocubanista poetry from exogenous cultural influences. The poetry, he argued, was not an artificial insert. It stemmed from an authentically Cuban black folkloric tradition that had been maintained uninterrupted throughout the history of the nation and had started with the oral traditions of the "poeta gayo" or "poeta de puya (güire)" of the African cabildos in Cuba. This tradition had continued later, he added, in funeral liturgical chants, *comparsa* chants, *décimas,* rumba drumming, and guarachas, as well as in plays written in African-sounding speech. In particular, Guirao wanted to distance afrocubanista poetry from European primitivism. According to him, the work of artists involved in this movement, such as Apollinaire, Cendrars, Morand, Modigliani, and Picasso, did not constitute anything more than a frivolous appropriation of black culture. He argued that the European interest in the black was not paralleled at the social level by more equality between blacks and whites. The objective of European primitivism, he concluded, was essentially to "add one more string to the bow of the Occidental artist, in order to shed some sunlight on his own art, which is dramatically disconnected from any new blood impulses and basic impurities. If blacks were invited to share the bread, if they were allowed to sit at the table for a few instants, it was only so that they could leave something original on the starched, white tablecloth" (1938, xix, xvi). The existence of an autochthonous Cuban black folklore pointed to the fact that in Cuba, unlike in the nations where European negrismo had emerged, blacks were a part of the social and cultural history of the nation. In Guirao's view, this factor had resulted in a wider, more exact, and more profound introspection of the "black soul" and in the production of more consolidated artistic products:

> We have acquired the dark merchandise in other aesthetic markets and we have examined it at the customs office without noticing our own black reality. When we found out that the local offered a way into the universal, we tried to assess the poetic potential of the black man. The most accomplished products of the Afro-Antillean modality come from Cuba because here we have at our disposal the living human document, which is racially and economically a part of our historical destinies. . . . The black mode, thus, was not born in Cuba in the same way as it was born in Europe, where it did not have a tradition and it was distanced from the human document. This bilingual poetry that combines African languages and Spanish has historical perspective and an indefinable future, and joined to our Creole sensitivity it can become part of the great vernacular poetry of which we speak. (1938, xviii, xix)

The degree of importance Guirao attached to this "poesía vernácula," which he earlier described as a Cuban folkloric tradition, led him to include at the beginning of the anthology a selection of folkloric eighteenth- and nineteenth-century texts entitled "Antecedentes folklóricos." By categorizing these texts as "antecedents" and placing them before the corpus produced by the afrocubanista poetic movement, Guirao created the impression that they were the earlier part of the same national literary tradition as afrocubanista poems. Through this essentialist image of afrocubanista poetry as the continuation of Cuba's "formidable tradición folklórica," the anthologist intended to make afrocubanismo appear rooted in the island's cultural past, thus distancing it from its European precursors. Almost three decades later, Óscar Fernández de la Vega would employ the same argument to distance afrocubanista poetry from non-Cuban artistic and intellectual movements (1977, 132). This essentialist understanding of folklore as a tradition that linked the nation to its origins also characterized previous European and Latin American approaches to the concept (García Canclini 1995a, 196–97). A similar conception of national culture is present in many nationalist discourses, where it is often closely linked to notions of origins, continuity, and tradition. As

Ernest Gellner has argued, the "national identity" is often conceived of as primordial, as forming the natural "essence" of most things. According to him, although this essence appears to be latent, it is always possible to reactivate it. In this way it is awakened from its "long persistent and mysterious somnolence" (Gellner, as cited in Hall 1992, 294).

Despite this essentialist aspect of Guirao's *Órbita,* it is important to remember that, as Mullen points out, previous anthologies of Cuban poetry presented Cuban literature as constituted solely by the literary practices of the educated elites (1998, 141–81). Consequently, by including this selection of folkloric texts, the poet also managed to introduce genuine transcriptions of Afro-Cuban oral forms in an anthology of Cuban poetry for perhaps the first time in history. For example, the titles of the first two texts, "Cantos de cabildo" (Cabildo Chants) and "Canto congo de cabildo para tres tambores" (Congo Cabildo Chant for Three Drums), clearly suggest that they are transcriptions of the lyrics of songs from Afro-Cuban cabildos de nación. Other clues indicate that, more specifically, they belonged to a cabildo of the Congo ethnic group, of Bantu origins. This is stated in the title of the second transcription and confirmed by references to drums of Congolese origin in the first. The references to Congo drums are the lines "Tumba cajero" and "jabla mula." The *caja* and the *mula* are characteristic of the Congo dance and music practices known as *yuka, makuta,* and *maní* (León 1984, 71). The fact that the two first texts in "Antecedentes folklóricos" belong to the Congo is significant because the *poeta gallo* or *poeta de puya* to which Guirao attributed the origins of Cuba's "formidable tradición folklórica" is characteristic of this particular ethnic group (León 1984, 78, 80).

Guirao's use of the label "Cantos de comparsa" (Comparsa Chants) to classify the next five texts in "Antecedentes folklóricos" suggests that they too belonged to a black cultural tradition. The comparsas were marching bands through which enslaved or free blacks in Cuban slave society represented their cabildos de nación during the Día de Reyes celebrations on the sixth of January (Ortiz 1992).[2] The text entitled "Mamá Iné," which Guirao presents as an anonymous composition from 1868, is certainly recognizable as a transcription of the comparsa song "Mamá Inés," which was first written by plantation slaves in Santa Clara in 1868 (Moore 1997, 108).[3] By including texts such as these, Guirao captured the perspectives of oppressed black sectors of colonial Cuba, who used song and oral poetry as a means of expression and self-affirmation. The text "Cantos de cabildo" is particularly representative. It probably belongs to the nonritualistic category of Congo songs known as *managua* or *makagua*. The texts of this type of song tend to be incidental and improvised and are often satirical and boastful, or they describe incongruent and enigmatic situations (León 1984, 77).[4] The speaker in this text is trying to cut a tree or tree trunk (*palo* in Cuban Spanish) that is too hard for his axe. He describes this situation in terms of a battle against an opponent, personifying the tree by attributing to it human attitudes, such as being angry ("brabbo") and talking without knowing ("Tu jabla y no conose"). The speaker defies the tree ("bamo be quie pue ma"), and when it seems to tell him that it is a *jocuma*, he responds that he is the much harder variety of tree known as *quiebra hacha*.[5] Through this theme, evidently the black author was expressing his worth, strength, and capacity to triumph in the face of impossible odds or a powerful foe. Thus, in a society where blacks were exploited, utilized, and treated as inferior by the dominant white classes, this song would have had clear connotations of black resistance to white domination:

> Dondó jachero
> pa un palo.
> Palo ta duro,
> jacha no cotta.
> Palo ta brabbo.
> ¿Qué son ese?
> Si palo so jocuma,
> yo so quiebrajacha.
> Bamo be quie pue ma.
> Dondó jachero
> pa un palo.
> Gayo cambia bo.
> Tu jabla y no conose.[6]
>   (Guirao 1938, 3)

The lyrics from the original comparsa song "Mamá Iné" also carry the perspectives of nineteenth-century slaves. In the song the speaker is a slave who complains to his master about the fact that the overseer has stolen his horse (Guirao 1938, 10).

But not all the texts in "Antecedentes folklóricos" were taken from Afro-Cuban oral forms such as these. Some of the texts were written by whites adopting black personae. A representative example is "Diálogo," which is a conversation between two black characters: a *negro criollo* and a *negro africano*. In his book *Los negros esclavos*, Fernando Ortiz uses this text as an example of how certain white writers in nineteenth-century

Cuba had imitated the language of the African-born blacks, or *negros bozales,* in popular poetry (Ortiz 1988, 222–23). The last text in Guirao's "folkloric" assortment, "Los novios catedráticos" (The Engaged Learned Couple), is actually an extract from a *teatro bufo* play by white playwright Ignacio Benítez del Cristo that is based on the characteristic figure of the genre known as *negrito*.[7] This figure was part of a tradition of representations of blacks by white authors in Cuban *teatro bufo,* where whites with artificially darkened skin and wigs normally played black characters.

The fact that Guirao conceived of Cuban folklore as made up of cultural forms produced by both black and white Cubans reflects the afrocubanista belief in the idea that whites can write black literature, which was discussed in the previous chapter of this book. Guirao's acceptance of this notion is made evident in the introduction to his anthology when he described the movement as "una introspección más cabal, amplia y profunda del alma negra" (a more thorough, wider, and profound introspection of the black soul) (1938, xviii). Since most afrocubanista poets were actually white, the use of the word *introspección* betrays his assumption that whites were as capable of understanding and representing the black soul as blacks. On the one hand, Guirao's comment clearly dismisses the singularity of the black experience all too easily. This tendency has led Kutzinski to argue that his perspective "falters quite miserably when it comes to acknowledging the cultural differences of Cuba's 'people of color'" (1993, 161). On the other hand, it is equally important to consider that, like Fernando Ortiz, Guirao was elaborating upon an antiessentialist awareness of the fluid interactions between black and white cultural elements. This is apparent in the introduction when Guirao argued that, despite containing stylistic borrowings from the poetry of Federico García Lorca, afrocubanista poetry could form part of Cuba's black folkloric tradition, because blacks themselves had often incorporated Spanish cultural elements into their folklore. As an example, Guirao cited certain blacks who in the nineteenth century sang in an Andalusian style and were immortalized by the Cuban painter Landaluce. Guirao brought attention to an even more complex and dynamic flow of cultural elements between Spanish and Cuban culture by adding that now Federico García Lorca had carried out the opposite process of cultural transmission by writing his Afro-Cuban inspired poem "Son" (1938, xx). The African/Spanish heterogeneity of Guirao's "folkloric antecedents" reflects equally intense processes of cultural interaction between African and Spanish cultural elements. For instance, many of the texts contain a mixture of African and Spanish lexicon and use call-and-response style phrasing characteristic of African oral forms. "Cantos de comparsa ta Julia" is a representative example (1938, 6–7).

There is a clear tension between this antiessentialist emphasis on the heterogeneity of Cuban folklore, on the one hand, and Guirao's earlier outlined conception of popular culture as an authentic national essence. The anthologist's antiessentialist approach to black culture also clashes with his statement in the introduction that "el negro . . . es una raza desligada de su centro nutricio que no ha podido apagar la llama quemante de la selva, ni ha logrado sustraerse al decreto de su sangre" (blacks . . . are a race that has been detached from the source from which it feeds and has not been able to put out the burning flame of the jungle or escape the dictates of the blood) (1938, xxii–xiii). Biological determinist ideas were equally in evidence in an essay that Guirao had written four years earlier entitled "Poetas negros y mestizos de la época esclavista" (Black and Half-Cast Poets of the Slavery Period). He argued there that the autobiography of black nineteenth-century poet Juan Francisco Manzano betrayed the traits that were inherent to his race: "resignación, pasividad, un sentido fatalista de la vida y una fácil adaptación al medio, así como una capacidad enorme de dolor; cualidades que van acompañadas de una resistencia física sobrehumana y de una servidumbre que parece nacer de sus almas debilitadas, entorpecidas" (resignation, passivity, a fatalistic view of life and an ability to adapt easily to the environment, as well as a tremendous capacity to endure pain; qualities that are accompanied by a superhuman physical resistance and a servitude that seems to emerge from their numb, weakened souls) (as cited in Mullen 1998, 163). Mullen uses this description from 1934 to argue that the anthologist still felt uneasy about blackness when writing the 1938 introduction, which was a reworking of the earlier text. According to him, at this point Guirao was, like his mentor Fernando Ortiz, still trying to write his way out of "a complex racial dilemma, with varying degrees of success" (1998, 163). In this way Mullen efficiently highlights the tension between contradictory conceptions of race that was a part of afrocubanista discourse, as shown in the previous chapter with reference to the writings of Fernando Ortiz. Nevertheless, like other North American Afro-Hispanists, Mullen is exclusively preoccupied with denouncing the racist elements of afrocubanista discourse, to the detriment of identifying its more productive aspects. As noted, Guirao's earlier reference to "the dictate of the black's blood" does suggest a biological determinist perspective, but, as Mullen himself notes, in the 1938 introduction the anthologist had actually edited out many other statements that reflected problematic notions about race. It seems necessary to acknowledge, then, that this could also reflect a degree of evolution in Guirao's thought toward a less biologically oriented understanding of black culture. Indeed, the 1938 text did not include the description cited by Mullen. Without it, the introduction to the anthology itself does not contain conclusive evidence to suggest that Guirao still "held . . . to the notion that race as an essentialist category affected writing" (Mullen 1998, 163).

To some extent, Guirao's belief in the idea that Cuban black folklore could be produced by both black and white Cubans was probably the reason why he did not consider it necessary to specify clearly the black or white origins of each of the texts in "Antecedentes folklóricos." In contrast to the care taken by the Sociedad del Folklore Cubano in establishing the origins of folkloric elements, Guirao provided only titles, occasionally a date, and, in the case of the only two nonanonymous texts, the names of the authors.[8] These scant details are misleading as to the racial origins of some of the texts. For instance, the title of the text "Son" suggests that it is a transcription from the musical genre *son,* which, in its urban variant, was developed by blacks in poor Havana neighborhoods in the early twentieth century (Moore 1997, 89). However, a more recent commentator has made clear that "Son" is in fact a transcription of a guaracha from the last third of the nineteenth century (Feijóo 1987, 65). In sharp contrast to *son,* guaracha seems to have been closely associated with whites. For instance, it was characteristic of the nineteenth-century *casas de cuna,* which, according to Moore, were "centres of musical entertainment where white men went to socialize and/or sleep with women of color" (Moore 1997, 49; León 1984, 173).[9] From the mid-nineteenth century on, the guaracha musical genre became part of *teatro bufo* representations, another typically white cultural tradition (Orovio 1994, 120). As Moore explains, these representations tended to be written by white playwrights and performed by white authors in front of white audiences (1997, 45–46). *Teatro bufo* plays in the nineteenth century tended to be performed in well-known establishments whose admission prices were high enough to confine them to white middle-class audiences (Moore 1997, 44–45; Leal 1980, 89). However, Moore also points out that by the late 1910s there were cheaper productions in smaller theatres all over Havana (1997, 45).

Another text that exemplifies the way in which Guirao's scant descriptions can mislead the reader is "Décimas," which follows "Son." At first sight the text would seem to belong to a black genre as well, since an explanatory note under the title indicates that the *décima* was a "género popular de los 'Negros Curros'" (popular genre among the *curros* blacks). Also known as *curros del manglar*, these were blacks from Seville who lived in colonial Havana and had a distinctive way of speaking, walking and dressing (Ortiz 1986a, 3). However, the last *décima* was actually written by a nineteenth-century white *costumbrista* writer called José de Jesús de Ocío. This *décima* was entitled "El negro Potoco," and it was part of a work entitled *Algarabía poética,* which was published in Matanzas in 1876 (Ortiz 1986a, 70, 251). Fernando Ortiz wrote in *Los negros curros* in relation to this text and two others that these texts were not written by "negros curros" but by *costumbrista* authors who were trying to portray them at a time when they had already become extinct (1986a, 70).

By concealing the white origins of these texts, "Antecedentes folklóricos" reinforced certain aspects of Guirao's discourse. One of these was his endeavor to distance the afrocubanista poetic movement from European primitivism. As explained earlier, for the anthologist the living presence of blacks and their traditions of African origins in Cuba decisively distinguished the two movements. In this sense, revealing the white origins of some of these texts may have brought excessive attention to the fact that afrocubanista poetry stemmed not only from poetic forms by Cuban blacks, such as oral traditions in Afro-Cuban culture, but also from white literary forms. For example, it would be hard not to find similarities of style, form, and subject matter between the antecedent "Son" and Nicolás Guillén's "Mulata" and "Mi chiquita" (Guirao 1938, 14, 90–91). Samuel Feijóo compares Nicolás Guillén's "Mulata" to another nineteenth-century guaracha that used to be sung in the 1885 *teatro bufo* play *El demonio en la guaracha* (The Devil in the Guaracha) by José M. de Quintana (Feijóo 1986, 302fn70, Guirao 1938, 90). There are further similarities between Guillén's "Mulata" and another fragment from Benítez del Cristo's *Los novios catedráticos* quoted by Feijóo (1986, 291).

The lack of detailed explanations as to the original contexts of the texts has another notable effect. By glossing over the widely different cultural traditions of these folkloric antecedents, Guirao conveyed the notion of a homogeneous, unified body of national folklore, which concurs with the afrocubanista vision of a single national culture. As was the case in Fernando Ortiz's discourse discussed in the previous chapter, in Guirao's anthology the idea of cultural unity was linked to a desire for the disappearance of racial conflicts in Cuba. The anthologist's urge to downplay racial divisions is reflected at various points throughout the introduction. It is evident in his argument that afrocubanista poetry implied "a sincere rapprochement between blacks and whites, as well as desire to lessen divisions and to overcome obstacles that, mainly due to economic, rather than racial, factors, had until now stood in the way of our mutual sympathy and brotherhood" (1938, xix). This comment played down the racial basis of discriminative practices and social conflicts in 1930s Cuban society. In fact, throughout the whole introduction the anthologist avoided addressing the issue of white-on-black discrimination in Cuba at the time. There was not even a mention of what is generally referred to as the "race war" of 1912, which, as explained in the first chapter of this book, culminated with the massacre by the Cuban armed forces of thousands of blacks who were demanding greater political representation. Such an omission provides a stark contrast to Guirao's detailed descriptions of the Spanish subjugation of blacks in Cuban slave society. This is a subject to which he dedicated more than a third of the introduction. In this way, the blame for the oppression of blacks was shifted onto the old colonizers, thus uniting black and white Cubans against another foreign oppressor.

"Décimas" provides an example of the way in which Guirao's decontextualized presentation of folkloric texts in "Antecedentes folklóricos" also contributes to downplaying racial conflicts. Commenting on this text, Ortiz pointed out in *Los negros Esclavos* that the imitation of black speech in this type of popular literature was intended to make fun of black people (1988, 222–23). Had Guirao explained this aspect of the text's original context he would have highlighted the presence in the nation's cultural history of a tradition of derisive white representations of blacks. The poem "Son" is also illustrative. As explained earlier, this text belonged to the musical genre known as guaracha. The following description by Robin Dale Moore illustrates how guaracha lyrics tended to reflect whites' negative perceptions of blacks: "In the *guaracha* and related genres, the mulata appears above all as the object of sexual desire, the epitome of wanton carnal pleasure. She is viewed as the source of familial discord, a 'danger' to married men, who pursues physical pleasure to the point of self-destructiveness. The *guaracha* transforms the socially oppressed and marginal status of most black and mulatto women at the turn of the century, suggesting that they were only interested in sex" (1997, 49–50). Seen as part of this Cuban tradition of white representations of black women, the racist connotations of the first five lines of "Son" become apparent:

97 Folklore and Poetry in Órbita de la poesía afrocubana

Mulatica colorá
aprende d'esa negrita
que se planchó la pasita,
se cotó la melenita
y tiene la bemba rosá.
    (Guirao 1938, 14)

Little red mulatto girl
Learn from that little black girl
Who straightened her hair,
And cut her mane
And has rosy lips.

These verses are part of a deeply entrenched Cuban tradition of deriding blacks' attempts at whitening. In her book *Sugar's Secrets: Race and the Erotics of Cuban Nationalism,* Vera Kutzinski provides other relevant examples of such representations. She reproduces a nineteenth-century lithograph that advertises a "whitening" liquid, showing a black man before and after applying it. The caption that accompanies the lithograph is "agua florida para blanquear la piel" (flower water for whitening the skin) (1993, 59).[10] Evidently, the comic effect of the lithograph relied on the author's and viewer's understanding that such whitening attempts were completely futile. The same ironic distance from the black protagonist is noticeable in "Son." In the last two lines the speaker indicates that the *negrita*'s attempts to whiten herself have made her "la reina d'el solá." In other words, all she has achieved despite her efforts is to become the "queen" of a lower-class urban slum. To white listeners, the pettiness of this accomplishment, along with the black speaker's admiration of it, would have seemed laughable. An awareness of the origins of "Son," then, shows how Cuban whites have often made fun of the social predicament of blacks, by which inalterable physiognomical markers determined their subordinate status.[11]

The text entitled "Los novios catedráticos" is a similar case. If Guirao had situated it within the tradition of Cuban *teatro bufo,* the reader would have been able to see that it reflects conflicts between nineteenth-century white Creoles and blacks. The following description by Rine Leal outlines the problematic aspects of the representation of the *negrito* by white authors in Cuban *teatro bufo:*

> If Afro-Cuban forms of expression "represent" the black through black eyes, performing in their own language, for black audiences, and offering a theatrical

image of their culture and their identity, then white authors achieve the exact opposite with the figure of the *negrito,* that is, the black character played by white actors, for a white public, acting in Spanish or in *bozal* (the parodied language), and of course reflecting the view point of the white slave owners. This is how the *negrito* deeply penetrates our history and covers up the black's own version in order to use it as a source of derision and ideological mockery. (1980, 30)[12]

This description suggests that in the text's original context the black characters of "Los novios catedráticos" would have served as an object of mockery for nineteenth-century white audiences. The *negrito catedrático* in particular was a semieducated black character who tried to copy white social and cultural customs in order to improve his status. Typically, he always confused many of the codes and conventions he was pretentiously trying to imitate.[13] Thus, again, the humor derived from blacks' hopeless attempts to "improve themselves." Guirao's extract from Ignacio Benítez del Cristo's play is a declaration of love by a *negrito* to the black woman he loves. The speaker tries to emulate the rhetorical conventions of erudite love poetry but in the language of semieducated black slaves, which is reflected in the incorrect spelling and grammar. The fact that the *negrito* combines vulgar expressions such as *mondongo* ("tripe") and *garrafón* ("demi-john") with romantic images typical of this kind of poetry would have also been a source of hilarity for white nineteenth-century audiences. The *negrito* himself inadvertently brings attention to his own pretentiousness at the end of the extract, where he seems to be telling his loved one that he has described what he feels "rhetorically" (Guirao 1938, 24–25).

Equally derogatory depictions of blacks appear in the text entitled "Diálogo," where the characters also mispronounce Spanish words. Even funnier must have been the Creole black's illusions of grandeur at having won the lottery, perhaps not as much as his blatant stupidity, evident in that he fails to realize that he cannot buy the other character a beer until he cashes his prize (Guirao 1938, 17–18). Stupidity and greed were among the many negative characteristics of the black characters of *teatro bufo* (Moore 1997, 45). Such associations were often intended to play down the threat of a Haiti-style black uprising (Leal 1980, 45). This may have also been the purpose of "Diálogo." The Creole black's stupidity would have certainly contradicted the notion that educated Creole blacks were potential black leaders, which was a widespread impression in nineteenth-century Cuba. This is evident in the following extract from an 1843 declaration by the authorities of the island's Eastern Department: "There is not much to fear from *bozal* blacks because of their total stupidity, but Creole blacks, who can often read and write and many are artists and craftsmen and many of them have considerable capital, can mix with the blacks from Saint Domingue and Jamaica and once they have amalgamated with the huge mass of *bozales* (who they will be able to lead at will), they will be ready to strike with fatal and perhaps irreparable consequences" (as quoted in Deschamps Chapeaux 1971, 44). This impression was also behind the 1844 repression of the Escalera conspiracy (Paquette 1988).

The origins of the last *décima* in "Décimas" also bring attention to a racist dominant-white discourse on blacks. The text was originally published in a nineteenth-century Cuban publication called *El Artista* (The Artist). The editor of this magazine specified that the *décimas* included were an essential concomitant to the *negro curro*. He explained that this was a Cuban black character who "la civilización progresiva del país ha borrado ya casi por completo" (has been almost completely obliterated by the progressive civilization of the country) (Ortiz 1986a, 304n1). Civilization and progress appear in his commentary as inherently irreconcilable with the *negros curros*. Thus, the editor obviously assumed that non-Western cultures and peoples would disappear as the colony progressed toward a Western model of social order. His attitude prefigured Fernando Ortiz's later conception of Afro-Cuban culture as incompatible with progress and civilization in *Los negros brujos* (1973a, 229).

It is interesting to note that Guirao's presentation of folkloric texts without detailed explanations of their original contexts mirrors a similar practice in previous approaches to folklore elsewhere. According to García Canclini, nineteenth-century European folklorists relied on a decontextualized approach to popular cultural forms that did not account for their socioeconomic functions (1995a, 195–96). He also explains that in Mexico the majority of studies of traditional music, crafts, and poetry by folklorists "enumerate and exalt popular products, without contextualizing them within the present logic of social relations." This is even more visible in museums of folklore and popular culture, which "exhibit pots and knitted fabrics without any reference to the daily practices for which they were devised" (1995a, 198). Rowe and Schelling find a similar flaw in a permanent exhibition of Latin American folklore in São Paulo. They argue that "although it is probably the best such exhibition in the world in terms of the quality of the objects displayed, it does very little to indicate the contexts of their production and use." As in Guirao's anthology, in appropriations of the idea of "folklore" in these other Latin American contexts, presenting popular culture in this way upheld nationalist concepts of national homogeneity by giving an impression of similarity between different objects (Rowe and Schelling 1991, 6).

Another feature of "Antecedentes folklóricos" worthy of analysis is the fact that it includes only eighteenth- and nineteenth-century texts, even when many of the cultural traditions from which these were taken were still alive at the time of Guirao's writing. The omission of contemporaneous oral forms of the Afro-Cuban sectors hides the connections between these and afrocubanista poetry. This contradicts Guirao's own emphasis in his introduction on the importance of the poetry's articulations to "el documento humano vivo" and undermines the contribution of these sectors to afrocubanismo (1938, xviii). This aspect of Guirao's discourse suggests a process of appropriation of Afro-Cuban culture similar to the one described by Brackette Williams in her definition of "transformist hegemony." She uses this concept, originally developed by Antonio Gramsci, to refer to the process in nationalist discourse by which, in creating the impression of a homogeneous cultural identity, elements from different human groups are assimilated through appropriations that devalue them or deny the source of their contribution (1991, 30). Peter Wade considers that Williams's approach is useful for the study of race and ethnicity in the nation-state because it directs attention toward processes of resignification by which particular cultural elements become incorporated or accommodated into nationalist versions of the national culture as long as their significance is defined within the central value complex of the dominant groups (1997, 87). As the explanations above illustrate, similar processes of re-signification are clearly at work in Guirao's anthology.

Guirao's exclusion of twentieth-century folkloric texts also plays a vital role in conveying an evolutionist image of Afro-Cuban culture similar in many respects to the one found in Ortiz's discourse, which was brought to light in the previous chapter. By not including the said transcriptions, Guirao promoted the impression that Afro-Cuban oral forms had become extinct. This concurs with Fernando Ortiz's descriptions of these forms as having disappeared, or as having solely a historical or "folkloric" value (1973b, 158). Furthermore, by placing folkloric oral forms from past centuries before contemporary afrocubanista poems, the anthology accommodates the notion that these "folkloric antecedents" have been replaced by or have "evolved" into afrocubanista poetry. This aspect of Guirao's use of "folklore" brings to mind the approach of the Sociedad del Folklore Cubano, which aimed to eradicate some Afro-Cuban traditions. For example, in one of the issues of *Archivos del Folklore Cubano,* Emilio Roig de Leuchsenring's tone throughout his article "Los velorios" (1924) suggests that he favored the total elimination of the practice he was writing about. This aspect of the Sociedad was directly specified in the "Actas de la 'Sociedad del Folklore Cubano,'" where one of its stated objectives was to carry out "a descriptive analysis that aims to serve as a kind of social therapy for certain morbid practices, like acts of sorcery and *ñañiguismo,* through which the lowest levels of popular life so eloquently express themselves" (Sociedad del Folklore Cubano 1924a, 78). It is worth noting that the Sociedad was based on elitist and condescending attitudes toward the popular sectors. For example, Chacón y Calvo's article "Cuestionario de literatura popular cubana" betrays a view of the populace as roguish and mentally slow (1924, 10).

The absence of transcriptions of lyrics from contemporaneous forms of Afro-Cuban culture may have also stemmed from Guirao's urge to maintain an impression of national homogeneity. The exclusion of such texts plays down the cultural diversity of the nation by hiding the fact that there were various types of Afro-Cuban poetry. By applying this category exclusively to afrocubanista poems, Guirao reinforced the notion that the literature of his movement was the only contemporaneous type of "Afro-Cuban poetry." In the introduction to the anthology, he referred to the afrocubanista poetic movement as "el cultivo afanoso durante el término de diez años de la poesía afrocubana" (the industrious cultivation of Afro-Cuban poetry over ten years). He added further on that Manzano's poetry, placed immediately before all the afrocubanista poems but after "Antecedentes folklóricos," "aparece al frente de esta antología de la poesía afrocubana" (appears at the beginning of this anthology of Afro-Cuban poetry) (1938, xi, xxiv). Even the title of the anthology reflects this understanding of the term by featuring the dates that mark the beginning and end of the movement.

It should be added that if Guirao had included transcriptions from contemporaneous Afro-Cuban musical traditions in his anthology, he might have brought attention to Afro-Cuban ideas of nationhood or identity that undermined the idea of national homogeneity. Indeed, through the lyrics of Afro-Cuban musical forms such as *son* many Cuban blacks of the 1930s asserted their African or black identities (Moore 1997, 94–95).

To conclude, Guirao's *Órbita de la poesía afrocubana, 1928–1937* illustrates that the concept of "folklore" was used in the afrocubanista poetic project with two main related objectives. On the one hand, it provided the means to redefine Afro-Cuban culture as part of a homogeneous black national tradition that was an intrinsic part of the nation's history and past. This made it possible to present afrocubanista poetry as emerging from an autochthonous and "authentic" Cuban culture, thus distancing it from European primitivism. On the other hand, by presenting Afro-Cuban folkloric oral forms as extinct, modern Afro-Cuban literature could be made to appear as constituted solely by afrocubanista poetry, an image that satisfied the elitist and evolutionist elements of afrocubanista discourse and hid the racial and cultural differences dividing the Cuban nation. At the same time, as has also been shown, through the concept of "folklore" Guirao brought attention to the African/Spanish heterogeneity of Cuban popular culture and introduced Afro-Cuban oral forms into the dominant literary canon.

5   The Black Rumbera

ONE OF THE themes in afrocubanista poetry that evokes the afrocubanista desire for racial fusion is that of the sexually desirable black female dancer. Undoubtedly, in conveying their wish for sexual union with the black rumberas represented in their poems, white afrocubanistas found another vehicle for expressing their vision of Cuban miscegenation as a symbol of black and white harmony in Cuba. This is part of the process by which, as Adriana Méndez Rodenas argues, "afrocubanista poetry incorporates African dance within the dynamics of poetry as a trope that projects the racial and cultural ideal of *mestizaje* and, consequently, also symbolizes Caribbean unity" (2002, 213).[1]

As is the case with Ortiz's and Guirao's discourses, it is important to remember that the afrocubanista representation of sexually desirable black female dancers carries with it a desire to gloss over black and white conflicts in Cuba. Afro-Hispanists have made a valuable contribution to the study of afrocubanismo by bringing attention to the problematic white sexist notions behind the poetry, which undermine the impression of a felicitous union between the white male and the black female. For example, Richard L. Jackson notes that afrocubanistas' obsession with the "uninhibited rump swaying and rhythmic hip-swinging of the black 'hembras' (females)" often conveys a "one-dimensional image of the black as an unintellectual sexual animal" (1976, 43). Ann Venture Young also attacks afrocubanistas' obsession with the black woman's anatomy, a preoccupation she suggests could be due to their refusal or inability to view her in terms "which accord her full human status." She sees "an almost total disregard for an essence which might transcend the color of the black woman's skin and the rotundity of her buttocks" (1977, 139). Claudette RoseGreen-Williams has interpreted the obsession with these erotic body signs as reflecting a white male dehumanization and reductive sexualization of the black woman (1993, 17).[2]

Nevertheless, these criticisms also convey the problematic idea discussed in the second chapter of this book: that afrocubanista poetry is disconnected from the reality of 1920s and 1930s Cuban blacks. In the case of the representation of the black female dancer, the emphasis in the poems on the physiognomy of black women is perceived as a result of their authors' ideology, rather than as a part of Afro-Cuban cultural reality. This is particularly evident in the comment by RoseGreen-Williams that these representations are "the creation of white male fantasy" (1993, 17).[3] It is also clear in Vera Kutzinski's analysis of the representation of mulatto women in the poetry as a product of a "masculinist imagination." In line with the widespread opposition in North American Afro-Hispanism to "false" and "derogatory" images of blacks in afrocubanista poetry, Kutzinski complains about the "stereotypical" representations of black women in the poetry (1993, 164, 180).

In this chapter I assess these critical approaches through an analysis of the portrayal of the black *rumbera,* or rumba dancer, in afrocubanista poetry. The first section focuses on the ideological motivations behind the emphasis on her sexuality and on its negative connotations. In the second section I analyze these afrocubanista representations in relation to Afro-Cuban choreographic features and their original Yoruba connotations. At the end of the chapter, I evaluate some general tendencies in feminist criticism of afrocubanista poetry.

On a basic level, afrocubanista representations of the black female reflect the interest of the 1920s and 1930s Cuban avant-garde in erotic representations of women. This interest characterized Cuban painting at this time, as illustrated by three female nudes featured in the 1927 Exhibition of New Art (*Revista de Avance* 1927, 112–13). The numerous images of nude women that appear throughout issues of the 1920s Cuban magazine *Revista de Avance* are illustrative as well. For example, in the editorial section of the 30 March 1927 issue, there is a drawing of a naked woman by Adía M. Yunkers that is completely unrelated to the content of the editorial text. In another issue, a nude drawing by Cuban painter Antonio Gattorno appears in the middle of an article about music by Francisco Ichaso (1927, 162). In point of fact, the appearance in *Revista de Avance* of sexually explicit poems by poets who would later take part in the afrocubanista poetic movement shows that their interest in erotic subject matter preceded their interest in Afro-Cuban culture.[4] Furthermore, as evident in the following lines from a 1927 poem by José Z.

Tallet, by this time these poets had already begun to represent black women as sexually desirable:

> ¡Oh, el deseo supremo!
> ¿Hay algo comparable, Marinello
> a la paralizante carcomilla
> que naciendo en el vientre
> poco a poco se extiende
> por todos nuestros miembros,
> ante los inefables, calipigios meneos
> de la ebúrnea o ebónica ninfa . . . ?[5]
>
> (Tallet 1927, 42)

> Oh, supreme desire!
> Marinello, is there anything that compares
> to the paralyzing, gnawing feeling
> that starts in the stomach
> and slowly spreads
> throughout our whole body
> when we witness the indescribable, callipygian swinging
> of the ivory or ebony nymph . . . ?

Fernando Ortiz's writings on the representation of black women in afrocubanista poetry effectively synthesize the reasons behind this obsession with black female nudity. It is interesting to note that, in sharp contrast to the criticisms outlined in the introduction to this chapter, Ortiz did not view this as a superficial fad or as the poets' intention to titillate with cheap sexual thrills. Instead, he saw it as an accurate depiction of the anatomy of black women and of the "vivo erotismo de la ondulante carnalidad de sus traseras pulpas" (vivid eroticism of the undulating flesh of her pulpous behind). The protuberance of this region was a somatic trait of the African race, he argued. In support of the representational accuracy of afrocubanista allusions to the black female's hips and buttocks, Ortiz made reference to the *culona*, a nineteenth-century *diablito* figure with an exaggeratedly large backside.[6] In addition, he referred to the hip swinging that characterized black Caribbean music (1973b, 162).[7]

Furthermore, Ortiz thought that, by portraying black female sexuality, afrocubanista poetry had managed to represent a type of active and dynamic sexuality that contrasted with the passivity of the white disembodied female prototype, as seen, for example, in traditional European Romantic poetry: "It is not a contemplative, suggestive, subtle, or spiritualist eroticism, but rather active, impetuous, dynamic, and copulative. It does not aim to be ethereal or spiritual; it is anchored in that reality of moving flesh. It reflects not only intimate states of mind but also external curves without avoiding carnality. It is not a swoon created by an ideal but by an orgasm. It is not the melodic expression of a thought, but, rather, rhythmic mimicry for the senses" (1973b, 161). The poetry had achieved in this way a more frank representation of sexuality, since the female body parts exalted in white eroticism were not the most important in human copulation:

> Decíamos que las emociones poéticas levantadas por la hembra mulata, más que a sus ojos, a sus senos y a su talle, se refieren a sus caderas, y, sobre todo, a sus nalgas. . . . Rara vez estos poetas miran las suaves curvas femeninas de los miembros radiales, ni aun las del rostro, creadas para articular las expresiones intelectuales con los infinitos acentos de la mímica fisonómica. Ni los pechos mujeriles, cuyas turgencias carecen de la movilidad funcional de las curvas copulativas; aquéllos son curvas para el santo amor materno de la humanidad ya fecundada, sin articulaciones sinérgicas para el rito de la cópula, ni cripta de la especie para el recóndito y divinal misterio de la creación de la vida. (1973c, 189)

> We were saying that the poetic emotions aroused by the mulatto female refer to her hips and, especially, to her buttocks, more than to her eyes, her bosom, or her waist. . . . Rarely do these poets look at the soft feminine curves of the radial members, not even those of the face, which have been created to articulate intellectual expressions with the infinite accents of physiognomical mimicry. They do not even look at the female breasts, whose turgidities lack the functional mobility of the copulative curves. Those [the breasts] are curves for the sacred motherly love of the already fertilized humanity, without synergic joints for the rite of copulation, and without the crypt of the species for the recondite and divine mystery of the creation of life.

Consequently, the unashamed sexual explicitness of afrocubanista discourse was for Ortiz a successful rejection of puritanical conventions that had in the past impeded a realistic representation of sexuality. It represented liberated sensuality and a break away from European codes of morality:

> The carnal metaphor of the brown female, anatomically distinct from the white woman, is a modern thing, of this century. In the past, poetry was not so devoid of conventions. The style of the poet, like the lives of freed blacks, was constrained by a kind of "patronage," of repression, which was not imposed

by the law but, rather, by a tradition that did not allow people to express things as they perceived them. Doing so seemed vulgar and harmful to the white Cuban and slightly delicate and even offensive to the newly freed black. (1973b, 163–64)

Ortiz's explanations reflect the fact that realistic or explicit female nudity was used by Cuban artists and intellectuals at the time as a means of defying contemporary bourgeois taste (López Segrera 1989, 191). The paintings by Carlos Enríquez in the earlier-mentioned Exhibition of New Art are a good example of this generation's defiance of bourgeois codes of morality. When members of the Asociación de Pintores y Escultores, which was hosting the exhibition, complained about the paintings' "exaggerated realism," the paintings were taken down for being too explicit. In their coverage of the exhibition, the editors of *Revista de Avance* explained that after a while the incident was resolved and the two paintings were exhibited again. They concluded that "hoy siguen todavía allá, implacablemente retadoras, pese a su 'realismo exagerado'" (today they are still there despite their "exaggerated realism"). Their mockery of this oxymoron, their defiant conclusion, and the incident itself illustrate what has been described as these intellectuals' rebellion against "the euphemistic bent of the bourgeois discourse on sexuality" (RoseGreen-Williams 1993, 17).[8] Undoubtedly, it is this intent that underlies many afrocubanistas' sexually explicit descriptions of black female dancers. Judging by the controversy that, according to Kutzinski, the overtly sexual language of Tallet's "La rumba" created, it is also clear that the poetry often succeeded in this respect (1993, 152).

At the same time, Ortiz's approach to afrocubanista representations of black women brings to light some of their problematic implications. Particularly significant is his reference to the "natural protuberance" of the black woman's buttocks. It is a clear reminder of racist European nineteenth-century discourse in which this physical feature was seen as one of the black woman's sexual anomalies. Sander L. Gilman's analysis of nineteenth-century representations of black female sexuality illustrates the European obsession with black women's buttocks with reference to the case of Sarah Bartmann, the "Hottentot Venus." Sarah, who came from the African Hottentots, was exhibited around Europe in the second decade of the nineteenth century. One of the main purposes of these exhibitions was to display a physical "anomaly" that fascinated European audiences: *steatopygia,* or unusually large buttocks. After her death at the age of twenty-five in 1815, Sarah Bartmann's sexual parts were preserved and exhibited in such a way as to allow the viewer to see the unusual nature of her labia. This hypertrophy, common among the Hottentots and other African ethnic groups, was caused by the manipulation of the genitalia for aesthetic purposes. In fact, as Gilman explains, the genitalia and buttocks became the central image for the black female throughout the nineteenth century. Discourses on these parts included conceptions of female sexuality (both black and white) as defined by the female genitalia, as anomalous (in particular as more anal than the male's), and as pathological. In addition, it featured ideas about black female sexuality as grotesque and comic, and about blacks as being physically different and, therefore, part of a separate, lower species. Furthermore, these parts came to represent the primitive sexual appetite and behavior of blacks as well as the aesthetic inferiority of their physical features (Gilman 1985, 213–19).

In view of these associations and Ortiz's comment about "natural protuberance," there is little reason to doubt that the afrocubanista emphasis on black women's buttocks was to some extent driven by similar notions. As Claudette M. Williams explains, "Their deromanticization of the *rumba* dancer's body showed remarkable continuity with the voyeurism in Victorian England's response to Sarah Bartmann" (2000, 53). Illustrative in this respect are the following lines from Ballagas's "Elegía de María Belén Chacón": "Ya no veré mis instintos / en los espejos redondos y alegres de tus dos nalgas" (I will no longer see my instincts reflected / in the round and merry mirrors of your buttocks) (Guirao 1938, 108). It is evident here that what the poet misses the most about the protagonist is that she brought out his sexual instincts. Thus, as in the nineteenth-century European perception of black female sexuality, María Belén Chacón's buttocks symbolized a more natural or animal sexuality. This is why they became a perfect instrument for bringing out the poet's "animal" desires.

Furthermore, Ortiz's emphasis on the "active and dynamic" sexuality of black women carried assumptions about blacks being more physical than whites, a notion that throughout history has been used to justify slavery,[9] as may be seen in Barbara Bush's analysis of representations of slave women in the intellectual discourse of nineteenth-century West Indies. Bush explains that, in the writings of plantocratic writers, black women appeared as a physically strong subspecies of the female sex, and this notion allowed for their economic exploitation (1990, 15). It is significant in this respect that various eighteenth- and nineteenth-century French writers repeatedly referred to the physical strength of African blacks in their travels through the African continent (Ortiz 1988, 69–74). Closely linked to the view of blacks as more physical than whites is the assumption that the former had an inferior intellect and, consequently, needed to be disciplined. The notion that the savage man's absence of discipline required repression and disciplinary restraint goes back to the late Middle Ages (Goldberg 1993, 23–24). In Cuba, merchant-planter Wencesleo de Villaurrutia subscribed to this idea as well. He argued in 1840 that the black's aversion to labor made him incapable of civilization, adding that "it is conferring on him a benefit to accustom him to labor, because it gives him and lets him hope for enjoyments, which he never knew, and never could know, in the state of barbarism in which he was vegetating in his own country" (as quoted in Paquette 1988, 98).

Admittedly, one could interpret the dynamism of black female dancers represented in afrocubanista poetry as resistance against oppression. For example, Julio Finn sees the representation of active black women in *Négritude* poetry as underscoring the values upon which racist societies are built. He argues that, because the society of the white poet is based on the exploitation of black men, images of active black women would threaten its stability. This is why in European poetry "the black woman tends to remain static—a statue which the poet dresses in his ideas and fantasies" (1988, 177–78). Nevertheless, if this was the idea behind afrocubanista representations, it is difficult not to find an inherent contradiction in the poets' tendency to present the sexuality of black Cuban women solely through the emotions that they experience at the sight of her dancing. The poem entitled "Caridá" by Marcelino Arozarena provides a suitable example. In this poem the speaker wonders why Caridad is not at the party, and he recalls the sexual appeal of her "grupa mordisqueante" (her biting rump), which is "tentadora del amor" (which tempts his love) (1983, 27–28). Thus, here the poet interprets the woman's dancing as sexually exciting, but it is not made clear whether she intends it as such or not. Thus, she may be physically active, but the only active aspect of her sexuality is her "grupa mordisqueante," a personification that is a projection of the poet's sexual excitement. She is not a subject but an object of the male gaze. Consequently, she remains reduced to an object of pleasure and desire and has no more agency than the white women represented in European poetry. A similar type of male projection is found in Arozarena's poem "Mulata rumbera." In this poem the poet transfers his sexual guilt onto the dancer's body movements when he argues that these provoke in him a feeling of remorse for the sins of her tasty flesh (1983, 123).

As RoseGreen-Williams points out, images such as these in afrocubanista poetry derive from long-standing universal myths created by men. She refers in particular to the Judeo-Christian tradition that has further entrenched the myth equating woman, sex, and sin, incorporating it into its ethical code (RoseGreen-Williams 1993, 18; Williams 2000, 46). Another example where these associations are evident is the representation of the mulatto woman in nineteenth-century French literature, where she appears as a demonic creature potentially responsible for the perdition of the innocent white male (Lamore 1987, 302–5). Similar perceptions underlie Leonardo's descriptions of his mulatto lover Cecilia in the following extract from *Cecilia Valdés,* a nineteenth-century novel by the Cuban Cirilo Villaverde: "She always drives me mad. . . . She is all passion and fire, she is a little devil in the shape of a woman, the Venus of the mulatto women. . . . Who can approach her without getting burnt? What man can hear her saying 'I love you,' without his brain becoming inebriated as if he were drinking wine?" (as quoted in Lamore 1987, 305).

Another problematic aspect of Ortiz's explanations regarding the inadequacy of facial features and breasts in erotic expression is a reductionist perception of female sexuality as predominantly centered on the act of copulation, which ties in with a long history of white images of the primitive *Other* as a childlike and sensual creature. This history can be traced back to medieval thought, where the image of the savage already represented sexual license as well as lack of civility and civilization (Goldberg 1993, 23). Sander L. Gilman mentions the twelfth-century Jewish traveler Benjamín de Tudela as an example. De Tudela wrote that "at Seba on the river Pishon . . . is a people . . . who, like animals, . . . go about naked and . . . cohabit with their sisters and anyone they can find. . . . And these are the black slaves, the sons of Ham" (Gilman 1985, 209). According to Bush, in the fifteenth and sixteenth centuries most Europeans who traveled to Africa remarked upon the nakedness of the native inhabitants. They were particularly shocked, offended, and fascinated at the same time by the nakedness of black women, which contrasted strongly with the modesty and propriety of respectable European women. The nakedness of Africans soon became a sign of their wantonness and lasciviousness (Bush 1990, 14). Gilman adds that, by the eighteenth century, the sexuality of the black male and female had come to symbolize deviant sexuality in general (1985, 209). Not surprisingly, according to Ortiz, nineteenth-century French ethnologists portrayed African blacks as "naturally indolent, overwhelmingly sensual, lacking foresight, exceedingly superstitious, of low intelligence and enemies of abstract ideas" (1988,

70). As Stolcke shows in her study of racism and sexuality in colonial Cuba, these notions were very much a part of white male perceptions of black female sexuality in Cuban slave society, where the belief in the immorality of the black woman was widespread (1992, 181–87). Consequently, Ortiz's explanations regarding the inadequacy of facial features and breasts in erotic expression reinforce widespread notions of black women as immoral and sexually promiscuous, notions that were long established in Cuba.

In addition, his explanations bring up a history of the black female being reduced to the sexual functions she could perform for white men. In Cuban slave society, black women were forced to prostitute themselves in order to make the money to buy their freedom. Furthermore, on the whole, in the nineteenth century it was they who often satisfied the sexual needs of the young white male. They were often motivated by the hope of marrying someone white, which in turn might enable them to have whiter offspring. Partly as a result of this, the idea of black women as immorally promiscuous was widespread among nineteenth-century Cuban whites, a fact that is reflected in the proverb "no hay tamarindo dulce ni mulata señorita" (there are no sweet tamarinds, just like there are no virgin mulatto women) (Stolcke 1992, 181, 186).[10] The notion that the 1920s and 1930s Cuban avant-garde was using black women in a similar way is supported by the fact that in the Exhibition of New Art there was also a painting of a naked black woman that, unlike Enríquez's, did not cause any upheaval. This suggests that RoseGreen-Williams may be right in pointing out that afrocubanista poets chose black women as vehicles of their sexual fantasies because such images, as opposed to those involving white women, were socially and politically nonthreatening (RoseGreen-Williams 1993, 17; Williams 2000, 58).

The Black Rumbera

Despite the problematic aspects of Ortiz's descriptions of afrocubanista poetry, his references to the *culona* bring up an issue that the critics cited at the beginning of this chapter have overlooked. The emphasis on the hips and buttocks of the black woman in afrocubanista poems occurs nearly always in the context of rumba. This Afro-Cuban dance offered afrocubanista poets a powerful image that would shake the puritanical discourse on sexuality. As Ortiz explains, the rumba had a very bad reputation. It was a "dance of ill repute that was only performed in the countryside or with great secrecy and in secluded premises in the city" (as cited in Habibe 1985, 74–75). While visiting Cuba in 1930, Langston

Hughes referred to rumba as "not a respectable dance among persons of good breeding" (as cited in Jacques 1998, 249). Fredrick Habibe explains that the erotic sensuality of this dance caused a scandal among Cuba's "civilized" middle classes. José Z. Tallet himself told Habibe in 1981 that when he recited his poem "La rumba" to a group of elderly women in the Liceo Lawn Tennis Club, they exclaimed, "How dare you!" Their reaction is not surprising considering that, as G. R. Coulthard has pointed out, in this poem the female dancer is presented solely through a description of her physical attributes (1962, 31–32). Nevertheless, this was not merely the product of Tallet's "perverted imagination," since in the actual dance itself prominence is given to the body parts highlighted in the poem. In fact, "La rumba" is a highly realistic rendition of the rumba dance episode known as *vacunao*. Usually, the *vacunao* takes place in the *guaguancó,* a fast type of rumba danced in couples. The *vacunao* normally commences after the chorus comes in, from which moment the dancers' steps become more disjointed. The couple initiates a game of attraction and rejection in which the female dancer teases the male dancer with gestures of sexual surrendering. However, every time he approaches her, she swiftly avoids him by covering her crotch with her skirt, a blanket, or a handkerchief. This continues until the woman fails to cover herself in time. At this point the male dancer thrusts his pelvis forward, a gesture symbolizing the consummation of his sexual desires. The female dancer responds to this with a sign of submission (León 1984, 158).

Tallet's "La rumba" was not the only afrocubanista poem to portray rumba dance accurately. Emilio Ballagas's "El baile del papalote" (The Dance of the Kite) reproduces in detail the rumba known as *Papalote* ("kite" in Cuban Spanish), which is a choreographic enactment of the game of flying a kite. It consists of tying an imaginary string to the waist of the female dancer through which the male dancer controls her movements. While she dances rumba, her partner may, for example, wind up the kite, thus letting her float in the distance. Alternatively, he may pull in the string and bring her closer to him (Cabrera 1926, 52; Daniel 1995, 71). Ballagas effectively reproduces these motions in the lines "Ponte frenillo[11] en los hombros, / mulata, y en el ombligo," "Ya flotas," "Empínate, papalote," "Baja," "Morena, ¡ven a mis brazos!" (Attach some strings to your shoulders, / mulatto woman, and to your belly button. You are already floating. Fly up, kite. Come down. Black woman, come to my arms!) (Guirao 1938, 115–17). Thus, Ballagas's mulatto woman does not "fly upwards because she is desirable but inaccessible to the poet," as Kubayanda claims, but simply because in the early part of the *rumba papalote* the female dancer enacts a choreographic metaphor for the ascent of a kite (Kubayanda 1974, 118). Similarly, the last lines of the above extract refer to the conclusion of the dance, which is brought about by the male dancer pulling the string in order to recover his kite. The female dancer's approach at this point of the dance has erotic connotations for the performers (Ortiz 1981, 432). This means that the sexual overtones of the concluding lines of the poem cannot be solely attributed to Ballagas's misinterpretation of "almost every Negro dance as an erotic social performance" (Kubayanda 1974, 118).[12]

The sexual gestures employed by female rumba dancers are similar to those present in many Yoruba dances. Peggy Harper explains that the knee and hip flexibility that characterizes the walk of Yoruba women carrying loads is a typical feature of these. She adds that "in the Delta region the dancing of the Nembe and Kalabari is characterized by a rapid shift of the weight in the hips and legs resulting in 'quivering' movement patterns of the buttocks accentuated by the forward inclination of the upper body" (1969, 289). The sociological factors behind the choreographic prominence of these regions of the female anatomy are delineated by Benedict M. Ibítókun in his analysis of Tédédè, an Efe Yoruba mask from Bénin (Cové region).[13] Ibítókun argues that "bulkiness is an aspect of Yoruba bodily attractive aesthetics." It is commonly believed to signify prosperity and affluence. Young men in their search for a prospective spouse favor women with "high hips, big buttocks and protruding breasts." Such preferences, he continues, have to do with the fact that, traditionally, Yoruba women carry their offspring on their backs; high hips and protruding buttocks fairly support the children before they are secured more firmly by swaddling cloths. Women with such attributes are thus symbolically regarded as mothers of many children because "nature has already endowed them, as it were, with procreational props." The parts of the female physique that Tédédè puts into bold relief are, therefore, the loci of procreation and fertility to which the Efe cult is linked. Hips and buttocks are seen as a "spatial metaphor/metonymy for sexuality, and child carrying, the breasts as terrains for infant feeding, femininity code and sexual appeal." But even more important, apart from these procreational overtones, Ibítókun sees in the dance "the ritualistic evocation of vitalistic forces." Tédédè's physique signifies not corporeality as such, but "the Yoruba code for transcendence, grandeur and extraordinariness." Thus the Yoruba dancer who represents Tédédè has a wooden prop fixed to his back that serves to enhance the size of the mask's hips and buttocks. Another physical feature of the Tédédè mask is its "roundish, longish and ponderous breasts with their nipples darting sensual codes." At one point Tédédè dances in the crowd "with breasts upright and hands raised to thrust more her breasts forward so as to deepen the emotional appeal" (Ibítókun 1993, 46, 47, 83).

These Yoruba bodily aesthetics seem to characterize the female's dancing style in traditional rumba. Although the following description of female movements in the *vacunao* does not specifically refer to the areas of the body made prominent in the Tédédè mask, it does refer to the physical motions that would put them in bold relief:

> Female energy is percussive when she escapes the *vacunao* by the swift slap toward her lower abdomen and groin area. . . . Her arms fling to an indefinite point when not holding her skirt edges, and her shoulders rotate in a forward direction as a result of the arm roll carrying the skirt. Undulation of the spine is almost constant: her torso can be divided into upper and lower sections and moves in forward to back swing energy. Her rib cage lifts with the undulation and alternates from side to side. Her knees are flexed and shift softly from side to side accommodating the polyrhythms above the feet. . . . The lower torso participates in the undulation by means of hip flexion and extension. (Daniel 1995, 77)

Not surprisingly, in Tallet's "La rumba," the female dancer Tomasa entices her male dancing partner Chepe Chacón with gestures that bring to mind Tédédè's dancing in the crowd "with breasts upright and hands raised to thrust more her breasts forward" (Ibítókun 1993, 83). For example, Tallet describes Tomasa as raising her arms, bringing her hands together, and throwing her head back, precociously offering her rotund breasts to the male dancer. After avoiding Chepe Chacón's *vacunao*, she walks away from him with the characteristic Yoruba hip and knee flexibility that brings her buttocks into bold relief (Guirao 1938, 66). Her walk is the same as that which Marcelino Arozarena describes in the earlier-cited poem "Caridá," where the poet refers to the black dancer's "grupa mordisqueante y temblorosa" (biting and shaking rump). A similar description is found in his "Liturgia etiópica," where the female dancer Mersé metaphorically dislocates her hip with her walk (1983, 32).

Thus, it is clear that these representations do not arise exclusively from a white racist and sexist imagination, since they also reflect traits of the cultural forms afrocubanistas were writing about. Nevertheless, in spite of the obvious choreographic analogies between Tédédè and the dancing movement in rumba, there is a difference between the transcendental meanings that Ibítókun attaches to the choreographic salience of these regions of the female anatomy and afrocubanista poets' apparent perception of them as, simply, erotic body signs. This perception could be interpreted as a sign of their lack of awareness of the Yoruba sociological connotations of these dancing movements. The connotations of fertility and procreation of the Tédédè mask's buttocks certainly contradict Ortiz's rejection of the maternal connotations of the buttocks. In fact, his entire description of the hips and buttocks as symbolic of the sexual act trivializes African concepts about these body parts. As Daniel explains, in African societies "the pelvic area is revered . . . because it contains the reproductive organs and body parts that have important effects on the person, the couple, and hence the extended family, the group, the community and the nation" (1995, 75). At first glance, this divergence in perception of black female sexuality would seem to suggest that afrocubanista poets distorted the meanings of these choreographic features of rumba in order to promote their own sexually uninhibited poetic discourse. In order to assess this notion fully, it is necessary to further specify the characteristics and meaning of the rumba performance in the Cuban context.

Unlike the Tédédè dance of the Efe cult, rumba is not a ritual that serves only to preserve and convey Yoruba religious and sociological values. Although it has often been used as a vehicle of religious meanings of African origin, as will be shown in chapter 7, rumba is often a profane dance and music form. It is, in the words of musicologist Argeliers León, "music for having fun and for entertainment that is used to occupy a period of free time." León argues that elements from the choreography employed in African ritual dances can, at times, lose their representational value when transposed to rumba and serve mainly to amuse and entertain its participants and observers. He argues further that this is due to the fact that rumba did not exclude that part of the white population with which lower-class blacks shared the lowest strata of Cuban colonial society. The white section of the lower classes was made up predominantly of Spaniards and their descendants who had usually moved from the Cuban countryside into the city. Thus, like the Africans, they found themselves estranged and dislocated. In order for these two groups of the population to cohabit, it became necessary for the Spaniards to break away from their peninsular cultural links and find new forms of social relations with which to relate to urban blacks. At the same time, their participation was made possible by the disassociation of this dance from a worldview and religion they did not share with their African-descended compatriots. Thus, dances such as those dedicated to Changó, the "baile del palero," or *makuta* and *íreme Abakuá* dances contributed movements and gestures but devoid of their religious significance, so that the physicality of the dancing became performative rather than representational. The rumba was thus the popular, cross-cultural performance that marked these new forms of social relations (León 1984, 151–52).[14]

Numerous explanations have been provided for a supposed shift from a sublimated sexuality in African dances to the more openly lascivious dancing present not only in rumba but also in other forms of Afro-Cuban dancing. Moreno Fraginals refers in particular to the effect that slavery had on certain African dances that originally had no sexual connotations. According to him, slavery infected such dances with an almost "lascivious meaning," which accounts for the fact that a great deal of the Cuban sexual lexicon originated in the sugar plantations (Moreno Fraginals 1977b, 21).[15] These processes undoubtedly had an effect on the posterior development of rumba dancing, but other sociological forces were present in the urban environments where, as Daniel explains, rumba began to evolve after the legal end of Cuban slavery in 1886 (1995, 64). Moreno Fraginals touches upon these forces in the analysis mentioned earlier. He explains that slavery distorted the sexuality of the slaves and that this was used by racists to invent the myth of the black's sadistic sexuality, black women's immorality, and the lasciviousness of mulatto women. Then he adds: "Todo ello independientemente de que en los núcleos urbanos, y en la casa solariega, la vida sexual fue el vínculo en que se apoyaron las mujeres para mejorar sus condiciones económicas" (All this aside from the fact that in urban areas and in the urban slums, many women used their sexuality as a means of improving their financial conditions) (1977b, 21). As Kutzinski points out, in particular light-skinned, socially ambitious *mulatas* made full use of their physique to attract the interest of white men in the hope that by marrying them their social position would improve (1993, 20). Gains were not always expected to be financial, as is made clear by Josefa's advice to her granddaughter Cecilia in *Cecilia Valdés:* "Tú eres casi blanca y puedes aspirar a casarte con un blanco. ¿Por qué no? . . . Y has de saber que blanco, aunque pobre, sirve para marido; negro o mulato ni el buey de oro" (You are almost white and can thus aspire to marrying a white. Why not? . . . You should know that even a poor white man is a better choice of husband. You should not marry a black or mulatto even if they have all the money in the world)(as quoted in Kutzinski 1993, 20).

Considering that the original ambience of rumba was made up of what Daniel describes as "whites and blacks, light and dark-skinned Cubans" who "found moments of recreation together in outdoor patio areas," the neocultural alteration of the meanings that originally shaped the choreography of female rumba dancing becomes clearer (1995, 64). Through movement, the mulatto female rumba dancer might capture the attention of the white men with whom they shared these recreational periods and who, although poor, represented a viable means of social improvement. This is not to say that, in sexualizing their dancing, rumberas eliminated all of the original African meanings of these movements. On the contrary, as will be shown in chapter 7, they often consciously enacted African concepts through movements that whites mistook as merely sexual. Thus, rumba is a flexible system of communication that its practitioners use to convey a variety of meanings in different contexts. In some contexts in the 1920s and 1930s, black rumba dancers and musicians used it as a vehicle of religious notions or social concepts but, in others, as a form of erotic expression. The afrocubanista representation of rumba as an erotic art form, thus, does capture some real characteristics of the latter version. More specifically, the poetry's emphasis on the anatomy of the black rumbera cannot be interpreted as solely the product of a "masculinist imagination" or "white male fantasy," since her intention was often to elicit desire.

It is worth noting that, like afrocubanista representations, these rumba movements themselves could have been shaped by white and European racist conceptions about blacks and, in particular, black female sexuality. The perspectives of the poor whites with whom black women shared these recreational spaces could have been influenced by the same history of representations outlined in the first section of this chapter. Therefore, they were already predisposed to view black women as sexy and available.[16] On their part, some black women must have played up to these preconceptions by sexualizing dancing movements of African origin. In this way, racist conceptions about blacks that have their roots firmly implanted in a history of European interpretations of Africans would have also played an important part in the development of rumba as an expression of sexual desire. In turn, this highlights the inappropriateness of Ortiz's view of afrocubanista poetry as representing the "African sexuality" of Cuban black women. As shown, the uninhibited sexuality that characterizes the dance was developed in Cuba from the social interaction between lower-class blacks and whites and was also influenced by Spanish cultural elements and European notions about black female sexuality. Consequently, the poetry's representation of the sexuality of female rumba dancing cannot be considered an incorporation of a "pure" African expression.

Nevertheless, Ortiz's analysis is a useful contribution to the study of the representation of black Cuban women's sexuality in afrocubanista poetry. With the above rectification in mind, Ortiz's interpretation shows that afrocubanista poets used aspects of Afro-Cuban sexual expression to produce a more realistic and frank eroticism than had characterized erudite Cuban poetry previously. By insisting on analyzing these poems as merely products of their authors' sexist imaginations, the critics cited at the beginning of this chapter gloss over the poets' utilization of this aspect of Afro-Cuban culture to correct a perceived weakness of the dominant literature.

In order to understand the full significance of the issue of the black rumbera's representation, it is necessary to outline similar feminist approaches to other features of afrocubanista poetry. This will effectively establish that this case is representative of a wider tendency in this type of criticism to overlook the poetry's incorporation of Afro-Cuban cultural elements. An illustrative example is the following interpretation by Kutzinski of the line "¡Por tí repica mi canto lo mismo que un atabal!" (my song vibrates through you like a drum) in Ballagas's "Nombres negros en el son": "The difference between 'por tí' (through you) and 'para tí' (for you) is a subtle, but significant, indicator of the poet's instrumental use of the *mulata,* who becomes what Evaristo Ribera Chevremont calls 'la morena rítmica y perfecta.' . . . Her stereotypical image also reappears in Marcelino Arozarena's 'Liturgia etiópica'" (Kutzinski 1993, 186). Indeed, in this poem by Arozarena, the way in which Caridad's physical movements are dictated by José Caridad's playing can be interpreted as "an instrumental use of the black woman" (Arozarena 1983, 33). However, these instrumental images reflect the relationship between drum and dancer in Afro-Cuban music. For example, in *columbia* (a very fast type of rumba) the dancer establishes a dialogue with the phrases that the drummer plays on the *quinto* (soloing high-pitched drum):

> Having responded with his movements to the rhythmic phrases played on the *quinto* drum, the dancer makes new movements to which the *quinto* must now respond. In this way, a kind of rhythmic dialogue is established, in which the rhythmic statements of one and the responses of the other become shorter, more precise and more pressing, until one of them manages to catch the other by surprise. The dancer resorts to gestures that are similar to the ones made in the *guaguancó* to symbolize the sexual possession of the dancing partner. (León 1984, 159)

The line from Ballagas's poem that Kutzinski refers to actually portrays the rhythmic effect that music has on the dancer in Afro-Cuban music. By linking Mersé's movements to José Caridád's playing, Arozarena is referring to this drum/dancer interdependency.

Similar arguments apply to the use of animal terms in relation to the black female in afrocubanista poetry. This type of imagery has been often condemned. RoseGreen-Williams sees the use of terms normally associated with horses, such as *grupa* and *ancas,* as a "discourse of bestialization" that puts forward a dehumanized image of Afro-Cuban women (1993, 17). G. R. Coulthard complains about the use of animal terms in Tallet's description of Tomasa, arguing that the poet reduces Afro-Cuban women to the status of "a sexual animal without thought or feeling" (1962, 31–32). Ann Venture Young remarks on what Julio Finn refers to as the "snakism" of the poetry (Finn 1988, 182). Young claims that afrocubanistas compared the movements of black women to those of the snake in order to present her as a creature that tantalizes the male with her "sinuous and slithering gyrations." The biblical fable is the origin of some of these poets' view of the snake and woman as evil influences on the good nature of man (Young 1977, 141, 139). It is important to remember that the notions about the physicality and lack of discipline of blacks outlined earlier were closely linked to assumptions about their animality, which also served to justify their enslavement throughout history. This is evident in Bush's analysis of descriptions of African women by Europeans traveling in Africa in the eighteenth and nineteenth centuries: "The connection between the physical strength and animality was quickly made. Comparisons between African women and female animals were not infrequent. Both Towerson and Sir Hans Sloane compared the breasts of African women who had borne children to the udders of goats" (1990, 15). In the West Indies, plantocratic writers supported their racist arguments by linking the black woman and the animal world: Edward Long, for instance, suggested that African females had a close, natural affinity with the orangutan. "An orang-outan husband," he declared, "would not be any dishonor to a Hottentot female" (1990, 15). In Cuba, members of the literary circle led by the nineteenth-century abolitionist Domingo del Monte also used the orangutan analogy: they referred to "the *apes* imported from Africa" and claimed that "even orangutans should be used [in the sugar plantations] where they are susceptible of domestication" (as quoted in Paquette 1988, 115).

Nevertheless, in respect to these objections to the afrocubanista use of animal terms, it is worth recalling Ibítókun's description of Tédédè's back view—"the hips and buttocks are in bold relief like a scorpion's tail on-end" (1993, 48). His use of the scorpion simile to describe the form of the hips and buttocks of a sacred figure suggests that animal comparisons in Yoruba culture do not have the same derogatory connotations that they do in Western culture. In point of fact, a conscious affinity with the animal world permeates many African dances. Geoffrey Gorer described an African dance in which the dancers performed a very realistic pantomime of the copulation of various animals while carrying cymbals in their hands and whistles in their mouths. Each man represented a different animal, for which each whistle had a particular sound. "These dances," wrote Gorer, "were extraordinarily impressive and serious; the old men mimed so well that they almost became goats, or cocks or bulls before our eyes" (1949, 223).[17] Animal allegories such as these can be found in Afro-Cuban culture as well. For instance, Ortiz explains that the Cuban descendants of the Congolese have a dance that reproduces all the stages of the courtship between the cock and the hen (1981, 210–11).

In view of the prevalent animal symbolism in African dance, it may be argued that the afrocubanista use of animal imagery in relation to Afro-Cuban performers is, to some extent, a representation of animal associations present in Afro-Cuban culture. Marcelino Arozarena's description of the female dancer's "grupa mordisqueante," for example, specifically brings to mind Ibítókun's description of Tédédè's behind. In a similar manner, in the context of Afro-Cuban culture, Tallet's use of the term *grupa* in relation to Tomasa cannot be considered exclusively a product of white imagination. Among Santería practitioners, possessed initiates are referred to as "horses," and it is said that the orisha "rides his horse" (Castellanos and Castellanos 1992, 92). Tallet's use of equine imagery in the context of Tomasa's possession, then, seems ethnographically appropriate. However, one must bear in mind that, according to Ortiz, there are no references in the *vacunao* of rumba to the courtship between the cock and the hen. Thus, his dismissal of this supposed allegory as "fantasías de blancos propincuos a la salacidad" (the fantasies of lascivious whites) could be seen as confirming the validity of the objections outlined above (Ortiz 1981, 433). This consideration aside, there is no denying that terms such as *nalga* and *ancas* in colloquial speech in Cuba and other Spanish-speaking countries are often used in relation to human anatomy without derogatory connotations.

Similar arguments can be made about the use of fruit imagery in afrocubanista poetry. For Young, it connotes a superficial image of Afro-Cuban woman in that fruits are grown not for their beauty but for their nourishing value. In the process of performing their function, fruits are "variously handled, savored, squeezed and devoured" (1977, 139).[18] It cannot be denied that fruit imagery suggests eating and therefore consumption, even devouring, and ultimately the assimilation of the female fruit into the male body. It is an image of carnal sexuality, unlike Platonic love, that suited the afrocubanista discourse on sexuality. The imagery suggests, furthermore, exploitation of black women as if they were one more product of the land.

Nevertheless, this semantic field reflects concepts found in Afro-Cuban culture. A suitable example is the musical style known as *son-pregón*. As musicologist Argeliers León explains, this musical form captures the verses shouted out by street vendors selling their merchandise (as quoted in Feijoó 1986, 50). The lyrics of the *son-pregón* can often be sexually suggestive, which is not surprising considering that many of these male peddlers must have been directing their products at housewives, whose husbands were probably at work. This suggestiveness is patent, for example, in the verses sung by the Trío Matamoros in their *son-pregón* "Frutas del Caney," in which the peddler compares the sweetness of his pineapples to the sweetness of a woman's lips (Matamoros 1992).

Any reader aware of the symbolism of fruit references in this musical genre would undoubtedly detect the sexual overtones in Guillén's "Pregón" (1990, 86–87). Kay Boulware certainly identifies the erotic connotations of the poem's fruit imagery. She argues on the basis of the line "trigueña de carne amarga" (black woman with bitter flesh) that Guillén blends sexuality with the fruits of the island (1977, 87). Thus, contrary to Young's objections, fruit imagery in afrocubanista poetry, at least in some cases, can be seen as yet another influence from the represented culture.

Young also unfavorably contrasts afrocubanistas' use of fruit imagery to the traditional portrayal of the "Euro-American woman" as "an object of adoration" whose beauty is likened to that of a flower (1977, 139). It could be argued, nevertheless, that equating women to flowers implies that they are conceived of as delicate objects whose only function is that of creating aesthetic and sensual pleasure. Both types of comparison, then, imply a conception of women as "objects"; whether they may be "of adoration" or "of pleasure" arguably makes little difference. One-dimensional presentations of women are not a peculiarity of afrocubanista poetry but rather are characteristic of male heterosexual love poetry in general. However, an important difference between these two images is that fruit imagery conveys a male desire for physical contact (one does not eat a flower), as opposed to the more Platonic connotations present in the flower image. This difference reflects again these poets' search for a more explicit and frank discourse on sexuality. In any case, one must not lose sight of the fact that, beyond its sexist connotations, fruit imagery responds to the urge of afrocubanistas to describe the *mulata*'s sensuality by using typically Cuban images rather than European ones. Tropical fruits and vegetables are better representatives of the *mulata*'s physiognomy than flowers are, because, like the *mulata* herself, they are specific to the Caribbean and function as cultural icons.

Thus, it is evident that the case of the black rumbera is only one of various cases in which, by insisting on analyzing these poems exclusively as products of their authors' sexist imaginations, feminist critics have missed the poetry's utilization of actual Afro-Cuban cultural elements. In this way, the influence of Afro-Cuban culture upon afrocubanista texts has been obscured. This is particularly serious in view of the fact that this influence was not merely thematic. As will be shown in the following chapter, Afro-Cuban cultural forms radically modify afrocubanista poetry from a formal point of view.

6 Afrocubanista Poetry and Afro-Cuban Performance

THIS CHAPTER analyzes the afrocubanista conception of the represented culture as oral and performative, as well as the ways in which afrocubanistas formally incorporated nonwritten Afro-Cuban cultural forms into their poetry. It also evaluates these incorporations in relation to other representations of blacks and black culture in Cuban literature and with respect to the afrocubanista belief in a process of increasing black and white harmony.

In his 1936 article "Más acerca de la poesía mulata" (More on Mulatto Poetry), Fernando Ortiz outlined the black aesthetic characteristics afrocubanista poetry focused upon: black sexuality (expressed through dynamic body movements such as hip swinging), the rhythm of African drums, and the phonetic peculiarities of black speech (1973c, 161–71). The afrocubanista emphasis on such modes of expression betrays a view of Afro-Cuban culture as oral and performative. Ortiz himself characterized it as being made up of religious rituals, secular dance, and music practices, which were essentially a rhythmic complex of dance, oral forms, and music (1973b, 156–57).

One aspect of this understanding of Afro-Cuban culture that cannot be ignored is that, in Fernando Ortiz's writings, it often appeared linked to cultural evolutionist and biological determinist notions. For example, as explained in chapter 3, the scholar described the oral forms employed in Afro-Cuban religions (in prayers, spells, and liturgical choruses) as being "part of a rhythmic complex of music, dance and chanting, like all primitive poetry" and as a genre of song characteristic of societies whose means of expression are not very developed (1973b, 157). These descriptions suggest a perspective similar to that which informed parts of Ortiz's *La africanía de la música folklórica de Cuba*, which was first published in 1950. He argued there that African culture was "preliterate." According to him, it had not developed a "superior" literate culture because it had not yet separated language from other modes of expression based on sound. This is evident in the following quotation: "La música del negro africano es aún música ingráfica y su literatura es preletrada, propia de los pueblos párvulos que aún no usan escritura. En éstos las artes sonoras casi siempre van juntas. . . . La escritura hace a los hombres más hombres pues a más del lenguaje hablado (que ya es una característica original de la humanidad), les da la fijación de ese lenguaje y su perdurabilidad y extensiones ilimitadas por el espacio y por el tiempo" (The music of the African black does not have a system of notation and his literature is preliterate, as is always the case with infant societies who do not yet use writing. In such societies, the sonorous arts are almost always joined together. . . . Writing makes men more human because it takes them beyond spoken language [which is an original attribute of mankind] by allowing them to lay it down. This makes it durable and opens up limitless possibilities in space and time) (1965, 161). Ortiz's perspective brings to mind nineteenth-century evolutionist theories in which, as Julien explains, contemporary Europe was seen as being at the adult stage of civilization while non-European cultures were viewed as being at the childhood stage (1992, 11).[1]

Despite his rejection of the concept of race, which was discussed in chapter 3, Ortiz often assigned anatomical causes to the characteristics of Afro-Cuban orality in his 1930s essays on afrocubanista poetry. An excerpt from his article "Más acerca de la poesía mulata" clearly reflects his belief that, to some extent, the phonetic peculiarities of black speech captured by afrocubanista poets were conditioned by the morphology of the black's vocal apparatus:

> Hay que admitir en este naturismo idiomático, sin los ropajes prosódicos y gráficos del castellano, los influjos anatómicamente étnicos de la conformación prognática del órgano negro de la expresión hablada, en esas gangosidades de narices y garganta que han hecho del fonema "ng" una característica negroide entrometida en el castellano vulgar; en esas explosividades labiales que dan al lenguaje antillano rimbombancias de tambor encuerado y oclusiones que oscurecen las vocales al salir por un tubo de bezos; y . . . esas morbideces que luden las aristas incisivas de los sonidos dentales. (1973c, 177)

> One has to acknowledge the anatomically ethnic influence of the prognathic configuration of the black's speech organ, in those nasal sounds that come from the nose and the throat and which have made the "ng" phoneme a negroid feature in everyday Castilian; in those labial explosions that give the Antillean

language the resonance of a skin drum and occlusions that darken the vowels as they come out through a tube of thick lips; and . . . those delicacies rubbed by the incisive edges of the dental sounds.

Similarly, in "Los últimos versos mulatos," he referred to the language of afrocubanista poetry as "un verbo cálido, de tropical erotismo, hecho más mórbido aún por las suavizaciones guturales, nasales y labiales, impuestas por la anatomía y por la imitación" (a warm poetry with tropical eroticism that becomes even more morbid due to the guttural, nasal, and labial softening imposed by anatomy and imitation) (1973b, 170). In light of these descriptions, the biological imagery employed by afrocubanistas to describe blacks in performance of Afro-Cuban dance and music practices could be seen to reflect the influence of biological determinist views. For instance, in "Lance de Juruminga," José Antonio Portuondo described the black female protagonist who is dancing rumba in the following way:

> Dominga, mi negra conga,
> hierve tu sangre mandinga
> en ritos de juruminga.
> (Guirao 1938, 139–42)

Similar notions are implicit in the lines addressed to the black female dancer of Teófilo Radillo's "La rumba (Bricomanía en blanco y negro)":

> Rumba de tus fetiches
> que tu instinto desata
> y desenfrena.
> (1939, 50–55)

It must be stressed that the biological determinism of these poems and of Ortiz's descriptions lies specifically in the attribution of certain cultural traits to the biological makeup of blacks. This is not to say, however, that such cultural traits were not a part of the culture afrocubanistas sought to represent. In fact, studies written long after afrocubanismo ended have continued to highlight the prominent role of orality in Afro-Cuban culture. Martinez Furé offers this explanation:

> Despite being in the diaspora, and despite being mistreated and humiliated, the captive Africans preserved their humanity and one of its most subtle creations: literature. Our Cuban people have been able to preserve that heritage through the oral tradition and today it is possible to compile from their spoken testimony, hundreds of myths, fables, legends, sayings, poems, ritual formulae,

etcetera, in their original languages or inserted into Cuban Spanish. This is a literature of astonishing richness and diversity and which remains on the whole unpublished. (1979, 209–10)

Martín Lienhard demonstrates how Afro-Cuban religious chants in the Palo Monte religion function as oral archives that preserve the Afro-Cuban view of the slaves' sea passage from Africa to the New World. One of the chants (or *mambos*) that he examines stresses the humanity, intelligence, and culture of the slaves being transported, which subverts the slave traders' view of their human cargo as mere objects from which to extract maximum financial gain (1999, 506–9). In Afro-Cuban culture, other nonwritten media apart from orality play an important role as well. As Brandon points out, for instance, "The use in *Santería* rituals of speech and song, along with such nonviable media as dance, acting out, graphic and plastic arts, and instrumental music, drastically increases the types of sensory data that have to be encoded in memory" (1993, 140).

Admittedly, it must be acknowledged that the written word did play a role in Afro-Cuban traditions. As Rogelio Martínez Furé points out, a considerable corpus of the oral literature of the Afro-Cuban ethnic group Lucumí was preserved in *libretas* (notebooks) by black practitioners of Afro-Cuban religions: "Although the whole complex of myths, fables, legends and poems of Yoruba origin is transmitted through oral tradition, there are manuscripts in which all this literature is preserved and the priests consult them in order to 'refresh their memories' in relation to the legends about the saints and other aspects of the cult." These *libretas* included, Martínez Furé adds, hundreds of myths and fables, lists of sayings, ritual procedures, and systems of divination.[2] Nevertheless, these literary forms do not constitute an autonomous written literary tradition, since they cannot be separated from Afro-Cuban oral and performative practices. Indeed, the fact that Martínez Furé describes the *libretas* as serving to "refresh their memories" suggests that their main role was to function as mnemonic devices in rituals and divination practices. Furthermore, it is evident that they were transcriptions of oral forms, and as such they presented traits that are characteristic of oral discourse. Martínez Furé refers to the "simple and direct style" of Lucumí oral literature, as well as to its use of reiteration as a stylistic device to increase the audience's interest in the plot (1979, 211, 216).[3]

Moreover, written forms such as the *libretas* were secondary to oral and other nonwritten forms in the preservation of the cultural memory of the Lucumí. This is reflected in the nature of the "acts that transfer memory and keep the images memory contains circulating within the group" in Santería. As Brandon explains, three of the main strategies that serve this purpose are "calendrical repetition, in the form of commemorative ceremonies for the saints; verbal repetition, through which the use of *Lucumí* as a sacred ritual language conditions communication between humans and the orisha; and gestural repetition as it relates to ritual dance and ceremonial spirit possession."[4] Brandon adds that "assistance from and access to the cultural memory of a group is one of the barest preconditions for the existence and persistence of culture and social life, as well as a sense of personal or group identity" (1993, 143, 132). From this point of view, it may be argued that it was precisely the nonwritten nature of Afro-Cuban culture that allowed many illiterate blacks to form a cohesive community at the margins of the dominant sociocultural order. Afro-Cuban religions, for example, offered an invaluable source of accessible nonwritten aesthetic practices (Benítez Rojo 1992, 159–60). Secular dance and music practices were another important form of expression for blacks without much formal education. In particular, it is worth highlighting the importance of rumba as a vehicle of Afro-Cuban empowerment. Martínez Furé states, "Rumba came from the *solares* and was 'a vehicle of liberation and protest.' From the *solares*, Afro-Cubans expressed their personal successes or failures in love relations, satirized government practices, and gradually fashioned the dance/music complex called rumba" (as cited by Daniel 1995, 19). In fact, according to Leonardo Acosta, in colonial society this dance and music form played the same fundamental functions for marginal sectors as the press did among the bourgeoisie. It was, he argues, an alternative "social chronicle" of the urban poor: "If the bourgeois media chronicled, for instance, violent crimes in the forms of versions directed at the poor, the same events narrated in a *guaguancó* reflected the perception of the dispossessed themselves" (1991, 54–55). In this sense, the role of rumba for marginalized blacks was comparable to that of similar collective dance practices in oral cultures. As Allegra Snyder explains: "Dance functions in some cultures, the non-literate cultures, with as broad a spectrum of functions as the written word includes for others. . . . Dance, in the ritual setting, is a literature of the non-literate cultures" (as quoted in Royce 1977, 154). The above considerations make it necessary to reexamine the widespread critical skepticism toward the "stereotypical" nature of afrocubanista representations of blacks in relation to Afro-Cuban dance and music practices. An example of this tendency in criticism is Lemuel Johnson's description of afrocubanista poetry as perpetuating stereotypes of blacks as simple-minded, sensual, and musical beings, which, he argues, date back to Golden Age Spanish literature (1971, 70–71). G. R. Coulthard also argues that much negrista poetry stereotyped the black man as "a grotesque dancing figure" (1962, 95). Along similar lines, Wilfred G. Cartey describes Emilio Ballagas's afrocubanista production as "a poetry that never quite presents the emotion of the Negro, but paints him with an external, somewhat stereotyped aesthetic." His poetry, Cartey concludes, "is hot, foamy poetry containing music and drums and the dancing forms of Negroes without spiritual dimension" (1970, 61, 72).

The predominantly oral and performative nature of Afro-Cuban culture demonstrates that even if afrocubanista representations of blacks in connection with dance and music practices are, to an extent, stereotypes, they nonetheless captured an important characteristic of Afro-Cuban culture. This confirms Barbara Bush's argument that "stereotypes can draw upon cultural traits and can contain 'a kernel of truth'" (1990, 13). Wade also points out that stereotypes can contain a kernel of truth in a purely descriptive sense (1991, 49).[5] Nevertheless, in accepting the afrocubanista understanding of Afro-Cuban culture as predominantly oral and performative, one must avoid assuming that the represented sectors were limited to nonwritten cultural practices. On the one hand, as explained in the second chapter of this book, these sectors were from the lowest social classes of the black population, where illiteracy was undoubtedly high. But with literacy rates among blacks rising rapidly and steadily throughout the first decades of the republican era, assuming that reading and writing were confined to the white and black middle classes would be unwise.[6] At least some educated blacks from the lower classes must have combined literary and other learned practices with Afro-Cuban ones. Indeed, Carpentier explained that the Cuban black of the late 1920s "peut porter des *over all* américains, lire les journeaux, et même danser le fox-trott," but "en cas de maladie il préférera toujours le sorcier au médecin" (can often wear American overalls, read the newspaper, and even dance the fox-trot, but whenever he falls ill he will choose to visit a sorcerer rather than a doctor) (1929, 92–93).[7] The following explanation by Martínez Furé is also relevant: "The fact that the Yoruba sub-culture has not remained static in Cuba is evident in the fact that the *libretas* contain many fragments of books on the African Yoruba published by Oxford University, which have been acquired by mail and obviously translated by university-educated *santeros*" (1979, 212). Martín Lienhard's definition of a sociocultural sector offers a way of conceptualizing the represented culture without confining the Afro-Cuban sectors to an exclusively oral and performative world. Lienhard acknowledges that the culture or the identity of an individual is made up of an array of diverse and contradictory practices. However, he specifies that a sociocultural group or sector is the ensemble of those who manage the same array of practices in the same contexts (1994a, 98; 1997, 193). Thus, in Lienhard's definition the emphasis is on the communicative contexts where members of the same groups converge, without denying the fact that some of these same individuals also participate in the cultural practices of other groups. From this perspective, the term "Afro-Cuban culture" can be understood as the array of oral and performative cultural practices through which the represented sectors became aware of the nature, the meaning, and the significance of their own lives as members of a distinct black Afro-Cuban community. This allows for the fact that members of these sectors must have taken part in many other practices that, as opposed to Afro-Cuban ones, did not serve this purpose.

As explained in chapter 3, Ortiz posited that the most accomplished afrocubanista poetry had to be formally mulatto, that is, it had to incorporate Afro-Cuban culture at the level of form. In this sense, the centrality in Afro-Cuban culture of the collective practices outlined earlier constituted a serious problem for afrocubanistas. Unlike written poetry, which is limited to the use of conventional graphic signs, these cultural practices conveyed messages through a much larger number of "sensory codes," including gestures and facial expressions, sounds, and even smells. Like all "cultural performances," Afro-Cuban rituals and secular celebrations were also composed of what Milton Singer calls "cultural media," that is, modes of communication that include verbal language but also nonlinguistic media such as music and dance. They were, as Victor Turner would argue, "orchestrations of media, not expressions in a single medium" (1986, 22–23). Thus, afrocubanistas felt that they had to formally incorporate into their poetry cultural forms based on nonwritten modes of expression and different sensory codes.

One of the ways in which they went about this was through the use of linguistic devices known as *jitanjáforas*. Fernando Ortiz defined these specifically in relation to afrocubanista poetry as "the poetic expression of a magical language, the literary survival of the mysterious expressions of the liturgies and sorcerers' spells" (1973b, 166). The term was first used in a poem by Cuban poet Mariano Brull. Mexican critic Alfonso Reyes then used it to refer to meaningless words that merely convey sensations (Ortiz 1973b, 166–69).[8] Examples of *jitanjáforas* in afrocubanista poetry include Guirao's "culembembé, / bémbere, / culembembé" in "Sólo hombre yo"; "Macucho con tu rumba, / . . . / te tiene cachumbambé" in "Macucho con tu rumba"; and "¡Jongolojongo / del Rey Congo!" in "Canto negro de Ronda." Others are Tallet's "Umabimba, mabomba, bomba y bombó" in "La rumba" and Guillén's "¡Yambambó, yambambé!" in "Canto negro" (Guirao 1934; 1938, 55–56, 65–68, 94–95).

Ballagas's explanation regarding his composition of an "African" poem using only names of African countries illustrates the kind of approach that guided the composition of these nonsensical phrases:

> I will finish this work with a few lines in pure African: *Bena-Kamba-Kilemba, Kalunga; Calabar, Katanga, Difúnda. Saranda, Musumba, Kabongo; Iyambuya, Uganda, Kasongo. Congo, Grave, Mokolo Boloko; Kamalongo; Lusambo, Basoko.* Is it a new African poem? Are they the magic words of a ritual? Gertrude Stein presented games of words similar to these in a magazine that she was directing. But what I have written here is not a poem. It is a list of names of African countries that I have copied from a map of this continent. Some black poems that we have seen do not have more meaning than this curious list. But the song of a nightingale does not have any meaning either and we still like it. It provides a stimulus to the ear and to the imagination. It makes us realize that man is not all logic and rational thought; that primitiveness is also a part of the mental organism of the civilized man. (1973b, 87)

This seemingly frivolous or superficial approach to African languages might lead some to assume that *jitanjáforas* were inventions by white dilettantes that did not actually capture any real characteristics of the represented culture. Nevertheless, it is important to bear in mind that the employment of made-up nonsense syllables for purely aesthetic purposes or with the intention of sounding African was actually a widespread practice in Afro-Cuban culture. According to Samuel Feijóo, the African-sounding lines of the songs of eighteenth-century cabildos de nación, for example, were merely pretexts for rhythm and song without any semantic meaning (1986, 230–31). The use of nonsense syllables for rhythmic purposes can be heard in classic rumba compositions as well, such as Carlos Embales's "Pim pam pum y blen blen blen" (1995). Furthermore, meaningless syllables have been traditionally used in rumba in the *lalaleo,* the melodic fragment by which the lead singer establishes the key and the harmony at the beginning of a song (Daniel 1995, 85). Thus, *jitanjáforas* can be viewed as an abandonment of the semantic logic of the dominant literature in favor of an Afro-Cuban verbal art form in which words may have a suggestive or musical function.

Percussive onomatopoeia was another of the verbal forms used by afrocubanistas in this way. Verbal reproductions of percussive sounds have a long history in Afro-Cuban culture. According to Fernando Ortiz, this type of music making or *música de bemba* was normally practiced by blacks "to imitate the rhythmic phrases of the drums when there is nothing else around that can replace them" (1996a, 33).⁹ A written example of *música de bemba* can be found in the text "Cantos de cabildo," which is featured in Guirao's *Órbita de la poesía afrocubana, 1928–1937*:

> Piqui, piquimbín,
> piqui, piquimbín;
> tumba, muchacho,
> yama bo y tambó.
> Tambó ta brabbo.
> Tumba, cajero.
> Jabla, mula.
> Piqui, piquimbín,
> piqui, piquimbín.
> Pa, pa, pa, práca,
> prácata, pra, pa.
> Cucha, cucha mi bo.
>   (1938, 3)

Singers from popular *son* bands during the afrocubanista vogue also interspersed musical onomatopoeia in their improvisations, and these undoubtedly influenced afrocubanista poets. For example, Tallet's "¡Tararíiii! / . . . / ¡Tararaaaá!" in his "Quintín Barahona" is reminiscent of the onomatopoeic "tarán tarantarantantan" by the lead singer of Sexteto Habanero in the song "Eres mi lira armoniosa" (You Are My Harmonious Lyre) (Sexteto Habanero 1992). Since, like *jitanjáforas*, these devices contradict the semantic and syntactic logic of Spanish, they modify a fundamental principle of the dominant literature of Cuba.[10] This is particularly evident when contrasted with Alfonso Hernández Catá's reproductions of musical sounds in the following extract from "Rumba," where the sounds of musical instruments are instead conveyed through the European poetic device of personification:

> Mientras la cuerda se queja,
> vocifera el cornetín.
> . . . .
> El galopar de los timbales
> pisotea todo recato.

. . . .
El bongó se ha vuelto loco.
(Guirao 1938, 127, 129)

While the string complains,
the cornet shouts.

. . . .

The galloping of the *timbales*
steps over all restraint.

. . . .

The bongo has gone crazy.

Afrocubanista poets also used lyrics from Afro-Cuban musical genres to alter high literary forms. Nicolás Guillén, for instance, used formal characteristics of *son* lyrics, as he pointed out upon the publication of *Motivos de son* in 1930: "He tratado de incorporar a la literatura cubana—no como simple elemento musical, sino como elemento de verdadera poesía—lo que pudiera llamarse *poema-son* basado en la técnica de esa clase de baile tan popular en nuestro país" (I have tried to incorporate into Cuban literature, not as a simple musical element, but as a component of genuine poetry, something that could be called the *son* poem, which is based on the technique of that type of dance, which is so popular in our country) (as quoted in Madrigal 1990, 62). The influence of *son* lyrics is evident in the structure of many of Guillén's *motivos*, which resembles that of early *son* compositions. As Alén Rodríguez explains, these started with the repetition of a four-line refrain sung by a chorus, and then moved on to a second section where the lead vocals improvised in response to a shorter, repeating chorus (1994a, 30). A representative example is the song "Yo no tumbo caña" (I Don't Cut Cane) by the Sexteto Habanero, a group whose influence on *Motivos de son* was directly acknowledged by Guillén (Sexteto Habanero 1992; Morejón 1974b, 41). There is a perceptible structural similarity between this song and Guillén's poem "Me bendo caro." The poem also commences with a four-line stanza that introduces the theme of the composition and continues by alternating a changing line with a repeating one. In this way the first stanza recreates the introduction of *son* compositions sung by a chorus, and the alternating lines the call-and-response singing between the improvised lead vocals and the repeating chorus (Guirao 1938, 85–86).[11]

Guillén was not the only one to make use of formal elements from Afro-Cuban lyrics. In Tallet's "La rumba," for example, the repetition of the lines "cambia e paso Cheché, / cambia e paso Cheché, / cambia e paso Cheché" (change your step, Cheché) can be viewed as reflecting the repetition that characterizes Afro-Cuban song forms. Furthermore, the lack of a fixed syllabic pattern or a fixed number of lines per stanza in this poem can be considered an influence of the free versification of rumba lyrics. Another illustrative example is Ramón Guirao's "Canto negro de Ronda." Although it is not made explicit, several factors suggest that the poem evokes the ritualistic sacrifice of a cock in the Bantu-derived religions known as *reglas congas*. For instance, the black speakers are repeatedly identified as being Congos in the second, third, and fourth stanzas ("Rey Congo," "conguito," "negricongo"). What further supports this notion is the mention of the Congo deity Babalú-Ayé, combined with the death of the cock at the end of the poem ("¡Babayú-ayé! / La gayo se fué"). Another revealing element is the word "jongolojongo" in the third stanza. It could easily be derived from the term "jolongo," which refers to an object (*nganga* or *prenda*) that plays a fundamental role in the magic of the *reglas congas* (Castellanos and Castellanos 1992, 140–41). Lastly, each of the poem's four stanzas is separated by the onomatopoeic "¡Quiquiriquiii!" (Guirao 1938, 55–56), which bears a strong resemblance to the following extract from a prayer that is recited after the cock has been sacrificed in present-day initiation rituals of the *reglas congas*:

> Kokorikó, kokorikó
> gallo va a cantar
> Kokorikó, kokorikó
> gallo va a cantar.
> (Castellanos and Castellanos 1992, 159)

> Kokorikó, kokorikó
> the cock is going to sing
> Kokorikó, kokorikó
> the cock is going to sing.

Afrocubanistas sometimes even managed to formally incorporate the nonverbal sensory codes of the represented performances. An example of this is Guirao's description of the black female dancer in "Bailadora de rumba," in which the texture of the *bongó* serves as a metaphor for the texture of the dancer's skin and the sound of the *maracas* for the sound of her laughter (1938, 53). Since metaphor is one of the essential formal devices of poetry, as Aviram explains (1994, 43), Guirao's description is an example of how tactile and sonic codes from an Afro-Cuban performance can formally influence afrocubanista poetry.

For afrocubanistas, another source of formal innovation was Afro-Cuban musical rhythm. Kubayanda has identified elements of Afro-Cuban music in the meter of Guillén's poetry, which he characterizes as "technically inspired by Afro-Cuban musical ingenuity." He has also brought attention to its use of "units of the African musical 'mixed metre,'" the "unstressed beats, the differences between stanzas, the clusters of identical vowel sounds (assonance), the buzzing, nasalized consonantal vibrations (mb in *bembón*), the visually and audibly uneven lines," and "the repeats" (as cited in Williams 1995, 51).

Afro-Cuban musical meters affect Tallet's "La rumba" as well. In this poem the predominantly dactylic meter of the first two stanzas is reminiscent of the 6/8 feel of the music of the *rumba guaguancó* being performed by the poem's protagonists. As Crook explains, in rumba "the basic accompaniment patterns of the percussion have a dynamic flexibility built into their structure that allows for duple-triple ambivalence" (1982, 101). However, because of the difficulties of transcribing this rhythmic feel, the *guaguancó* is often written in 2/4 or 4/4 time (Daniel 1995, 83; Crook 1982, 99–100; Ortiz 1973b, 170). Despite its incorporation of the triplet feel of rumba, Tallet's poem is often dismissed for its "superficial" and "stereotyped" representation of black culture. For example, Moore stresses the fact that Tallet wrote few Afro-Cuban-inspired poems and that the impetus to write "La rumba" actually came from a friend who dared him to make the nonsensical phrase "Mambimba, mabomba, mabombo y bombó" part of a poem. Moore also cites Néstor Baguer's comment that "La rumba" represented for Tallet no more than poetic gymnastics (1997, 199–200). Some may argue on the basis of Tallet's seemingly superficial approach that the poem's incorporation of rumba rhythm was not a deliberate formal accomplishment. Nevertheless, becoming aware of the rhythmic peculiarities of rumba did not require painstaking research on Tallet's part. The journal *Archivos del Folklore Afrocubano* had regularly included articles on Afro-Cuban cultural traditions, mainly by Fernando Ortiz, from as early as 1924 (Ortiz 1924b, 1924c, 1924d). In fact, in this same year Ortiz had explained in *Glosario de afronegrismos* that "the syncopation found in the music of this dance [rumba] is characteristically in a 2/4 time signature, with interspersed crotchet triplets that bestow on the music an unmistakable flavor" (1924a, 410). Tallet could have read about this aspect of rumba in any of these publications and decided to try to incorporate it into the meter of his poem. On the other hand, the dactylic meter of Marcelino Arozarena's "Liturgia etiópica" reflects the 6/8 meter of many of the rhythms that are traditionally employed in the *bembé,* a celebration dedicated to the orishas in which the poem takes place (Guirao 1938, 151–53).[12] These explanations greatly undermine Mónica Mansour's analysis of the meter used in afrocubanista poetry, in which she concludes that "the poets of the *negrista* movement resorted to the models of popular Hispanic poetry, not to the analysis and application of African or even Afro-American music" (1973, 151).

Afrocubanistas also incorporated aspects of Afro-Cuban dance into the formal texture of their poetry. For instance, Tallet's use of language throughout "La rumba" displays the formal influence of the represented dance. In writing this poem the poet was faced with the difficulties of describing dance movement through the type of language traditionally employed in written poetry. As Aviram explains, this language draws attention to its rhetorical features, such as style, images, and figures. By contrast, the main purpose of expository language, which is used in other literary genres, is to draw the reader's attention to the subject matter (Aviram 1994, 49). As can be appreciated in the following extract, expository language is used to describe dance movement in academic studies: "The male dancer holds his back very straight with a forward tilt and with shoulders raised slightly. The head retains a raised position and alternates between side right and side left. The elbows are raised extremely to moderately high in middle range. . . . Arm movement is from side to forward, in an arc" (Daniel 1995, 76). Tallet's descriptions do make ample use of poetic rhetorical figures such as similes and metaphors. Nevertheless, the language is at the same time expository in that its main purpose is to convey to the reader the exact movements of the two dancers (Guirao 1938, 65–66).

A poem that exhibits deep formal influences from an Afro-Cuban dance is Emilio Ballagas's "Rumba." This poem uses the image of the cyclone to convey the black female dancer's movements (Guirao 1938, 108–9). Since the poem conveys the idea of movement through metaphor rather than describing it directly, it could be argued that the kinesthetic codes of the rumba performance have been processed through a poetic formal device. Nevertheless, other factors suggest a very different process, one by which Ballagas's "Rumba" was formally determined by the dance of the orisha Yemayá of the Lucumí tradition. The use of the metaphor "olaespuma" to refer to the dancer's dress in the second line of the poem already suggests the presence of Yemayá, because her colors are the blue of the sea and the white of the waves' foam. Furthermore, other images in the poem present close similarities with the outfit worn by the performer who represents Yemayá in this dance. As Ortiz explains, this dancer "viste una bata blanca, como las otras *orichas* hembras, ceñida con una especie de ancho cinto de tela con un peto o ampliación de forma romboidal sobre el ombligo" (wears a white robe, like the other female orishas, tied with a wide belt made of cloth with a rhomboid shape over the belly button) (1981, 345). The use of the word *olaespuma* to refer to the *bata* suggests that the dancer in the poem may be wearing a white dress. Also, in view of the "rhomboid shape" over the performer's belly, the simile in the last stanza of Ballagas's poem, where the black dancer's belly button is likened to a single eye that looks at Changó, cannot be merely a coincidence (Guirao 1938, 109). In the same way as the eye simile could have been inspired by the rhomboid shape of the dancer's belt, the use of the cyclone metaphor to describe the dancer's movements could be an influence from the movements that are employed in the dance of Yemayá, as made evident by Ortiz's description of this orisha's dances: "Her dances begin with soft undulations, like waters that move languidly in the breeze, but soon they become more vigorous and more passionate, just as the sea becomes excited when there is a storm. The female dancers symbolize the furious waves with their movements and with their wide and fast gyrations they imitate the whirlwinds of the sea that are caused by hurricanes" (1981, 345). Since in the dance of Yemayá the hurricane presumably symbolizes her uncontrolled and unbridled character,[13] the dancer's movements are an example of the metaphoric mode of signification in dance, which "expresses one thought, experience or phenomenon by another which resembles the former and is somehow analogous to it, such as dancing a leopard to refer to the power of death" (Hanna 1977, 224). Thus, Ballagas's poem uses a formal characteristic of the represented dance as an important rhetorical device.

A similar formal borrowing from rumba can be found in Ballagas's "El baile del gavilán" (The Dance of the Blackbird). This poem deals with a pantomimic rumba called *Gavilán* in which, as Daniel explains, dancers enact the hunting of blackbirds (1995, 174). In the dance, a dancer imitates one of these birds through his or her dancing movements, an association that becomes the basis for the central metaphor of Ballagas's poem, where the woman is equated to a flying blackbird (Ballagas 1984, 89–90). A similar judgment can be made in relation to this poet's "El baile del papalote." As explained in chapter 5, in the rumba variety on which this poem is based, the male dancer impersonates a man flying a kite, and the female dancer is the kite. At the end of the dance, as the male dancer winds up the string, he tells the female dancer to approach him and embrace him, which reflects his desire for her. According to Ortiz, the fact that this part of the dance has erotic connotations for the performers themselves strongly suggests that the dance of the kite is a metaphor for the courtship between man and woman (1981, 432). In "El baile del papalote," the dancers' game of retreat and approach is recounted by the male dancer, who talks to the female dancer as if she were a kite. In this way, the association of the act of flying a kite with human courtship, which constitutes the metaphoric mode of signification of the dance, becomes the poem's central metaphor. Considering the importance of metaphor in poetry, this means that the poem's form has been determined by that of the represented dance. Consequently, like "Rumba" and "El baile del gavilán," "El baile del papalote" is an example of how afrocubanista poetry can formally incorporate stylistic features of an Afro-Cuban performance by capitalizing on formal similarities between dance and written poetry.

The afrocubanista poems that have been analyzed above achieve Ortiz's goal of incorporating Afro-Cuban culture from a formal point of view. This feat sets afrocubanista poetry apart from other literary representations of Cuban blacks and their culture. A relevant point of contrast is nineteenth-century Cuban abolitionist literature, which as William Luis explains was part of a movement to abolish slavery and the slave trade. Its initiator was Domingo del Monte, who encouraged other younger participants of his literary circle, such as Félix Tanco y Bosmeniel, Anselmo Suárez y Romero, and Cirilo Villaverde, to write a realistic type of literature that denounced the evils of slavery. On the one hand, these abolitionist authors could not entirely avoid being influenced by problematic ideas about blacks, as is made clear in various studies.[14] On the other hand, as Luis also points out, they did challenge the dominant image of the decent and honest white versus the wicked and immoral black. They did this by portraying blacks as powerless victims of the white masters' cruelty and, often, as also being more virtuous than whites, from both a moral and a religious point of view (Luis 1990, 27–28; 2003, 393). In addition, some critics have identified in abolitionist writings an impulse to acknowledge the potential value of African cultures. As Adriana Méndez Rodenas points out, Félix Tanco y Bosmeniel at one point described blacks as being "the poetry of the Cuban nation" and, foreshadowing Ortiz's work on processes of transculturation in Cuba, he recognized the African as an active ingredient in the formation of Cuban and Caribbean culture (1999, 89, 97).[15] Another relevant example can be found in an 1853 chronicle entitled "La casa del trapiche" (The House of the Sugar Mill) by Suárez y Romero. In this text the author remarked on the way in which the slaves constantly updated their songs to deal with everyday occurrences. Furthermore, he defined the context of enunciation of these songs and their dialogic structure (Lienhard 1996, 20–21). In addition, African concepts were occasionally incorporated in abolitionist literature. In his *El cántico del esclavo* (The Song of the Slave), Padrines included African ideas and religion in the composition. Death, for example, was associated with the African belief that, after death, slaves go back to their place of origin, rather than with the Christian concept of burial and resurrection (Luis 1990, 43).

Yet abolitionists on the whole did not engage in such a conscious effort to formally incorporate Afro-Cuban culture into their literary works as afrocubanista poets did. As Paquette points out, to abolitionist liberals "progress" implied retaining much of the culture inherited from Spain and Western Europe, and African influences on Cuban vernacular culture horrified many of them (1988, 102–3). One of the main objectives of Domingo del Monte's project in his literary *tertulias* was to produce "culture of European level and with a solid Spanish base" (Otero 1990, 729). Accordingly, Del Monte encouraged abolitionist writers to read French literature. He thought that the historical novel was the best model for them to follow, and Félix Tanco favored the literature of Balzac (Luis 1998, 12; Méndez Rodenas 1999, 90).[16] Not surprisingly, then, in abolitionist literature, unlike in afrocubanista poetry, the formal characteristics of Afro-Cuban culture did not generally become guiding principles in the author's discourse.

Other examples of contrasting attitudes toward Afro-Cuban oral forms can be found in Rómulo Lachatañeré's *¡Oh, mío Yemayá!* and Fernando Ortiz's *La africanía de la música folklórica de Cuba*. As Lienhard shows, Lachatañeré makes use of a realist-naturalist mode characteristic of nineteenth-century European narrative in relating the *patakíes,* the religious short stories of the Lucumí. Thus, argues Lienhard, there is nothing left of the enunciation, the rhythm, the humor, or the vocabulary normally used in these narrative forms. In a similar way, the formal peculiarities of the song forms Ortiz deals with in his famous treatise on Afro-Cuban culture do not visibly affect the authorial discourse. As Lienhard points out, the former are presented in the form of transcriptions of lyrics that interrupt the learned exposition, thus creating a kind of vertical dialogue between the scholar and his cultural subjects (1996, 25–28).

It is important to note that by incorporating the formal principles of a particular culture into his or her discourse, an author inevitably acknowledges its legitimacy and, at least to some extent, the worth of its members. Significantly, afrocubanista poems that do not formally incorporate the forms of the represented cultural practice at all often betray a derogatory attitude toward blacks. This is the case with Hernández Catá's "Rumba," in which, as argued earlier, the poet fails to incorporate the sound of musical instruments formally through onomatopoeia, resorting instead to the European literary device of personification. The personifications of musical instruments in this poem have the effect of denying the agency of the musicians who play them. Furthermore, the juxtaposition of these personifications with the description of the black woman as a statue—"la negra estatua se agita" (the black statue shakes)—has the effect of granting less human status to her than to the musical instruments. Her dehumanization continues in the synecdoche "risa feroz que no sabe / que el bien puede ser el mal" (ferocious laughter that does not know / that goodness can be evil), which presents her as a ferocious animal, incapable of distinguishing between good and evil. The poet's animosity toward the black female is equally in evidence in his reference to her "sesos huecos tras de la frente" (hollow brains behind her forehead). Although the dancer succeeds in eliciting the desire of the event's participants ("Cien ojos buscan los caminos / que conducen a sus entrañas" [A hundred eyes look for the paths / that lead to her insides]), images such as "Ojos de concha marina, / labios de crudo bisté" (Eyes like a sea shell / lips like a raw steak) and "nariz desparramada" (scattered nose) reveal the poet's disgust with her physiognomy. By contrast, in "El baile del papalote," which formally assimilates elements of the represented cultural practice, Ballagas displays an entirely different attitude toward the black protagonist and her dance. As explained earlier, Ballagas participates in the dance rather than remaining a detached observer, and, in line with the poem's overt sexuality, he directly communicates to the black woman his desire for her.

Nevertheless, the fact that some afrocubanista poems formally incorporate Afro-Cuban cultural forms does not justify interpreting afrocubanista poetry as reflecting the harmonious coming together of blacks and whites in Cuban society. A significant consideration in this respect is that some afrocubanista poems actually emphasize the formal differences between Afro-Cuban cultural practices and written poetry. For example, in Hernández Catá's "Rumba," verbal forms from the event appear as quotations in italics that interrupt the poet's learned discourse without directly affecting its form. This division is exacerbated by metric differences:

whereas the poet's discourse takes the form of four octosyllabic lines, those representing popular speech do not present a fixed pattern, thus reflecting the free versification that characterizes rumba lyrics.[17]

While formally incorporating several nonwritten elements, some of the poems discussed earlier at times also bring into relief differences between the written poem and the live performance. For instance, there is a perceptible detachment from the represented cultural practice in "Bailadora de rumba," where Guirao uses quotation marks to quote the chorus sung in a rumba event. The chorus "¡Arriba, María Antonia, / alabao sea Dió!" was clearly taken from the Sexteto Habanero composition "Eres mi lira armoniosa" (Sexteto Habanero 1992). Like Hernández Catá, Tallet uses italics when reproducing a phrase from a rumba song in "La rumba." The phrase is found in the line "se acabó la rumba *con con, co, mabó*" (the rumba is finished *con con, co, mabó*), and Marcelino Arozarena also uses it in italics in "Caridá," defining it in his glossary as a phrase from a popular rumba (1983, 27–28, 169).[18] Tallet further accentuates differences between the poem and the represented practice by dividing the former into long stanzas, which describe the dancing movements of the performers, and short ones, which attempt to reproduce the sound of instruments. Admittedly, no poem could ever effectively reproduce the simultaneity of audio and visual rhythms in rumba. As argued earlier in this chapter, all Afro-Cuban practices include a wide array of sensory codes that work at various levels of signification. Consequently, the written reproduction of these practices could never be a substitute for the experience of the live performance or convey the multiple meanings of its different sensory codes. Nevertheless, by delivering these musical and choreographic codes in clearly separated stanzas, Tallet's "Rumba" actually emphasizes differences between the written text and the live performance.

In fact, it could be argued that in general all afrocubanista poetry brings into relief differences between the literary culture of afrocubanistas and the oral and performative culture of the Afro-Cuban sectors. The very preoccupation of afrocubanistas with reproducing the multiplicity of media of Afro-Cuban collective practices betrays the strictly written nature of their poetry by drawing attention to the fact that it was intended for an individual reader and not as part of a live Afro-Cuban performance. In this sense, afrocubanista poetry reproduces the sociocultural fractures of the society in which it emerged. As will become evident in the following chapter, the notion that afrocubanista poetry reflects a united mulatto Cuban culture and identity crumbles even further when one considers Afro-Cuban interpretations of the poetry.

7 The Subversion of Afrocubanista Discourse

IN "RE-PRESENTATIONS of Afro-Caribbean Folklore in Spanish Caribbean Poetry," Claudette RoseGreen-Williams analyzes the way in which elements from Afro-Caribbean folklore are "made to function within the discursive-ideological system of the poetic text." In doing so she relies on the notion that "in the process of literary production, the author ... does not merely reflect or reproduce a given reality that is given, but rather re-presents it" (1992, 121). In *Sugar's Secrets: Race and the Erotics of Cuban Nationalism,* Vera Kutzinski also focuses on the way in which afrocubanistas appropriated black cultural forms to further their ideological objectives. She argues that "what is at issue in *poesía mulata,* then, is the aesthetic commodification of blackness and the depersonalization of race and of racist social practices. Represented as pure rhythm, blackness could easily be appropriated by Cuba's literati and, at a distance from the squalor of Havana's ill-famed 'Afro-Cuban underworld' and similar urban ghettos, be assimilated into a poetics of *mestizaje*" (1993, 180). RoseGreen-Williams sees afrocubanista poetry as "designed to ward off discontent, to create a sense of social well-being, and ensure conformity with the *status quo* of social inequality" (1993, 17). She further claims that in the poetry the "bestialization of the sexual physiognomy of the folk performers served, ironically, to further entrench the ideology which had degraded blackness" (1992, 126). In his article "Negrismo: Hibridez cultural, autoridad y la cuestión de la nación" (Negrismo: Cultural Hybridity and the Issue of the Nation), Jerome Branche seeks to demonstrate that "far from constituting a racial democracy [*negrismo*] is part of the process of creation of a new consensus or definition of reality that ultimately aims to preserve the status quo" (1999, 484).

By focusing on the ways in which afrocubanismo furthered the ideological interests of the dominant sectors, these criticisms promote the impression that afrocubanista poets could easily adapt the Afro-Cuban cultural forms represented in their poetry to their versions of Cuban culture and identity. The main aim of this chapter is to assess this notion by exploring Afro-Cuban meanings that penetrate afrocubanista representations. The discussion is based on an analysis of the history of Afro-Cuban dance as a means of cultural resistance.

Afro-Cuban Dance as Cultural Resistance

It is evident that for a long time whites in Cuba did not attribute complex meanings to Afro-Cuban dance. This can be gathered from Esteban Pichardo's comment in the nineteenth century that in their *cabildos de nación* blacks sang and danced in confusion and disarray (as cited in Castellanos and Castellanos 1988, 111). Generally, most nineteenth-century observers assumed that these dances were simply forms of courtship or that they served only as a vehicle to express sexual desire. A suitable example is Fredrika Bremer's description of the slave dances that she witnessed on a nineteenth-century Cuban plantation: "Each *nación* uses different variations; but they all present a fundamental similarity in the main characteristics of the dance. It is always performed by a man and a woman, and it represents a kind of flirting or courtship, during which the male lover expresses his feelings, partly by shaking his limbs so intensely, that he almost looks as if he were coming apart" (1981, 94). Anselmo Suárez y Romero interpreted nineteenth-century rumba as a "baile muy obsceno en pareja, cuyo atractivo principal son las indecorosas contorsiones de cintura" (very obscene dance performed in couples, whose main point of attraction is the unseemly hip movements) (as cited in Ortiz 1924a, 406). This perception continued in the republican era when Fernando Ortiz argued that the rumba was "sensual" and "agitadísima" (very agitated) and that its only purpose was to imitate "the chase and final conquest of the woman, which sometimes takes the form of a live sexual act between the dancers." "This happens," Ortiz explained, "when the dancers, with their sweat-drenched bodies, have been overly excited by the violent exercise, the alcohol, the nudity and the physical contact with members of the opposite sex, and, as a consequence, the dance culminates with a wild orgy" (1924a, 406–7). Specifically in relation to the female dancer, Ortiz explained that her hands raise her skirt according to the extent of her sexual arousal (1924a, 406–7).

Whites made similar assumptions about the dances of the nineteenth- and early-twentieth-century Afro-Cuban comparsas on the Día de Reyes festivities in Havana. For example, a 1925 ordinance by president Gerardo

Machado denounced the way in which comparsa performers marched through the streets "ejecutando movimientos lascivos en una inconcebible promiscuidad de sexos" (making lascivious movements and with men and women all outrageously mixed together), as well as the fact that "con insolente impudor toman parte niños y ancianos" (children and elderly people participate with a shocking lack of propriety) (as cited in Moore 1997, 231). The notion that the elites perceived comparsa dances as sexually suggestive is further illustrated by Harold Courlander's interpretation of the dancing of the *íreme abakuá* or *diablito* as reproducing the movements of a cock in the sexual act (cited in Ortiz 1981, 489–90). Another appropriate example is Ortiz's description of a black female member of a comparsa pictured in a *costumbrista* drawing as a "mulata de rumbo," a term which means "loose mulatto woman of the street."[1]

In fact, it is evident that Afro-Cuban dances were often tolerated and even encouraged by whites precisely because their overt sexuality satisfied some of their own needs. This was clearly the case in nineteenth-century plantations, where Fredrika Bremer witnessed a dance in which "the overseer, a short, ugly man (I often saw the women work under his whip) often took advantage of his authority, sometimes kissing the most beautiful girls with whom he danced, and other times interrupting the other men when they were dancing with the most beautiful black women or with the best dancers, and taking their place" (1981, 94). The fact that, according to Bremer, in the nineteenth century sailors gathered outside cabildos de nación in the hope of catching a glimpse of their dance and music practices is equally indicative of the attraction that outsiders felt toward this aspect of Afro-Cuban dance (1981, 154). Whites' fascination with provocative black dances continued throughout the republican period. Robin Dale Moore has written the following in relation to 1920s and 1930s *son:* "The very fact that middle-class society as a whole continued to condemn *son* music and to discourage its performance in public areas seems if anything to have increased its appeal for many of Cuba's elite. A perception of the *son* as an overtly sexual dance attracted them, as did the prostitutes who taught them new steps." The popularity of rumba in the 1930s also owed much to its eroticism. During this time a more sexually explicit version became widespread in Havana's cabarets, and similar versions were also included in afrocubanista musical spectacles (Moore 1997, 100, 177–78, 184–85).

After the end of Cuban slavery, whites also often allowed the performance of overtly sexual Afro-Cuban dances because they benefited from them financially. In *Los bailes y el teatro de los negros de Cuba,* Ortiz explained that at the time he was writing the people who banned religious Afro-Cuban dances because they delayed blacks' assimilation into Catholicism were the same who turned a blind eye to the more lascivious dances of the island's cabarets. They did this, he explained, because the latter attracted tourism and, thus, financial prosperity (1981, 255–56). Ortiz described this phenomenon as part of an ongoing process by which capitalism had corrupted the "pure" and "primeval" sexuality of African dances. These explanations are revealing, because they illustrate that often it was precisely the whites' conception of Afro-Cuban dances as erotic forms of expression that allowed blacks to perform the dances in public contexts.

Significantly, this perception was not based on an awareness of what these dance forms meant for their practitioners, but on a preestablished and Eurocentric conception of dance. Jahn establishes a distinction between European and African dance that helps to explain the divergence between the ways blacks used their dances and whites' understanding of them: "European dances always have an objective: the physical contact with the female partner, or expressing the dancers' state of mind and their enjoyment through movement, or becoming inebriated during it, etc.; African dance always has a meaning. It activates the order of the world . . . and in this way it is necessary and indispensable" (1970, 100). Indeed, in African societies dances carry out a much wider range of social functions than they do in European ones. The importance of dance in West Africa, for instance, is brought to light in the following extract:

> Dance was (and is today) of central importance in West Africa. It is . . . an integral part of ceremonies that bind groups together as a people. It links one's personal identity to that of the group; events throughout the life cycle of the individual and the community are commemorated in dance: fattening house dances, fertility dances and rite-of-passage dances. Dance also serves as a mediating force between people and the world of the gods. Specific dances and rhythms were appropriate for particular deities. . . . Indeed, dance is so much a part of the philosophy, customs and sense of place that eliminating it would radically alter the African view of the universe. (Hazzard-Gordon 1990, 3–4)

In Cuba, as in West African culture, Afro-Cuban dances represent deities. The dances of the Afro-Cuban ethnic group Lucumí recreate different orishas through specific movements, gestures, and attitudes. In the dance to the deity Elegua, for example, the dancer moves a small, sinuous stick from side to side, pretending to be opening a path in the bush—an allegory of this orisha's ability to "open the way." Another example is the dance to Changó, in which a series of erotic gestures allude to his tremendous virility. Similarly, the dances to Yemayá and Ochún—goddesses of the sea and the rivers, respectively—incorporate gestures that attempt to recreate the movement of sea waves and the flow of the river (Ortiz 1981, 228; Urfé 1977, 221).[2] The pantomimic *rumbas del tiempo de España* (rumbas from the time of Spain) are highly representational as well, their main purpose being to recreate a variety of themes, such as a woman taking a shower, a grandmother reprimanding her grandson, or the hunting of blackbirds (Daniel 1995, 70–71).

As in all forms of nonverbal communication, effective communication in all these dance forms can take place only when the viewer is aware of the preestablished symbolism of the sender's movements and gestures. As Judith Hanna explains, nonverbal communication is successful when the sender's intended message fits with the receiver's reception. Thus, the encoder actively conveys data to the decoder by means of a shared code (1984, 375). It is unlikely that many whites could understand all the kinesthetic codes of Afro-Cuban dances. The degree of immersion in Afro-Cuban culture that this requires is underscored in the following description by Ortiz of Lucumí religious dances:

> The most curious thing about these dances is the way in which the dancers always evoke the spirits that have possessed them, with their pantomimes, their steps and gestures; and they even enact the specific state of a particular spirit in line with the specific attitude in which it has chosen to manifest itself. Consequently, the spectators can deduce from the movements and the performance of the possessed which deity is possessing them and in what modality. The spirit will dance differently depending on which way it chooses to enter or ride the mind of the possessed; and all this choreography responds to a preestablished symbolism. (1981, 229)

Thus, whites' conception of Afro-Cuban dances as merely erotic owed much to their inability to understand them fully. Significantly, Fredrika Bremer did not attribute religious meanings to any of the dances she observed. For example, she failed to remark upon the possibility that the performer dressed in brilliant red who flirted with her in a Lucumí celebration may have been impersonating the precocious Changó, whose dance is also performed by a dancer wearing his characteristic red color (Bremer 1981, 155–56; Ortiz 1981, 333).[3] Fernando Ortiz's approach to Afro-Cuban culture in *Los negros brujos* provides another perfect example of how the religious symbolism of these dances was often mistaken for sexual allusions. In a passage from this book, Ortiz's description of Lucumí dances does not include a single reference to their religious dimension. Instead, he focuses on their overt eroticism, dwelling on the frenzied sexual arousal of the participants and claiming that these rituals often conclude with a wild orgy (1973a, 82–83).

Blacks may not always have objected to such misinterpretations of their dances. Whites' attraction to their imputed eroticism often allowed them to enact essential African myths. Blacks must have taken advantage of this misconception in the first Cuban plantations, where the white masters allowed slave dances because they considered them nonsubversive and cathartic forms of entertainment (Ortiz 1981, 255).[4] It is possible that slave owners also thought that these dances could stimulate their slaves' sexual activity. This would have suited them, since, according to Moreno Fraginals, slave owners were often keen to encourage their slaves' sexual reproduction in order to increase their workforce (1978, 38–57). It is unlikely that they would have approved of the real religious purpose of these dances considering the subversive role that religions of African origins played in the Cuban slavery period (Castellanos and Castellanos 1988, 198–200).[5] Cuban slaves certainly used their collective dances to plot rebellions, and this led to severe restrictions of their dance and music practices after an uprising in 1846 (Bremer 1981, 116–17). They used their songs as forms of protest as well.[6] Significantly, when Fredrika Bremer inquired about the meaning of the words of a slave song, she was told by the slaves that they were insignificant and not worth quoting (1981, 188–89). Bremer may have been right to feel skeptical about this explanation. The slaves were reluctant to explain probably because the lyrics were hostile to their white masters. Alternatively, these songs may have had religious meanings that they wanted to keep secret. In a similar way, members of ethnic groups of African origin used the comparsas to communicate complex religious meanings through a series of linguistic, choreographic, and percussive codes that were incomprehensible to the elites. Examples of these codes are those used in the comparsas of the Abakuá by the character or figure known as the *morúa,* who communicated with the *íreme* or *diablito* in Abakuá sacred language and by making symbolic gestures with two sugar canes or bananas (León 1984, 86, 91).[7]

Julia Cuervo Hewitt identifies a reference in Cuban fictional narrative to the way in which blacks may have taken advantage of whites' misconception of African music as simply erotic entertainment in order to use it as an instrument of rebellion. In a short story entitled "El otro cayo" (The Other Key), written in 1946 by Cuban writer Lino Novás Calvo, a white character describes African music as "carne para el sexo" (flesh for sex). In reality, Cuervo Hewitt comments, "for the African, the drum beat was the language through which human beings communicated with the gods." Thus, a mulatto character in the story who has, according to Cuervo Hewitt, "plena conciencia de las dos culturas" (full awareness of both cultures) replies to the white character that "la música también es pólvora" (music is also gunpowder) (1988, 44).

Ortiz, then, was probably wrong in thinking that the popularity of erotic Afro-Cuban dances in the island's cabarets was destroying their religious meanings (1981, 253–66). Like the slaves in the first Cuban plantations, blacks in the republican period seem to have taken advantage of this popularity to maintain African religious notions. For example, black *son* musicians at this time used elements of Afro-Cuban religions in their popular compositions, thus introducing them into the public sphere (Moore 1997, 93–94). Rumba seems appropriate for a similar stratagem because, whereas whites see it as a form of erotic expression, its practitioners often view it as a vehicle of religious notions. For example, a rumbera from Matanzas told dance ethnographer Ivonne Daniel that sometimes she is talking to Changó while dancing. She said that at other times the dance is like Oshún and she wants this orisha to dance with her partner (1995, 100). Not surprisingly, then, although possession never occurs, female rumberas often make symbolic gestures to the orishas that could be easily mistaken as sexual (Daniel 1995, 100, 132–35). For instance, a rumbera's raising her skirt could be interpreted as sexually enticing, but a Santería practitioner will know that this might be a reference to Changó. As Lydia Cabrera explains, the female *caballos* (possessed initiates) of this orisha often raise their skirts to make clear that "'él tiene, y muy grandes, ¡Ekuá, etié mi okko!' algo que le falta a su caballo" (he [Changó] has very large things [testicles] that are missing in his *caballo*) (Cabrera 1975a, 34; Ortiz 1981, 234). Thus, in a move parallel to that of *son* performers, cabaret rumberas must have used sexually suggestive choreographic elements from religious dances in front of black and white audiences.[8] In doing so, they were introducing essential aspects of their subaltern cultural traditions into Cuban popular culture by exploiting the fact that the erotic qualities of rumba satisfied the needs of the popular sectors.

The Religious Potency of the Afrocubanista Rumba

The proliferation of rumba-inspired afrocubanista poems throughout the 1920s and 1930s is another indication of the success of this Afro-Cuban strategy. Like many other whites, some of the participants in the afrocubanista poetic movement were attracted to the eroticism of this dance form and believed it to be essentially a secular form of entertainment. These perceptions are reflected in the following extract from Teófilo Radillo's "La rumba (Bricomanía en blanco y negro)," which echoes Ortiz's distaste for cabaret rumba:[9]

> Lúbrica tu cadera
> cuando bailas la rumba
> rumba caliente de tu carne fresca.
> . . . .
> Ya tu rumba no es santa;
> ya tu rumba no es negra;
> ya se ha descolorido
> en el ácido turbio
> de tus noches perversas.
> (1939, 50–55)

> Lewd is your waist
> When you dance rumba
> Hot rumba with your live flesh.
> . . . .
> Your rumba is no longer sacred;
> Your rumba is no longer black;
> It has already lost its color
> In the turbulent acid
> Of your perverse nights.

And yet, in describing rumba, afrocubanistas often unknowingly introduced Afro-Cuban religious elements into their poetry. For example, in "Bailadora de rumba," Ramón Guirao's purpose seems to be solely to convey the idea of a rumbera dancing the *guaguancó*, describing her appearance and the audiovisual sensations of the rumba event. Nevertheless, references to the dancer's "collar de jabón" (soaplike necklace) and "bata blanca" (white robe) indicate that she is an initiate of the Regla de Ocha or Santería. The first ceremony of initiation in this religion is the bestowal of a necklace known as *eleke,* which is made of shiny glass beads. After becoming a *santo,* the initiate or *iyawó* must dress in white for a whole year, thus the dancer's "bata blanca" in the poem (Castellanos and Castellanos 1992, 89, 97; Canizares 1993, 32–33).

Emilio Ballagas's "Rumba" is another relevant example. This poet's use of the imagery of the Yemayá dance, which was explained in the previous chapter, suggests that the poem may have been based on a rumba performance in which the dancer was making use of the symbolic movements of the dance to this orisha. Whereas this imagery would clearly recreate the figure of Yemayá in the mind of an informed reader, it is doubtful that this was the author's intention, since the poem does not contain any direct references to this female orisha. In point of fact, the sexually suggestive nature of the images indicates that Ballagas was more interested in the erotic aspects of the dance than in its religious connotations. Most notably, the line "emerge de la olaespuma de su bata de algodón" (she emerges from the sea foam of her cotton robe) suggests that the black woman is stripping (Guirao 1938, 108). This is consistent with the references to her belly button, which suggest it is in full view. It also fits with the clear Venus imagery identified by Boulware (1977, 21), since in classical representations such as Boticcelli's *The Birth of Venus* this goddess emerges naked from the sea. The notion that Ballagas conceived of rumba as a striptease is supported by the drawing of a naked black woman that he included along with his afrocubanista poems in his anthology *Mapa de la poesía negra americana* (1946, 135).

Nevertheless, by evoking Yemayá, the represented dance would suggest meanings other than sexual ones to an informed reader. For instance, since this orisha is considered the mother of Changó, the poem could symbolize his birth, because at the end of the poem the dancer's belly "opens up" like an eye in order to look at him.[10] From this perspective, the cyclone metaphor in the poem could be seen as reflecting the turbulent state of Yemayá's womb prior to the birth (Guirao 1938, 108–9).[11]

Another way in which Yemayá introduces meanings into the poem is by reminding Regla de Ocha initiates of the complex of myths, legends, and proverbs featuring the deities alluded to in the poem. This process of association also operates in the dances to the orishas. For example, Antonio Benítez Rojo points out that the dance to Changó "carries within itself the profuse cycle of myths, legends, and proverbs that tell about Changó, and whose purpose in the Yoruba culture is a double one: to provide the child and the adolescent with didactic examples of what he should and should not do according to tradition" (1992, 169–70). In view of this, it can be argued that the poem could remind the reader of a particular *pataki* that features Changó and Yemayá in conjunction with the sea.[12] In this legend, as recounted by one of Lydia Cabrera's informants, Changó tries to seduce Yemayá at a party without knowing that she is his mother. Yemayá reacts by provocatively inviting him back to her house, the sea. They get on a boat, and when Changó, who cannot swim, falls in the water, Yemayá refuses to help him. Eventually, Obatalá appears and urges her not to let her son drown, so she helps him out of the water and tells him to respect his mother in future. The conclusion reflects the didactic purpose mentioned by Benítez Rojo: "Changó y Yemayá se abrazan en el mar y cuando hay batá y bajan estos dos ocha, Changó, que dice que después de Dios, en el mundo no hay santo más grande que él, layé layé mi ságguo, se achica ante sus madres. Las respeta a las dos y las dos lo amansan cuando se arrebata" (Changó and Yemayá embrace in the sea, and when there is a *batá* both these *ocha* come down; Changó, who claims that apart from God there is no one in the world who is more saintly than he, *layé layé mi ságguo,* shrinks in the presence of his mothers. He respects them both and they both appease him when he becomes angry) (Cabrera 1975a, 236–37). Changó's respect for his mother is central to Regla de Ocha mythology, where Yemayá is considered an exemplary mother figure (Ortiz 1973b, 161; 1973c, 189). Illustrative of her role as a quintessential mother is the fact that she is associated with Mariana Grajales Cuello, the mother of black nineteenth-century hero Antonio Maceo, whose motherhood was not only that of "the protective nurturing mother" but also that of "the motherhood of total and selfless dedication to a cause, sacrificing home, husband and children to war and making it good" (Stubbs 1995, 312–13).

The presence of an orisha in José Z. Tallet's "La rumba" would also suggest a myriad of meanings to an informed reader. Changó's possession of Tomasa at the end of the poem suggests that, like the female dancer of Ballagas's "Rumba," some of her dancing gestures are references to this orisha. This could apply to Tomasa's use of the traditionally male pelvic thrust known as *vacunao,* because the dance to Changó is characterized by an emphatic pelvic movement (Benítez Rojo 1992, 169). In fact, one cannot help but wonder whether Chepe Chacón himself (Tomasa's black dancing partner in Tallet's poem) is mistaking religious allusions for sexually enticing gestures. Like many whites, he may have thought that rumba was only a form of sexual expression. By contrast, to a reader versed in Regla de Ocha traditions, Tomasa's pelvic thrusts could symbolize not only sex but also violent resistance, irreverence, and transgression. As Benítez Rojo points out, in the dance to Changó "the accentuated hip movement . . . refers at once to Changó's erotic character in the Yoruba pantheon and also to his warrior attributes: the two-headed axe in the shape of a pelvis. It also refers to the color red, to blood, to fire, to anger, to pleasure, to nonreflection, to the *fiesta,* to wine, to transgression, to incest, to suicide" (1992, 169). The religious connotations of these poems demonstrate that afrocubanista poetry is another example of how the explicit sexuality of Afro-Cuban dance served to introduce Afro-Cuban religious notions into dominant culture. It is equally evident that in the poetry this process often took place without the knowledge of the whites who made it possible, as in the examples cited in the previous section. It could be argued that Afro-Cuban deities that penetrate afrocubanista texts play a role similar to that of the Signifying Monkey, a trickster figure from Afro-Cuban culture that, according to Henry Louis Gates, mediates and challenges all figurations of discourse (1984, 286–87). For example, in his analysis of afrocubanista poetry, José Piedra uses this figure to argue that, in poems by Nicolás Guillén and Teófilo Radillo, certain Afro-Cuban concepts "are protected and thrive by their subtle intrusion into Cuban literature" and "African traditions are preserved beyond the temporary compromise of the enslaving text." Other Afro-Cuban cultural elements "signify recklessly upon the integrity of Cuban discourse" (1985, 375, 379, 390).

The Afrocubanista Rumba as a Vehicle of Female Empowerment

Other meanings that the representation of rumba in afrocubanista poetry could suggest to an informed reader have to do with the dance form's potential as a vehicle of female empowerment. Before illustrating this, it must be pointed out that the role which black rumberas played in the process of cultural resistance that was described earlier reflects their subordinate position in relation to the black men of their own communities. In a male-dominated society it was particularly their sexually enticing dancing that guaranteed the popularity of rumba and, thus, the continuation of symbolic religious dancing. It was black women, consequently, who had to sacrifice their integrity in order to salvage the culture of their group, a sacrifice that also included undressing in the more explicit versions of rumba performed in 1930s Havana strip clubs.[13] This point brings to mind José Piedra's comparison between the rumbera and the figure of Sikán, who, according to the foundational legend of the Abakuá, also had to sacrifice her body for the sake of her male-dominated community (1991, 657–59).[14] In the myth, Sikán is killed by the men of her community so that she can inhabit the drum *ekue*, through which the male Abakuá dignitaries communicate with their supreme deity Ekue.[15]

Nevertheless, this myth can also serve to illustrate the notion that the role played by these rumberas reflects the central position of women in

Afro-Cuban culture. According to Cabrera, in the legend, Sikán became united with Ekue and was inseparable from him from then on, which means that the supreme deity of the Abakuá is part woman (1975b, 6). Furthermore, in the rituals of the Abakuá it is Sikán's spirit that makes Ekue speak. Jorge and Isabel Castellanos point out that this feature reflects the essential role of women in Abakuá rituals, which cannot be carried out without the presence of Sikán (Castellanos and Castellanos 1992, 219). For Piedra, on the other hand, the relation between genders in the Abakuá myth is a "mythological exchange between the two" in which "the man is condemned to create and procreate through the woman." He adds that "his voice is forced to be lodged in a part of her, skin, hip, vagina, womb" (1991, 658–59). In the same way that Abakuá men could not preserve their culture without Sikán's body, the strategy of resistance behind rumba would not have worked without the rumbera's sacrifice. Therefore, in both cases, the continuation of the cultures and identities of men depended crucially on the intervention of women.

A similarly ambivalent relation between genders is present in the choreography of rumba. Undeniably, the dance of the *guaguancó* strongly reflects values of male domination. As Daniel explains, the dance includes a controlling male figure that takes advantage of his partner's vulnerability to possess her. Thus, she adds, "notions of accommodation and subservience to men which reside deep within Cuban culture are maintained." Nevertheless, not all aspects of the dance put forward an image of women as submissive. The percussive energy that characterizes female movement can suggest a daring, playful, and even aggressive mood. Furthermore, the female dancer can avoid possession by the male by swiftly covering her crotch with a garment. Thus, given that she has the reflexes and dancing skills to do so, the female dancer can conceivably be the one who determines when and how the possession takes place. Since women in rumba often do not want to be seen to be "taken" in public, the *guaguancó* can often conclude without a single successful *vacunao*, the pelvic thrust through which the male dancer tries to possess his female partner (Daniel 1995, 121, 124, 77, 98). José Piedra describes the potential for female empowerment in this aspect of *guaguancó*: "In spite of the improvisational virtuosity reserved for men rumba performers, women overtly set the grammatical pattern of the dance and covertly that of the song, including the manipulation of their partner's 'triumph' and the choreography of their own joint defeat as a 'get down' or 'break'" (1991, 641).

José Z. Tallet's "La rumba" reflects some of the characteristics of rumba that suggest female empowerment. For example, in the extract below, the poet presents an image of the female dancer as powerful, furious, and defiant, whereas the male dancer, Chepe Chacón, appears as an almost comical rigid puppet or dummy, a hopeless victim of his libido desperately chasing after Tomasa:

> Las ancas potentes de niña Tomasa
>
> . . . .
>
> desafiando con rítmico, lúbrico disloque
> el salaz ataque de Che Encarnación:
> muñeco de cuerda que rígido el cuerpo,
>
> . . . .
>
> a saltos iguales, de la inquieta grupa
> va en persecución.
> (Guirao 1938, 65)

> Tomasa's powerful legs
>
> . . . .
>
> challenge in rhythmic and lewd disarray
> the salacious attack of Che Encarnación,
> a wind-up dummy with a rigid body,
>
> . . . .
>
> who chases after her unsettled rump
> with even leaps.

In the ensuing two stanzas it becomes evident that Tomasa's teasing and lascivious breast-shaking severely inflames Chepe Chacón. She appears cool and in command and actually performs the traditionally male *vacunao*. By contrast, the male dancer is frenetic, as if possessed by a devil, which suggests that he has lost control of his body (his voice falters) and of his actions. Significantly, Tomasa's unorthodox *vacunao* subverts notions of male dominance inscribed in the gesture (Guirao 1938, 66).

In the following stanza Tomasa avoids Chepe Chacón's *vacunao*, and while she is described as courageous and defiant (she turns away from him, suggestively swinging her hips), he is described as defeated. Tomasa's superior skill and composure allow her to avoid being symbolically possessed by Chepe Chacón and, instead, at the end of the poem she is possessed by Changó. In this way, as Jiménez has argued, "Tomasa counteracts the committed role of the typical submissive *rumbera*" (1993, 33). Thus, José Z. Tallet's poem presents an image of the *guaguancó* as an art form that allows women to use their sexual allure to dictate the actions of men. On the other hand, the idea that the rumbera's movements could actually serve as an offensive weapon against white men can be found in Alfonso Hernández Catá's "Rumba." In this poem, images of ferociousness and aggressiveness applied to the rumbera, her dancing, and Afro-Cuban music combine to create an image of her sexually charged movements as an instrument of black revenge against the injustices of slavery (Guirao 1938, 127, 128–29).

Rafael Esténger's poem "Coloquio" is a particularly interesting example of how a cultural practice characteristic of rumba contributes to promoting an empowering image of black women. Unlike other poems analyzed in this chapter, "Coloquio" does not focus on a particular performance of rumba. In this case the dance and music form is the object of a disagreement between a black mother and her daughter. The mother feels that since her daughter has become a schoolteacher and, consequently, reached a high status in society, it is unsuitable for her to continue participating in vulgar rumba events. Estrella, the daughter, asks her not to scold her any more, because she is simply incapable of controlling her body when she hears rumba music. She then proceeds to express her inherent rhythm through a series of biological images, the last one being a comparison between her heart and a drum (*atabal*). After this, as if language alone could not adequately express the extent of her affinity to the music, Estrella's speech breaks into percussive onomatopoeia that accurately reproduces the high-pitched notes from the soloing drum employed in rumba:[16] "Príquiti-príquiti-príquiti, / príquiti-príquiti-prá" (Guirao 1938, 164).

By making Estrella vocalize the onomatopoeia, Esténger was inadvertently distorting the gender biases that permeate most Afro-Cuban traditions. Indeed, every aspect of the *batá* drumming of Santería or Regla de Ocha seems sexist. Fernando Ortiz explains that although the name of the biggest *batá* drum that leads the ensemble translates as "mother" (*Iyá*), all three drums (*Okónkolo, Itótele,* and *Iyá*) are considered by *santeros* to be masculine, and even their skin must come from a male animal. He adds that among the foremost personal attributes that a *batá* drummer must possess are masculinity, physical strength, and endurance. The importance of masculinity for the correct execution of the drumming is such that drummers (*olúbatá*) give up playing when their sexual cycle is over. *Santeros* even believe that if a woman touches the drums they lose their tension and their adequate pitch (1996b, 215–16). In fact, playing drums has been traditionally forbidden for women in most Afro-Cuban traditions. As Rogelio Martínez Furé explains, "Even in secular music, drumming is considered to be for men only. It is regarded as inconceivable that a woman beat the head of an instrument whose creation is attributed to Changó, god of lightning and fire, who changed the divining boards and the sedentary life with his wild drumming which had imprisoned the rumbling of the turbulent clouds" (1991, 40).[17] Changó's extreme masculinity and his ownership of all drums may well be the reason behind these restrictions. On the other hand, they may also derive from the idea of keeping from women the secret of divine communication that relies on percussive codes of signification. This is probably the case among the Abakuá, in view of Sikán's betrayal of the secret to the enemy tribe of the Efik in their foundational myth. Indeed, the *batá* drums themselves contain a secret (*afóuobó*) that gives them their sacred and magical strength and that is only known by the *omoaña batá* drummers (Ortiz 1996b, 209).

These restrictions must also be seen in relation to images of women in Afro-Cuban culture that suggest the role of a passive instrument, rather than that of an active player. These connotations are present in the practice of dividing binary drums into male and female according to the tuning. The highest-pitched drum is perceived as being more "energetic" and, consequently, male. By contrast, the lower-pitched drum is more "passive" and therefore female. Sometimes the distinction depends on the role of each of the instruments. In the case of the *clave*, for example, the striking stick is male and the passive stick is female (Ortiz 1996b, 18–19; 1984, 15). The idea of women as an instrument to be played, struck, or used by men is sharply in evidence in Abakuá rituals. In these, the high priest (Iyamba) produces the voice of the Supreme Being by wetting his fingers with water or the blood from one of the sacrifices and then rubbing a stick (*güin* or *yin*) on the edge or the center of the drum known as *ekue*, which Sikán is believed to inhabit (Cabrera 1975a, 212, 282; Ortiz 1996b, 383–409).[18]

Afrocubanistas themselves seemed particularly keen on this Afro-Cuban conception of women. An important semantic field in their poetry is that of instrumental imagery, in which parts of the female anatomy are likened to Afro-Cuban musical instruments. These associations may be based on shape, as in the image of a female waist that becomes a guitar in Emilio Ballagas's "Piano" (Ballagas 1984, 77). Similarly, the *maracas* become breasts in his "Nombres negros en el son":

> Libres altas las maracas
> saltan como dos redondos, duros senos de mulata.
> (Guirao 1938, 114)

The *maracas* are free and jump up high,
like the round, hard breasts of a mulatto woman.

Alternatively, these associations can be based on tactile sense, as in Guirao's "Bailadora de rumba," where the line "tersura de bongó" metonymically relates the texture of the dancer's skin to the texture of the skin of the *bongó* (Guirao 1938, 53). In Ballagas's "Nombres negros en el son," the skin of a woman named Rita Barranco is also compared to the texture of this drum:

de carne tostada, a fuego quemada al sol,
de tersa carne templada al fuego como un bongó.[19]
(Guirao 1938, 113)

of toasted flesh, burnt with fire under the sun,
of soft flesh tuned on the fire like a *bongó*.

The presence in Afro-Cuban culture of this conception of women's bodies as instruments suggests that these poetic images are yet another afrocubanista utilization of Afro-Cuban cultural elements. It is evident, then, that in this case the sexist principles characteristic of Afro-Cuban traditions served afrocubanistas in conveying their own sexist conceptions of women.

In view of these explanations, Estrella's onomatopoeia challenges important aspects of Afro-Cuban and afrocubanista male sexist discourse. In Esténger's poem it is a woman who produces percussive codes of signification without the need of a guiding male hand. She thus reappropriates an instrument of communication that was central to Afro-Cuban culture and had been denied to members of her sex. In this way the poem challenges the image of women and their bodies as passive instruments of men, an image that is present in the traditions outlined above and in much afrocubanista poetry.

Rumba in the Poetry of Marcelino Arozarena

As in the poems analyzed in the previous section, rumba introduces Afro-Cuban religious meanings in Marcelino Arozarena's "Caridá" as well. The poem consists of various descriptions centered on a rumba performance. These include images that recreate the singing and drumming of the collective event and Caridad's skilled and provocative dancing, as well as the electrifying emotions she feels while dancing a *guaguancó*. In between these descriptions the poet repeatedly wonders why Caridad is absent (Arozarena 1983, 27).

In spite of the poem's seemingly limited subject matter, a series of clues that a reader familiar with Lucumí lore would detect introduces other themes into the composition. These clues suggest that the protagonist of "Caridá" is in fact an orisha, in this case Oshún. First, although the line "la hija de Yemayá" (Yemayá's daughter) could simply mean that Caridad is Yemayá's *omó* or protégé,[20] it could equally suggest that she is actually Oshún, because this orisha is the daughter of Yemayá in some legends (Castellanos and Castellanos 1992, 54).[21] The fact that Oshún's Catholic alter ego is the Virgen de la Caridad del Cobre, as Cabrera indicates, lends further weight to this interpretation (1975a, 81). Furthermore, Oshún shares with Caridad a love for dancing to the music of drums. A *pataki* reproduced by Mercedes Cros Sandoval makes clear that "Oshún, hermosa mujer, gustaba de ir al *güelimere* a bailar ante los tambores sagrados" (Oshún, a beautiful woman, enjoyed going to the *güelimere* to dance in front of the sacred drums) (Cros Sandoval, as quoted in Castellanos and Castellanos 1992, 51).[22] Like Caridad, Oshún is a very seductive dancer, as evident in a *pataki* where she manages to entice Ogún out of the forest with her dancing (Castellanos and Castellanos 1992, 51). Just as Oshún is shown as bewitching Ogún, Caridad is described as "la maga del embó." Since "embó" means spell, according to Arozarena, Caridad is being presented as a sorceress who casts spells over men (1983, 169).

An important difference between "Caridá" and the poems seen earlier is that, unlike Guirao and Ballagas, Arozarena must have been aware of the symbolic dimension of his poem. Arozarena came from the black lower classes of Havana, in which, as explained in the second chapter of this study, involvement in Afro-Cuban traditions was common. As Arozarena's daughter Georgina Arozarena Himely and Celia Pinto explain, "Marcelino Arozarena was born on the 13th of March of 1912, in a *solar* . . . in Vedado, a neighborhood of Havana. His father was a builder and his mother was a washerwoman. His ancestors were *Lucumí* on his mother's side and on his father's side too, with the exception of one of his great grandfathers, who was Spanish" (1998, 3). Since Arozarena's family proudly retained the memory of their African ethnic origins, they probably practiced Lucumí cultural traditions as well. The fact that the poet was born in a *solar* certainly points to a direct involvement with Afro-Cuban traditions. As De La Fuente explains, the *solares* were tenement houses (normally old colonial mansions) where many low-income families lived in conditions of extreme poverty. Although the *solares* housed both blacks and whites, the former were vastly overrepresented (2001,

114). In the communal patio areas of these large houses, poor blacks could gather and perform their dances, songs, and rituals of African origins.[23] Because of this, the *solares* became centers of preservation and development of strongly African-influenced forms at the time Arozarena was born. Rumba, for example, emerged from the *solares* of urban areas in the early republican period, according to musicologists.[24]

Arozarena's poetry certainly reflects a profound knowledge of Afro-Cuban culture. The poet made use of a much larger array of Afro-Cuban cultural traditions and forms than other afrocubanistas did. Whereas most afrocubanista poems deal with better-known dance and music genres, such as *son* and rumba, Arozarena's poetry features many others. He represents the *conga de comparsa* in "La conga" and "Ensayando la comparsa del majá" (Rehearsing the Comparsa of the Snake), the *bembé* in "Liturgia etiópica" (Ethiopian Liturgy), and the *toque de santos* in "Amalia" (Arozarena 1983, 46–48, 61–63; Guirao 1938, 146–49, 151–53). In addition, he deals with Abakuá culture in "Cumbéle Macumbéle" and with a varied number of orishas, including Ogún in "Evohé," Changó in "Bongó," and Babalú Ayé in "Liturgia etiópica" (Guirao 1938, 149–53, Arozarena 1983, 38–40). The way in which some of these poems elaborate upon very specific aspects of Afro-Cuban cultural traditions is equally revealing. For instance, "Bongó" constructs images around Changó's status as the creator and owner of Afro-Cuban drums. More specifically, the image "lágrimas de cintura" (tears made with the hips) in this poem is based on this orisha's characteristic pelvic movement (Arozarena 1983, 40).

Arozarena's poem "Amalia" is equally revealing of the poet's familiarity with the figure of Changó. Here, Arozarena describes the dancing of a woman called Amalia who is dancing at a *Toque de santos* and fears that Changó might be officiating in the ceremony.[25] Arozarena's knowledge about Changó is evident in that he refers to the orisha's strength and characteristic red color. Furthermore, Amalia's fear would only make sense to someone familiar with the orisha's bad temper, which is such that only Obatalá can pacify him (Castellanos and Castellanos 1992, 45). In this poem Arozarena also creates an ethnographically correct representation of spiritual possession by Changó. The gradual possession is conveyed by making use of Changó's lascivious qualities as the poem moves from a romantic description of the protagonist,

Amalia, ¡mulata santa!,
las almendras de tus ojos encerraron dos cocuyos

y son tuyos
en la negrísima pulpa de tus radiantes pupilas

Amalia, saintly mulatto woman!
the almonds that are your eyes contain two fireflies
and they belong to you
in the very black pulp of your radiant pupils,

to a more sexually charged description of her dancing movements—"sus tachos de sabrosura / que van lujuria quemando" (her buckets of delight / which burn lust)—as the final possession approaches (1983, 48).

In "Caridá," by contrast, Arozarena uses a more openly erotic tone in representing secular dance and music practices. The type of sexual jesting that takes place in profane Afro-Cuban dance forms is also portrayed in his poem "Ensayando la comparsa del majá":

Saca e pié,[26]
. . . . .
Si nos miran de frente a los do,
paresemo uno;
si no miran de lao,
oh!
no no miren de lao, por Dió!
(1983, 55)

Stick your foot out,
. . . .
If they look at us from the front
it looks like there's only one of us;
if they look at us from the side,
oh!
Please, don't look at us from the side.

Thus, it is evident that Arozarena's treatment of the female dancer's anatomy is substantially subtler in the context of a religious dance than in the context of profane dances. This reveals an ability to appreciate a more sublimated type of sexual expression in the former.

"Cumbéle Macumbéle" further illustrates the poet's familiarity with the represented culture. In this poem the image "y sangre de son espeso / deja un hilo de temblores en la piel de los tambores" (blood of thick *son* / leaves a trail of shivers on the skin of the drums) is based on the contact between blood and the drum, which is central to the foundational

160 *The Subversion of Afrocubanista Discourse*

myth of the Abakuá. The poem captures the myth's emphasis on female betrayal as well, since it recounts the shock experienced by an Abakuá dignitary at discovering that his girlfriend is not as white as she had led him to believe. Understanding the poem fully also requires knowledge of Santería or Regla de Ocha traditions and of the specific attributes of the orishas. What betrays the blackness of Cumbéle's woman is the fact that she is wearing the "coyá de la Mesé" (*collar de la Merced*):

> ya no es tan blanca como su risa
> . . . .
> ¿quién ha bito niña blanca,
> . . . .
> con coyá de la Mesé?
>   (1983, 36–37)
>
> She is no longer white like her laughter
> . . . .
> Who has ever seen a white girl
> . . . .
> wearing the necklace of Mesé?

As in Guirao's "Bailadora de rumba," this is a reference to the *elekes*, the beaded necklaces that are conferred to initiates of Santería. An informed reader would understand that the line "coyá de la Mesé" is a reference to the white necklace of Obatalá, since this orisha is generally identified with Nuestra Señora de las Mercedes (Our Lady of Mercy) (Castellanos and Castellanos 1992, 26; Canizares 1993, 34). In the poem, the characters that sing the chorus conclude that Cumbéle's woman is black upon seeing her with the white necklace of Obatalá. Thus, it is obvious that they associate attachment to Afro-Cuban religious traditions with this racial category. Since they identify the Afro-Cuban religious significance of the necklace because of its white color, only an informed reader would understand the irony that it was precisely the whiteness of this woman's necklace that disproved her own.

In view of the familiarity with Afro-Cuban traditions that his poems reveal, it is likely that in "Caridá" Arozarena consciously hid the figure of Oshún under a secular guise. The poet may have intended his ode to this orisha to be understood only by other Lucumí. Furthermore, just like rumba was tolerated because it satisfied certain needs of the white elites, the erotic tone of "Caridá" would have secured its publication by making it popular among whites. Unbeknown to them, however, the poem, like rumba, introduced important Afro-Cuban religious notions into the dominant culture.

The Subversion of Afrocubanista Discourse

It is clear that by incorporating elements from rumba, the afrocubanista poems analyzed in the previous sections would suggest Afro-Cuban meanings that would undermine or transcend afrocubanista concepts and assumptions. For instance, the *patakí* that the presence of Yemayá brings to mind in Ballagas's "Rumba" conveys notions that contrast sharply with the way some of the afrocubanista movement's participants approached black women. This approach was brought to light in the chapter dedicated to the representation of the rumbera with reference to Fernando Ortiz's writings on the afrocubanista representation of black women. It was shown that, for Ortiz, afrocubanista poetry successfully represented the black female body as a source of carnal pleasure divorced from any maternal notions. By contrast, as illustrated earlier in this chapter, Yemayá introduces into Ballagas's "Rumba" exemplary notions about motherhood that are a part of Afro-Cuban culture. In addition, the connotations of fertility and procreation in the dance of Yemayá further undermine Ortiz's descriptions (Ortiz 1947, 621). In fact, this orisha is considered the goddess of fertility, which is why she is often represented as a pregnant black woman or black mermaid with protruding breasts (Castellanos and Castellanos 1992, 54). Her imputed chastity differs from the image of black women as lewd that is present in so many afrocubanista poems. Nevertheless, it is worth pointing out that this aspect of Yemayá's personality would not necessarily stop a Lucumí reader from enjoying the sexually suggestive tone of Ballagas's poem. Unlike in Catholicism, in Afro-Cuban religions virtue and sexuality are not mutually exclusive qualities (Ortiz 1981, 345; Canizares 1993, 4).

Paradoxically, "Rumba" subverts a negative dominant attitude toward blacks through the use of an Occidental cultural reference. The image of the black dancer coming forth from the sea in the first two lines of the poem can be related to similar classical portrayals in, for example, Homer's sixth hymn, "To Aphrodite," and, in classical art, in Botticelli's earlier-mentioned *The Birth of Venus* (Boulware 1977, 21).[27] This association elevates the physique of black women to the same status as Western icons that determined dominant aesthetic norms in Cuba. Consequently, it subverts established ideals of beauty in Cuban republican society, where the ideal phenotype was white skin, wavy hair (but not excessively curly or woolly), thin lips, and a narrow nose (Castellanos and Castellanos 1990, 423).

The presence of Changó in José Z. Tallet's "La rumba" would also subvert essential afrocubanista concepts. For instance, by introducing notions of black protest, violent resistance, and transgression of established norms, it could bring to mind a history of slave resistance against white oppression. It was argued earlier that Tomasa's pelvic thrusts could evoke these associations by suggesting the figure of Changó. Evidently, Chepe Chacón's *vacunaos* could bring up these notions as well, which is significant in view of Tallet's use of a whipping metaphor to convey the male dancer's pelvic thrust in the line "¡Ahora!, lanzando con rabia el fuetazo, aulla." As Luis A. Jiménez has argued, this metaphor "conveys what can be clearly traced to slavery and the punishment of the slaves, victims of the cruelties of the system" (1993, 32).

By suggesting the idea of suicide, the dance also carries connotations of slave resistance, since slaves often resorted to suicide as a means of escaping the oppressive world of the slave plantation (Ortiz 1991d, 106; Castellanos and Castellanos 1988, 106). The fact that rumba commenced as a dance among black slaves suggests that its choreography has other subversive connotations. These have to do with its emphasis on shaking different parts of the body, a quality which, as Ortiz argues, Tallet captured effectively in "La rumba" (1973c, 189). At the same time, rumba dancing is characterized by restrained feet movement within a contained, narrow space (Daniel 1995, 75). It is popularly believed that this characteristic derives from the fact that, when slaves were developing this dance form in the nineteenth century, they were chained up by the ankle at night. Because of this, they had to channel their kinetic energy onto other parts of the body, primarily the hips (Delgado 1997b, 11). Consequently, this characteristic of the dance could be interpreted as symbolic of the slaves' success in overcoming the physical restrictions imposed by the slave system or, as Celeste Fraser Delgado and José Esteban Muñoz have argued, as "the triumph of motion over constraint" (Delgado 1997b, 11). Similarly, this history invites an interpretation of hip movement in rumba along the lines of Bastide's approach to Brazilian samba, which he views as "one of the means by which resistance to reduction of the body to a productive machine was expressed" (as cited in Rowe and Schelling 1991, 123). Consequently, for an informed reader the afrocubanista emphasis on hip-swinging female dancers in general could bring up a history of slave resistance. These associations would clearly go against the ideals of black and white unity that guided the afrocubanista poetic movement. More specifically, they undermine the afrocubanista tendency to gloss over a history of conflicts and divisions between Cuban blacks and whites, which was illustrated with reference to Ramón Guirao's anthology in chapter 4.

The potential of the *guaguancó* for female empowerment reflected in Tallet's "La rumba" undermined aspects of afrocubanista discourse as well. One of these aspects was the poets' conception of female sexuality as inevitably leading to the sexual act. This notion can be appreciated in Arozarena's description of the rumbera as lascivious in "Mulata rumbera" and in "Liturgia etiópica" (Arozarena 1983, 123; Guirao 1938, 151–53). Another example is Guillén's "Rumba," where the lines "ya te cogeré domada, / ya te veré bien sujeta" (I will catch you when you are tame / I will see you being held firmly) convey the speaker's assumption that he will soon be sexually possessing the rumbera (Valdés-Cruz 1970, 109–10). Similarly, the connotation of the lines "Con tu cuchillo de rumba / he partido en dos tu carne" (with your rumba knife / I have split your flesh in two) in José Antonio Portuondo's "Rumba de la negra Pancha" is that the poet has violently penetrated the dancer after her performance (Guirao 1938, 136). Equally, the overtly erotic tone of Tallet's references to an "ebónica ninfa" (an ebony nymph) in a poem from 1927 suggests that his interest in *rumba guaguancó* derived from a conception of it as leading to the male's sexual possession of the black female. Nevertheless, Tallet obviously chose to recreate a rumba performance in which the female dancer had used her sexual allure to manipulate and triumph over her male counterpart, thus clearly subverting these perceptions. In addition, it is worth noting that the very idea of women using their sexual allure to exert power over men forms the basis of the *patakíes* mentioned earlier. This suggests that by representing rumba, Tallet introduced into his poem an empowering conception of woman found in Afro-Cuban culture. As shown, Esténger also subverted sexist assumptions in Afro-Cuban traditions and in afrocubanista discourse.

Like Ballagas and Tallet, Marcelino Arozarena undermined several aspects of afrocubanista discourse by using rumba as subject matter. The appearance of Oshún in "Caridá" subverts dominant representations of women as sexual objects by introducing the connotations of love that are attached to this orisha. Significantly, the name Caridad is derived from the Latin *caritas*, which means "love" (Jahn 1970, 112).[28] Furthermore, the presence of Oshún means that Arozarena's sexually charged references to her dancing movements cannot be seen solely as an expression of the male poet's desire for the protagonist, since they also play a role in determining her divine identity. Therefore, the sexuality of black women in this case is endowed with religious symbolic power. Another way in which the presence of Oshún could challenge dominant perceptions of black women is by bringing to mind positive qualities associated with this orisha, such as her status as savior of human kind (Castellanos and Castellanos 1992, 50).

Finally, all three poems challenge Fernando Ortiz's assumption that afrocubanista poetry hardly included any Afro-Cuban religious elements, which was illustrated in the chapter dedicated to his writings. It was also shown there that the Cuban scholar used afrocubanista poetry as confirmation of the gradual disappearance of Afro-Cuban religion (1991e, 169, 173). The afrocubanista poems analyzed in this chapter demonstrate that, through strategies of resistance such as the ones outlined at the beginning, Afro-Cuban religion would continue to survive and spread through new cultural products and interactions. The case of Marcelino Arozarena and his poem "Caridá" is particularly significant in this respect. It exemplifies how black practitioners of Afro-Cuban religions such as him were not abandoning their beliefs as they became educated. While, as shown in chapter 3, Ortiz claimed that "los poetas mulatos del día ya no creen en los dioses de sus abuelos negros" (the mulatto poets of today no longer believe in the gods of their black grandparents), Arozarena used afrocubanista poetry to introduce Afro-Cuban religious notions into the dominant culture (1991e, 162). Furthermore, since, as Brandon explains, Afro-Cuban religions have always played an important role in conceptions of African ethnicity amongst Cuban blacks, his poems could have served many practitioners of Afro-Cuban religions to reassert their Afro-Cuban or black identities (1993, 56, 74–78).

It can be concluded that the arguments put forward in this chapter challenge the assumption in the criticisms cited at the beginning that afrocubanistas could easily adapt Afro-Cuban cultural forms to their version of national culture and identity. This notion undermines the symbolic and signifying potency of these cultural forms by overlooking their capacity to carry the perspectives of their practitioners into the texts, perspectives that, as shown, would often contradict the afrocubanista discourse.

Conclusion

THE 1920s and 1930s poetic revalorization of Afro-Cuban culture known as poetic afrocubanismo took place in Cuba after a period of discriminative policies against blacks and their African-derived cultural practices. In this period the anthropological studies of blacks by prominent Cuban intellectuals provided a justification for these policies by presenting Afro-Cuban culture as inferior and primitive. Views of this kind were undoubtedly part of the reason why there were no conscious attempts to incorporate Afro-Cuban elements in the erudite cultural production of this time. The subsequent and radical shift in erudite culture toward afrocubanismo was a reaction to a series of social, political, and cultural concerns. One of these was the United States' economic and political dominance of the island. In response to it, Cuban intellectuals began to emphasize the need for a distinctive and authentic Cuban Creole art. Afro-Cuban culture was a perfect source of raw material for the production of this type of art because it was assumed that it had remained uncontaminated by U.S. cultural influences. At the same time, it offered the possibility of distancing Cuba from Spain, whose colonial occupation of the island had only ended in 1898. By introducing Afro-Cuban cultural elements into erudite forms of Spanish origins, afrocubanista arts could foreground the African/Spanish hybridity that made Cuba distinctive. Another important motivation behind the emergence of afrocubanismo was a desire for the disappearance of racial conflicts and divisions in Cuba.

This book has dispelled the widespread notion in criticism that afrocubanista poetry was disconnected from 1920s and 1930s blacks in Cuba. It has demonstrated that the poetry focused upon the African-derived cultural practices of specific sectors of the black population. Although most afrocubanista poets, including Nicolás Guillén, were not themselves members of these sectors, they were able to introduce many elements of that culture into their poetry by drawing upon a combination of ethnographic research and reliable secondary sources.

Afrocubanista poetry also drew upon the thought of Cuban scholar Fernando Ortiz Fernández. Ortiz's writings on Cuban national culture and identity reveal important concepts behind the afrocubanista project. They show that it was based on a productive questioning of the idea of race and on an antiessentialist conception of cultures as dynamic and fluid. His writings also bring into relief the fact that in afrocubanista poetry, Afro-Cuban culture was playing a counterhegemonic role by radically transforming the dominant literature from a formal point of view. At the same time, it is important to recognize that the scholar advocated a type of afrocubanista music and literature that remained erudite, even if it was based on Afro-Cuban formal principles. His failure to grant the Afro-Cuban cultural forms of lower-class blacks the same value as afrocubanista forms is linked to his view of Cuban development as a process through which the former would gradually disappear to be replaced by the latter.

An important element in afrocubanista discourse was the concept of "folklore." The first generation of Cuban republican intellectuals had already used this notion in order to redefine popular cultural forms as repositories of the nation's original essence. The afrocubanista use of the concept, as reflected in Ramón Guirao's 1928 anthology *Órbita de la poesía afrocubana, 1928–1937,* continued this view of popular culture as an authentically national tradition. More specifically, Afro-Cuban folklore served Guirao as a way to implant afrocubanismo in the nation's black cultural traditions, thus distancing it from European primitivism. Another way in which he used the concept of folklore was to bring together texts from black and white cultural traditions under a single category. While undermining the distinctiveness of black literature to some extent, this seemingly indiscriminate blending of black and white literary forms partly stems from an antiessentialist awareness of the fluid interactions between black and white cultures. At the same time, by omitting descriptions of the original contexts of the texts, Guirao put forward an image of a unified body of Afro-Cuban folklore that glossed over racial conflicts. His use of the notion also reproduces Ortiz's evolutionist view of Afro-Cuban literature as being replaced by afrocubanista poetry.

In this study, afrocubanista representations of sensuous black women and explicit references to their erotic body parts have been shown to carry problematic notions from nineteenth-century European discourses on black female sexuality. They equally reproduce problematic conceptions of blacks that emerge from Cuba's history of black exploitation. But these sexually charged representations are also an accurate depiction of the sexually suggestive dancing through which black rumberas at times consciously sought to attract males. From this perspective, afrocubanistas used a form of black sexual expression to introduce a more frank representation of sexuality into the dominant literature.

The oral and performative nature of Afro-Cuban culture led afrocubanistas to explore ways of formally incorporating into their poetry elements from dance and music forms. They managed to achieve this feat by capitalizing on formal principles that poetry shares with music and dance. The fact that afrocubanista poetry uses Afro-Cuban culture as a guiding formal principle sets it apart from other representations of Afro-Cuban culture. This fact also reveals that afrocubanistas granted a degree of validity to Afro-Cuban culture and its practitioners. Nevertheless, it has been stressed that the formal incorporation of Afro-Cuban culture that takes place in some afrocubanista poems does not warrant a reading of afrocubanista poetry as reflecting a harmonious unity between blacks and whites in Cuba. In point of fact, to some degree all afrocubanista poems bring attention to differences between written literature and the oral and performative culture of the Afro-Cuban sectors.

Finally, this study has shed light on the way in which, by incorporating elements from rumba, many afrocubanista poems would suggest Afro-Cuban meanings that transcend afrocubanista concepts and assumptions. It has been suggested that this phenomenon calls into question the assumption that Afro-Cuban culture could be easily appropriated and adapted by afrocubanista poets to their own visions of Cuban culture and identity.

To sum up, the heterogeneous nature of afrocubanista poetry that has reemerged in all the analyses in this book undermines interpretations of the poetry that reduce it to the discourse of one racial or ethnic group, be it white or mulatto. On the one hand, the presence of Afro-Cuban cultural elements in negrista poetry undercuts the tendency in Afro-Hispanism to describe it as being predominantly the product of white racist ideologies. On the other hand, partly elaborating upon this Afro-Hispanist perspective, this book has also challenged interpretations of afrocubanista poetry that derive from a conception of Cuban culture as a felicitous mulatto or *mestizo* fusion of black and white culture. Through such an approach, the present study has established that afrocubanista texts, whether written by whites or written by blacks, are spaces where discourses from different Cuban racial and sociocultural groups converge and interact in various ways.

Several important factors emerge from this book that are of relevance to future research on afrocubanista poetry and Afro-Hispanic literature in general. The commonalities of black and white afrocubanista poets that have been outlined in this study call for a reassessment of the division of afrocubanismo into two separate movements along racial lines. It has been shown that all of these poets undertook the collective task of incorporating Afro-Cuban culture into Cuban poetry at the same point in history and in response to common nationalist concerns. They were all members of Cuban cultural associations that had a specific aesthetic program aiming to emphasize Cuban black and white unity. They all took as their subject matter a specific stratum of the black population in which Afro-Cuban cultural traditions were still practiced, excluding in the process other sectors of the black population. None of the poets, with the exception of Marcelino Arozarena, came from the represented sectors, but from the middle classes. In addition, the separation advocated by critics such as Jackson has been shown to rely on essentialist notions about black authenticity.

To acknowledge the cohesiveness of afrocubanismo is not to deny the distinctively black perspectives of its black participants. In fact, it is hoped that this book will serve as the basis upon which to analyze new aspects of the black distinctiveness of Guillén's and Arozarena's poems. A substantial part of Arozarena's poetry has not been analyzed in this book because it was written after the end of the afrocubanista poetic movement. Consequently, his treatment of Afro-Cuban culture throughout his poems of the 1950s, 1960s, 1970s, and 1980s remains to be studied in depth. This is an important issue, because Arozarena's knowledge of Afro-Cuban culture clearly allowed him to give it a highly sophisticated treatment. One other issue to explore is his attitude toward the other afrocubanista poets. Interestingly, he maintained an overtly critical stance toward their representation of blacks exclusively in relation to Afro-Cuban music. This is noticeable in his poem "Canción negra sin color" and in his short essay "Nicolás Guillén, antillano domador de sones" (Nicolás Guillén, an Antillean Who Tames *Sones*) (Arozarena 1983, 29; 1974, 326; Jackson 1976, 41). One productive approach could be to investigate the ways in which Arozarena distinguished his own representation of Afro-Cuban music from that of other afrocubanistas. His discourse on Cuban national identity is another topic worthy of research. It has been argued that he viewed Cuban culture and identity as a syncretic unity of African and Spanish cultures and that, like Guillén, he disapproved of the term *afrocubano* because it suggested African/Spanish cultural differences (DeCosta-Willis 1998, 12–13; Arozarena Himely and Pinto 1998, 10). Nevertheless, the extent to which Arozarena accepted this unifying discourse is yet to be studied through in-depth analysis of his poetry and critical essays.[1]

One line of inquiry in relation to both Arozarena and Guillén would be to investigate whether their own discourse of racial and cultural fusion responded in any way to a desire to resolve their mulatto identities, which is something that Antonio Benítez Rojo has already suggested in relation to Nicolás Guillén (1992, 127–28). A wider comparative approach in this respect could take into account the notion of double consciousness that W. E. B. Du Bois employed to refer to the difficulties experienced by blacks in postslave populations when attempting to internalize an American identity: "One ever feels his twoness,—an American, a Negro; two souls two thoughts, two unreconciled strivings, two warring ideals in one dark body whose dogged strength alone keeps it from being torn asunder" (as cited in Gilroy 1993, 1, 126, 188).[2] By highlighting the problems of the Cuban nationalist discourse on *mestizaje*, it is hoped that this book will contribute to future definitions of Cuban identity that move away from the essentialism that characterized many previous approaches.[3] These should attempt to convey a multiplicity of black, white, mulatto, or Cuban perspectives. They should equally avoid glossing over the fragmented and conflictive nature of Cuban culture and society. It should not just be a question of bringing to light the interaction of "African" and "Spanish" cultural units. The heterogeneity of all Cuban cultural forms makes it problematic to understand Cuban identity as the interaction of such purified essences. Like the portrait of procreation painted in W. E. B. Du Bois's *Dark Princess,* Cuban identity should appear, according to Gilroy, as a meeting of heterogeneous multiplicities (1993, 144). Thus, one important task, which Kaliman has already suggested in relation to categories like *mestizaje* and hybridity, will be to start formulating sustainable definitions of the interacting units that do not rely on preestablished "genetic" categories (Kaliman 1995, 1998).

Finally, it is worth noting that by revealing the presence of Afro-Cuban elements in afrocubanista poetry written by whites, this book demonstrates that the analysis of poetry by white authors on black themes can further the understanding of black culture and identity. Like afrocubanista poetry, blackness is constituted by the dynamic renegotiation of cultural elements, identities, and discourses of different origins. On the basis of this understanding, future researchers of literatures about blacks and black culture in Latin America will hopefully pay more critical attention to the works of white authors.

Notes

Introduction

1. Examples of critics who term this movement *afrocubanismo* and *afrocubanista* are Morejón 1974a, 42; Castellanos and Castellanos 1994, 157; Moore 1997; and Carpentier 1961, 172.

2. Two relatively recent studies dealing with the pictorial and musical offshoots of afrocubanismo are, respectively, Martínez 1994 and Moore 1997.

3. For a detailed analysis of some of the main intellectual debates that have taken place in Latin American cultural criticism, see D'Allemand 2000. The key characteristics of this critical tendency can also be found in Rowe 1996, 43–44.

4. The 1999 special issue of *Revista Iberoamericana* constitutes an important step toward redressing this imbalance, since it is exclusively dedicated to recent studies of black literatures throughout Latin America.

5. Notable exceptions are Branche 1998 and 1999; and Phaf 1999.

6. For an analysis of Afro-Peruvian literature that draws upon Antonio Cornejo Polar's theory on indigenista literature, see Orihuela 1996.

7. Unless otherwise indicated, all translations are mine.

8. Examples of book-length studies on Nicolás Guillén include Smart 1990, Williams 1982, Ellis 1983, Kutzinski 1987, and Branche 2003.

9. For an analysis of Guillén's prose writings on Cuban blacks, see Fernández Robaina 2003.

10. For an analysis of the representation of this ideology in these two poems, see Animan 2003, Aponte-Ramos 2003, and Zielina 2003.

11. On Guillén's desire for a mulatto Cuba, see Benítez Rojo 1992 and Duno Gottberg 2003a.

12. Examples of critics who assess afrocubanista poetry or black Latin American literature in general in terms of its "authenticity" include Jackson (1978, 43; 1984, 5; 1988b, 37, 51; 1995, 104–7) and Williams (1982, 142).

13. In her 1993 book *Sugar's Secrets: Race and the Erotics of Cuban Nationalism*, Vera Kutzinski makes a similar criticism of the "thematic bias of most current approaches to Afro-Hispanic American writing" (1993, 15).

14. Jackson 1976, 43; Lewis 1983, 2; Mullen 1998, 155; Moore 1997, 200; Kubayanda 1982, 23.

15. Important exceptions are Kutzinski 1993 and Mullen 1998. Kutzinski pays close attention to essays by afrocubanistas Emilio Ballagas and Ramón Guirao, shedding light on how their discourse was partly based on racist and cultural evolutionist notions. Kutzinski also shows how these intellectuals undermined blackness and glossed over Cuba's racial divisions in promoting an impression of national unity (1993, 155–62). Mullen analyzes Ballagas's and Guirao's introductions to their anthologies of afrocubanista poetry, emphasizing their acceptance of biological explanations of racial and cultural differences and their tendency to dilute Afro-Cuban cultural distinctiveness. He also shows how their anthologies modified the dominant literary canon, which had until then excluded works of literature by blacks and literature with African constituents (1998, 141–64). In addition, Mullen dedicates a whole chapter (the fourth) to the writings of Fernando Ortiz, although he concentrates exclusively on the writer's 1906 *Los negros brujos* (The Black Sorcerers), leaving aside Ortiz's many other important contributions to afrocubanismo. I am referring here to the various essays Ortiz wrote on afrocubanista poetry during the 1930s and to his thought on national Cuban identity during the afrocubanista period, which culminated with his renowned definition of Cuba as an *ajiaco* (a traditional Cuban stew) and his influential definition of the concept of "transculturation" (Ortiz 1991b, 14–30; 1978, 92–97).

16. Apart from the fundamental studies of Cuban literature mentioned earlier (Pérez Firmat 1989 and 1999; Benítez Rojo 1989), studies of Cuban, Caribbean, or Latin American literature that do not dedicate detailed attention to afrocubanismo include Arrom 1985; Fernández Retamar 1954; Feijóo 1986; Fornet 1967; and Pereda Valdés 1970. An exception among recent studies of Spanish Caribbean literature is Claudette M. Williams's 2000 *Charcoal and Cinnamon: The Politics of Color in Spanish Caribbean Literature,* which pays considerable attention to the deconstruction of the racist and sexist notions that underpin afrocubanista poems written by whites. Studies dedicated to individual afrocubanista poets that do not carry out a detailed analysis of the movement as a whole include Morejón 1974a and 1982; Orovio 1969; Pallas 1973; and Pryor Rice 1966.

17. See Cornejo Polar 1978, 1980, 1994a, and 1995; Lienhard 1992; and Kaliman 1994 and 1995. Some of the most recent approaches to indigenista literature are found in Moraña 1998.

1. Redefining the Mulatto Nation

1. Jorge and Isabel Castellanos provide statistics of literacy rates among the black population from 1898 to 1943, based on official population polls and Alberto Arredondo's *El Negro en Cuba* (1939). In 1898 the percentage of black Cubans who could not read was as high as 72.06 percent. By 1907 it had decreased to 54.97 percent, further decreasing to 46.86 percent by 1919. By 1931

only 31.3 percent of the black population was illiterate, and in 1943 the percentage decreased to 25.4 (1990, 356). See also De La Fuente 2001, 141–42.

2. See also Luis 2001, 7–8.

3. See Benítez Rojo 1992, 68–69, for a comparison of figures of black populations in different Caribbean islands.

4. Howard 1998 is the first book-length study of the *cabildos de nación*. Other publications that include information on these associations include Ortiz 1992; Scott 1985; Helg 1995; Paquette 1988; León 1984; Cabrera 1975a; and Alén Rodríguez 1994b.

5. The question of whether the cabildos de nación were prohibited or simply subjected to new restrictions is not clear in most sources. Moore affirms that the associations were prohibited in 1888 (1997, 66). Scott argues that from about 1883 on "the *cabildos* faced hostility but no legal ban and persisted in their special role as patronized Afro-Cuban organizations subject to government supervision of their elections and meetings" (1985, 268). Since Ortiz lists five cabildos de nación as being registered in 1909 in the *Registro de Asociaciones del Gobierno Provincial de la Habana* (Register of Associations of the Provincial Government of Havana), it can be assumed that what the 1888 decree aimed to decrease was their level of independence (1992, 12).

6. For an analysis of the reasons for the large increase in the numbers of blacks migrating from rural to urban areas in the first three decades of the twentieth century, see De La Fuente 2001, 110–15.

7. On the migration of rural ex-slaves and their African-derived cultures, see also Helg 1995, 29. For a more detailed analysis of the economic recession of the 1880s, see Pérez 1988, 129–33.

8. Writing in Brazil only eight years after Ortiz, the intellectual Edgar Roquette Pinto also claimed that, with proper education, Brazil's blacks were capable of progress, as evident in the United States (Skidmore 1998, 186–87).

9. In Brazil the work of the French poet Blaise Cendrars in particular is seen as the main stimulus for the 1920s Brazilian modernist valorization of the black (Vianna 1999, 67; Brookshaw 1986, 87). According to Brookshaw, in Brazil the interest in the black did not result in an autonomous literary movement, as was the case in Cuba. Brazilian primitivists focused predominantly on the figure of the Indian, drawing upon a well-established tradition of literary Indianism in Brazilian cultural nationalism (1986, 88; 1988). However, some poets in the Northeast of Brazil did write poetry on black themes. See Brookshaw 1986, 99–108, for an assessment of their literary production.

10. Ortiz's opposition to U.S. imperialism at this time was one of the reasons that he supported President Grau San Martín (1933–34), whose overtly anti-U.S. policies forced him from power in the same year as this publication appeared. Ortiz would maintain his anti-imperialist stance and his support for Grau San Martín after 1934, despite the fact that Cuba's economic relations with the United States improved considerably (Roig de Leuchsenring 1935, 211–19; Pérez 1988,

267, 279–81; Moore 1997, 144). However, it is interesting to note that, like other Cuban intellectuals, the scholar had been in favor of U.S. interventionism before 1931 (Le Riverend 1978, xvii). In 1927 he had actually demanded that the U.S. government, in compliance with its obligation to guarantee good government, put pressure on President Gerardo Machado to resign (Pérez 1988, 259).

11. Like Aznar, other intellectuals continued to belittle the distinctiveness of Cuban and other Latin American cultures in the 1930s. A good example can be found in Salazar 1938, 6–7.

12. Ortiz describes the near extinction of the culture of the Cuban Taíno Indians in *Contrapunteo cubano del tabaco y el azúcar* (Cuban Counterpoint: Tobacco and Sugar) (1978, 94). He also provides an outline of Taíno cultural elements that survived in Cuba (1991b, 20–21). A detailed analysis of Cuba's indigenous ethnicities can be found in Ortiz 1991g.

13. For a more detailed analysis of Martí's discourse on the "racelessness" of Cuba, see Ferrer 2000.

14. See also Helg 1995, 190, 145, 219.

15. An example of a 1930s Cuban intellectual who used Martí's notion of a *mestizo* Cuba is José Antonio Ramos (1937, 107, 112). Medardo Vitier also used Martí's ideas (1937, 133). A particularly celebratory review of Martí and his work by a Cuban intellectual at the time is Campoamor 1937. On Martí's influence on 1920s Cuban intellectuals, see Schwartz 1977, 112–14; Cairo Ballester 1976, 71; and Ripoll 1968, 69–85.

16. An overview of the rhetorical strategies employed by political parties in competing for the black vote can be found in De La Fuente 2001, 60–66.

2. "Rumbas, guarachas y solares"

1. Tieles Ferrer makes a similar criticism about a tendency in Cuban musicology to privilege African-influenced culture as the sole representative of Cuban black music (1994, 91).

2. For a similar perspective, see Ellis 1988, 19.

3. For a detailed description of Gilberto Valdés's orchestra and one of his concerts, see Departamento de Turismo del Municipio de la Habana 1937, 140–41.

4. For other examples of how nonphenotypical criteria can influence racial classifications in Latin America, see Wade 1997, 38. Skidmore provides an example of how in Brazil the color attributed to an individual can be a function of his/her social position (1996, 9). On race relations, black culture, and black identity in Brazil, see Wade 1997, 68–73; Agier 1995; and Hanchard 1999.

5. See also Alén Rodríguez 1994a, 50, and Daniel 1995, 81.

6. See also Jenkins 1986, 170–71.

7. On the idea of maintenance of ethnic boundaries, see Barth 1969, 15–16, and Eriksen 1993, 37.

8. Palmié agrees with Pichardo on the need to adopt an emic perspective in the study of Afro-Cuban Santería. "The question," he writes, paraphrasing

Pichardo, "is not whether objects identifiable as pertaining to the symbolic repertoire of other religions grace the altars of priests of *Regla de Ocha,* but what their owners themselves think they represent" (1995, 84). In relation to the study of the syncretism of Latin American cultural objects, Lienhard makes a distinction between the etymology or history of an object carried out by the detached observer and the practices in which the object is used as an instrument. An analysis of these practices may often reveal that, for the practitioners, the object in question is not syncretic at all (1997, 187–88). In relation to indigenismo, Kaliman makes a similar point (1995, 93). See Canizares 1993, 38–47, on the issue of whether Santería should be considered a synthesis of African religions and Catholicism (syncretism) or a deliberate disguising of African orishas in order to preserve African traditions.

9. See also Thompson 1974, 29–41, for an overview of descriptions throughout history of collective dance and music practices in different African societies.

10. Julien describes African verbal art as mainly oral, without denying the existence of African writing prior to the arrival of Europeans in the continent. See Julien 1992, 159, for examples.

11. Other examples of the elitist attitude of black professionals toward the black lower classes can be found in De La Fuente 2001, 154–55, 165–66.

12. De la Serna's privileging of Jesús María over the New York neighborhood of Harlem suggests a perspective similar to that of Regino E. Boti regarding the relationship between Guillén's poetry and the work of Harlem Renaissance writer Langston Hughes. In an article published in the same year (1932), Boti bitterly criticized those who saw the influence of Hughes in Guillén's poetry (90). On the relationship between Langston Hughes, the Harlem Renaissance, and Guillén's poetry, see Mullen 1998, 115–40; Ellis 1998; and Schwartz 1977, 223, and 1998, 109. The extent of Hughes's influence on Guillén is part of an ongoing debate in criticism. See Ellis 1997 for a brief outline of different perspectives.

13. See Helg 1995, 29; Moore 1997, 30; Alén Rodríguez 1994a, 47; Deschamps Chapeaux 1971, 43; and Paquette 1988, 33–34.

14. The 1934 edition of Guirao's *Bongó: Poemas negros* does not have page numbers. Therefore, page references cannot be provided.

15. See Ortiz for a definition of *cheche* and *chévere* (1986a, 21–24).

16. Other racially based definitions are those used by Fernando Ortiz, which include "versos del género blanquinegro" (poems from the black and white poetic genre), "poesía de tema negroide" (poetry with negroid themes) and "poesía mulata" (mulatto poetry) (Ortiz 1973b, 156; 1973c, 173, 178).

17. As I will explain in chapter 7, the black poet Marcelino Arozarena was the only afrocubanista poet who came from the Afro-Cuban sectors.

18. For an outline of the social background of the members of this generation, see López Segrera 1989, 190.

19. In a different context, Peruvian critic José Carlos Mariátegui used the term *indigenista* in a similar way when he argued that "*indigenista* literature

cannot yet give us a veristic version of the Indian. It has to idealize him and stylize him. It cannot give us his soul either. It is still a literature written by *mestizo* authors. This is why it is called *indigenista* and not *indígena*. A truly indigenous literature will only come when indigenous people themselves are able to write it" (1968, 265).

20. See Jackson 1988b, 51.

21. Emery makes a similar statement regarding criticism on José María Arguedas, arguing that "critics who posit for Arguedas an 'insider's view' based on physical and/or emotional proximity, are in danger of eliding the problematic nature of the eye in his work, and in his life" (1996, 69).

22. See also Williams 1982, 142.

23. See also RoseGreen-Williams 1991, 121.

24. No page reference can be provided for the photograph because it is situated in a section of Orovio's book, between pages 21 and 23, that has no page numbers. Orovio does not mention the date this picture was taken. Nevertheless, the film in which Berta Singerman carries out her performance of Tallet's poem was shown in Cuba in 1934, and Tallet's poem was first published in 1928 (Fernández de la Vega and Pamies 1973, 22; Guirao 1938, 68). Consequently, the photograph must have been taken either in the late 1920s or in the early 1930s. It is worth noting, incidentally, that afrocubanista composer Alejandro García Caturla would also use Tallet's poem as the lyrics for his own composition "La rumba." A transcription for piano featuring some of the verses from the poem can be found in Eli Rodríguez 1994, 102–3.

25. Ruiz del Vizo 1972, 75.

26. Vianna undertakes a similar analysis of the interactions between the Brazilian elites in Rio de Janeiro and *samba* musicians or *sambistas* in the 1920s and 1930s. He explains that "the lower class neighborhoods where the *sambistas* lived (such as the *favela* of Mangueira) exercised a certain fascination on the Carioca elite, but the 'authentic' *samba* came from a territory they perceived as dangerous, too." And yet, just as Cuban middle-class intellectuals attended live performances of rumba in the *solares,* some Brazilian middle-class musicians such as Mário Reis actively sought to come in direct contact with the mysterious world of *samba* (Vianna 1999, 85).

27. Another available nineteenth-century collection of lyrics from guarachas and other popular songs was R.V. (*sic*) 1893. On the first page of the introduction to this collection, the editor refers to a previous compilation of guaracha lyrics from 1883 that may have also inspired afrocubanistas. For other written sources of research on popular Cuban culture available to them, see Trelles 1924. Among those who refer to Hallorans's compilation are León 1984, 176; Fernández Retamar 1954, 47; and Moore 1997, 50. León reproduces several of the songs featured in the anthology (1984, 166–84).

28. While probably based on Ortiz's description, "Sensemayá" includes a specific reference to the Congo Mayombe religious sect of the ethnic group of Bantu

origins known as Congo. This reference is found in the first lines: "¡Mayombe-bombe-mayombé! / ¡Mayombe-bombe-mayombé! / ¡Mayombe-bombe-mayombé!" Nevertheless, although the role snakes play in Congo Mayombe rituals does not seem to involve their death, Guillén writes: "Tú le das con el hacha y se muere / dale ya!" (You hit it with the axe and it dies / hit it already!) (Guirao 1938, 102, 103–4). Consequently, Guillén's inclusion of the name of an Afro-Cuban religious group in his poetic reworking of Ortiz's description resulted in a pastiche of different traditions that was not consistent with any one specific ritual practice. On Congo Mayombe and the role snakes play in its rituals, see Orozco and Bolívar 1998, 215–16; León 1984, 78; Castellanos and Castellanos 1992, 393; Cabrera 1975a, 296; and Brandon 1993, 169. For a useful summary of other approaches to "Sensemayá" and an imaginative interpretation of the poem, see Kutzinski 1987, 133–44. See Matibag 1996, 157–58, for an analysis of the Afro-Cuban meanings of some of the words used in the poem. An analysis of the musical version of the poem by Mexican composer Silvestre Revueltas can be found in Hoag 1987.

29. The date of Antonio Bachiller y Morales's 1887 treatise *Los negros* is not provided in *Los negros brujos,* but all its publication details can be found in the bibliography of Ortiz's *Los negros esclavos* (The Black Slaves) (1988, 493). Ortiz does not provide the details for the source of his claim that the dance was no longer in use after the second half of the nineteenth century, apart from the date (1862) and the author's surname, Pichardo. Again, the bibliography of *Los negros esclavos* indicates that Ortiz was using Esteban Tranquilino Pichardo Tapia's 1862 *Diccionario provincial casirazonado de vozes cubanas* (Almost-Reasoned Provincial Dictionary of Cuban Expressions) (1988, 507).

30. See, for instance, Ortiz 1965, 257–58, 287, 290, 305; 1996a, 29, 48; and 1996b, 347.

3. Transculturation and the Cuban Stew

1. Although these critics are more critical of Ortiz, some of them also acknowledge some of the scholar's positive contributions. For example, Jorge Duany interprets Ortiz's definition of "transculturation" as "ultimately indefinite insofar as it posits fluidity and hybridity as keys to Cuban identity" (2000, 22). Coronil concedes that despite reproducing certain biases "concerning primitive and advanced civilizations," Ortiz "significantly revalorizes contemporary Latin American cultures." He also argues that Cubans appear in *Contrapunteo* as "transient creatures with fluid identities," and he asserts that the concept of "transculturation" breaths life into reified categories (1995, xv, xxx).

2. See also Hall 1992, 277.

3. Ortiz would later use the term "acculturation" with this meaning (see 1996b, 380–81). Since Ortiz's definition of "transculturation," the term "acculturation" has been widely used in the sense he advocated. For example, Peruvian writer and anthropologist José María Arguedas used it to refer to the idea

of assimilation (as cited in Rama 1982, 37–38). Even the 1982 edition of the *Concise Oxford Dictionary* defines acculturation as "the adoption of a different culture."

4. For an analysis of the ways in which Malinowski tried to assimilate Ortiz's work into functionalism, see Coronil 1995 and Santí 2002. Santí's recent study of Ortiz's *Contrapunteo cubano del tabaco y el azúcar,* which analyzes the book in relation to its historical context, looks in detail at the relationship between Ortiz and Malinowski, on the basis of the correspondence they exchanged during the preparation of *Contrapunteo.*

5. Despite the effectiveness of Ortiz's definition as a correction of this use of the term "acculturation," Ángel Rama describes it as being based on an incorrect interpretation. In support of this, Rama cites Gonzalo Aguirre Beltrán's explanation of "ad-culturación" as indicating in anthropology "unión o contacto de culturas" (1982, 33). Friedhelm Schmidt argues that Rama's criticism is that Ortiz misinterpreted the term "acculturation" as referring to the replacement of the culture of one group by that of another. Ultimately, Schmidt accuses Ortiz of misunderstanding this term as signifying "a process of unilateral assimilation" (1995, 193–94). More recently, Enrico Mario Santí also accuses both Ortiz and Malinowski of misrepresenting the meaning of the term "acculturation" as defined by Refield, Linton, and Herskovits (2002, 68–70). These critics distort Ortiz's contribution. When the Cuban scholar argued that the term "acculturation" indicated the acquisition of a different culture, he did not mean that in anthropology this term was used to refer to this process, as Rama, Schmidt, and Santí claim. What Ortiz was saying was that the term suggested this notion from an etymological point of view. Coronil perfectly captures this nuance. He writes that Ortiz "explains that acculturation is being used to describe the process of transition from one culture to another and its manifold social repercussions, but asserts that transculturation is a more fitting term" (1995, xxv). In any case, as explained above, Ortiz's emphasis on the counterhegemonic potential of dominated cultures was most effective as a critique of the tendency in anthropological studies to analyze predominantly the effects of dominant cultures on dominated ones.

6. See, for instance, Ortiz 1991f, 191–92. It is interesting to note that the counterhegemonic role of black culture in Brazil had been described by Brazilian intellectual Gilberto Freyre in his 1933 *Casa Grande e Senzala.* According to Skidmore, in this work Freyre "dwelt on the manifold ways in which the African and mulatto deeply influenced the life style of the planter class, in food, clothing, and sex" (1998, 191).

7. Patricia D'Allemand provides a useful analysis of some of the other uses of Ortiz's concept in Latin American cultural criticism. She questions the recent tendency to focus solely on the reductionist aspects of the concept and stresses the importance of exploiting its productive potential as well (1999). Other critics who have made use of Ortiz's notion of "transculturation" and have not been

mentioned so far include Pratt 1992, De la Campa 1996, Emery 1996, Vianna 1999, Pérez Sarduy and Stubbs 2000b, and Martínez Furé 2000.

8. Ernest Gellner explains that the tendency to homogenize the different cultures present in a given nation is often present in nationalist discourse, where culture becomes "the necessary shared medium, the life-blood, or perhaps rather the minimal shared atmosphere, within which alone the members of the society can breathe and survive and produce." "For a given society," he continues, "it must be one in which they can all breathe and speak and produce; so it must be the same culture" (as cited in Hall 1992, 296).

9. The differences Ortiz established between *cubanidad* and *cubanía* can be found in Ortiz 1991b, 14.

10. On the issue of Morejón's uncritical approach to the ideology of *mestizaje* in the poetry of Guillén, see Duno Gottberg 2003a, 160–62.

11. For a definition of identity in postmodernist thought, see Wade 1997, 80–81, and Hall 1992, 277.

12. According to Jesús J. Barquet, Lezama Lima described the mulatto identity put forward by afrocubanistas as a "rushed synthesis." For him, instead of amalgamating, it excluded "certain elements from integration into the national identity because these will resent the violence of this enforced synthesis" (Barquet 1996, 3).

4. Folklore and Afrocubanista Poetry in Ramón Guirao's *Órbita de la poesía afrocubana*, 1928–1937

1. These are Ballagas 1935, 1946; Pereda Valdés 1936; Ruiz del Vizo 1972; and Valdés-Cruz 1970.

2. For a more detailed analysis of the *comparsas*, see Moore 1997, 62–86, and Urfé 1977, 216–19.

3. The song was subsequently turned into a popular *teatro bufo* piece by Eliseo Grenet in the 1920s, and the Septeto Nacional then rerecorded the song as a *son* piece in 1930 (Moore 1997, 95; Orovio 1992, 225–26).

4. See León for transcriptions of the lyrics of *makagua* songs (1984, 79–80).

5. A description of these trees can be found in Cabrera 1975a, 460, 532.

6. It is worth clarifying the meaning of some of the Afro-Cuban terms and expressions in this text, since a translation alone would not bring out their full cultural significance. The word "dondó" in the first line could be a number—for example, twenty-two (*dos con dos*) or two hundred and two (*doscientos dos*). This would convey the hyperbole that the wood of the tree is so hard that it would take the combined effort of many woodcutters to bring it down. The title of the song "Setenta y dos hacheros pa' un palo" (Seventy-two Lumberjacks for One Tree) by 1930s *son* composer Arsenio Rodríguez further supports this interpretation by showing that this image was common in Afro-Cuban culture. In this song, which also deals with the theme of a tree that cannot be cut, further similarities are palpable in the lines "Qué cosa tiene ese palo / que no lo puedo

tumbar. / Quizás sea quiebra hacha / quizás sea guayacán" (What is it with this tree? / I can't cut it down. / It might be a *quiebra hacha* / It might be a *guayacán*). In the sixth line of Guirao's "Cantos de cabildo," the question "¿Qué son ese?" means "¿Qué es eso?," that is, "What did you say?" Presumably the tree has just told the speaker that he is a *jocuma*, which is why he defiantly answers that he is a *quiebra hacha*. According to Jorge and Isabel Castellanos, the use of the third-person plural of the verb *ser*, i.e., *son*, as the only conjugation of *ser*, irrespective of number, was characteristic of the speech of Cuban black slaves known as *bozal*. It is often reduced to *so*. In old *bozal* the term *ese*, with which the line ends, was the only demonstrative adjective or pronoun (1992, 344, 338–39). Finally, in the last line of the poem, the expression "*cambiar voz*" can mean "to change one's mind" in Cuban Spanish. For example, according to Lydia Cabrera, Cuban *paleros,* practitioners of Congo religions, refer to the Cuban *cuaba* as "palo cambia voz" because this tree "hace cambiar a las gentes de opinión y de rumbo" (makes people change their minds and their direction) (1975a, 501). "Gayo" could refer to the *gallo* or *insunsu,* i.e., the solo singer in Congo music practices (León 1984, 78). As Fernando Ortiz explains, "The solo singer or *gallo* frequently improvises his song, which is called *inspiración,* and once he has finished this he repeats it to the sound of the instruments, accompanied by the chorus of the dancers or the audience. A rival *gallo* usually responds to the song, thus forming a counterpoint" (1982, 394–95). In view of this practice, the last two lines of the second stanza could have been addressed to the next *gallo*, asking him to take the lead. The goading tone of these last two lines ("Gayo cambia bo. / Tu jabla y no conose") also supports this interpretation, since in the traditional martial-art dance contest of the Congo known as *maní,* "cada 'gallo' lanzaba a su antojo sus 'puyas' y fanfarronadas que enardecían a los rivales" (each *gallo* professed his challenges and boastful remarks at will, thus inflaming the rivals) (Ortiz 1996b, 68).

7. See Castellanos and Castellanos 1994, 228, for a summary of the plot of *Los novios catedráticos*. Feijóo 1986, 290, includes another extract from Benítez del Cristo's play. On the origins of the *negrito,* see Leal 1980, 31, and Castellanos and Castellanos 1994, 224.

8. The Sociedad's meticulous approach in this respect is demonstrated in Chacón y Calvo's "Cuestionario de literatura popular cubana," where he outlined the procedure to be followed by folklorists in collecting material. This included noting not only the name, age, and place of birth of the informant but also whether he had learned the data through listening or through reading, how long ago he had learned it, who told him, and what his nationality was (1924, 10).

9. Manuel describes the guaracha as "an up-tempo dance piece, popular in the nineteenth century, with a picaresque and often bawdy text" (1987, 166). In relation to the guaracha, see also Galán 1983, 302; Orovio 1992, 227; and Feijóo 1977, 201.

10. Other examples of representations of blacks in nineteenth-century lithographs can be found in Cámara Betancourt 2000, 107–10.

11. It is only fair to clarify that not all guaracha lyrics were so unkind to black women. In a nineteenth-century guaracha entitled "Tus ojos" (Your Eyes) the speaker addresses a *prieta* (dark-skinned black woman) in the following way:

> Son tus ojos, linda prieta
> dos luceros refulgentes
> que brillan resplandecientes
> con magnífica atracción.
> Negros mis pesares,
> negros como mis tormentos
> mis amargos sufrimientos
> y mi acerbo y cruel dolor.
> . . . .
> Porque son tus ojos bellos,
> prieta del alma querida,
> los que a mí me dan la vida
> y los que me hacen feliz.
>   (R.V. 1893, 72–73)

> Your eyes, beautiful dark woman,
> are like two shiny bright stars
> that glisten and sparkle
> with magnificent allure.
> Black are my sorrows,
> Black like my torments
> My bitter troubles
> And my sour and cruel pain.
> . . . .
> Because your beautiful eyes,
> My loved dark girl,
> give me my life
> And they give me my happiness.

Notice the curious contrast between the writer's use of the negative associations of the color and his infatuation with the blackness of her eyes. Admittedly, these references to the color may have been humorous, tying in with a long tradition in Spanish literature of using blacks' skin color to comic effect. See Young 1987, 22, for examples. Another guaracha full of loving references toward a black woman (this time a *mulata*) is "La mulata Celia" (R.V. 1893, 136–37).

12. See Leal 1982, 235, on the representation of the *mulata* in *teatro bufo* as a loose woman or prostitute dangerous to white wealthy young men.

13. On the *negrito catedrático,* see Castellanos and Castellanos 1994, 24, 224, and Leal 1980, 77. Other *teatro bufo* plays featuring black characters can be found in Feijóo 1961, 13–44, 83–150, 217–55.

5. The Black Rumbera

1. Adriana Méndez Rodenas provides an outline of different representations of African dance in Cuban culture at various historical moments. In particular, she focuses on representations in the anthropological writings of Ortiz, the writings of nineteenth-century abolitionist intellectuals, afrocubanista poetry, and the black poetry of Nancy Morejón (2002, 211–28).

2. In relation to the Brazilian Jorge de Lima's 1927 poem "Xango," which is based on an Afro-Brazilian religious ritual, Brookshaw interprets the emphasis on the physical sexuality of the black female protagonist along similar lines (1986, 101–3).

3. See also Williams 2000, 57, 61.

4. Most afrocubanista poets contributed to *Revista de Avance,* including Emilio Ballagas, Alejo Carpentier, Ramón Guirao, Alfonso Hernández Catá, and José Z. Tallet. Intellectuals who wrote extensively on afrocubanista poetry, such as Juan Marinello and Fernando Ortiz, published in *Revista de Avance* as well. See Domínguez Alfonso 1969, 26, 29, 44, 63–66, 74, 83, for articles published in the magazine by these intellectuals. On *Revista de Avance,* see also Barquet 1992, 15–17; Ripoll 1964; Pallas 1973, 18–24; and Marinello 1969, 1977. The Exhibition of New Art was sponsored by *Revista de Avance* and held at the Asociación de Pintores y Escultores (Association of Painters and Sculptors) in Havana in May 1927. See Martínez 1994, 6, for more details.

5. Another poem that shows the interest in erotic themes of an author who would later write afrocubanista poetry is Esténger's "El poema de las narices" (1927).

6. Examples of afrocubanista poems focusing on the hips and buttocks of the black female protagonists are Ramón Guirao's "Etoy diparao" (1934), Teófilo Radillo's "Tú y yo en la comparsa" (1939, 58), Emilio Ballagas's "Elegía de María Belén Chacón" and "Comparsa habanera" (Guirao 1938, 108, 119), Nicolás Guillén's "Rumba" (Valdés Cruz 1970, 109–10), and José Antonio Portuondo's "Lance de Juruminga" (Guirao 1938, 140).

7. See Ortiz 1924b, 69–70, for a description of the *culona.*

8. See also Williams 2000, 52.

9. Lorna V. Williams identifies similar notions about blacks in Guillén's "Balada de los dos abuelos" and "Madrigal" (1982, 20).

10. The predicament of black women in Cuban slave society is perfectly illustrated in Cirilo Villaverde's *Cecilia Valdés.* The protagonist of this novel is a young mulatto woman wooed by a white man from a respectable family who, in order to seduce her, promises to marry her and then breaks the promise by marrying someone from his own class. For Cecilia as for many other black women,

a whiter partner constituted a better means of *blanqueamiento* than a black husband; thus the popular Cuban maxim "Mejor querida de un blanco que mujer de un negro" (It is better to be the lover of a white than the wife of a black) (Stolcke 1992, 181, 186). On the predicament of the black Cuban woman in Cuban slave society, see also Montejo Arrechea 1998.

11. *Frenillo* are the strings that hold the ends of the kite in order to make it fly and control its movements (Cabrera 1926, 56).

12. With reference to this poem, Kubayanda further argues that Ballagas regarded most Afro-Cuban dances merely as erotic social performances, concluding that the way Ballagas described blacks in relation to their dances betrays his lack of understanding of the fundamental elements of Afro-Cuban dance (1974, 118–19). Nevertheless, Kubayanda's own lack of understanding of Afro-Cuban culture is evident in his criticism of a poem entitled "Rumba" by the Mexican poet Miguel N. Lira. He argues that, although the poet's descriptive details effectively reflect the celebratory euphoria that characterizes rumba, the appearance of Changó mars the cumulative effect of the poem because it is odd to include a war god in a poem about a love dance. He concludes that "even though the poet was attracted by the growing respectability of Negro dances in the twenties he was not in a position to acquaint himself with the complexity of his subject" (1974, 115–16). Kubayanda disregards the fact that, aside from being a war god, Changó is also extremely virile (Amira and Cornelius 1992, 8). His appearance in Lira's and Tallet's poems, then, is not thematically at odds with the sexuality underlying their renditions of rumba. Thus, Kubayanda's comments illustrate how overlooking the poetry's representation of choreographic features can lead to serious misinterpretations.

13. The purpose of the Efe cult was to combat sorcery and "the many magico-religious practices that endanger the traditional equilibrium and traditional customs" (Huet and Savary 1995, 132). Masks such as the Tédédè are a part of the many ritualistic symbols (costumes, musical instruments, particular objects such as fly whisks, amulets, and magical objects) employed in the course of African rituals. Masks "introduce characters drawn from the village society, and are used to depict the principal episodes from the myth of creation and the history of the group through the oral tradition. The masks represent humans or animals and are often hybrid forms. They are worn in front of the face or on top of the head, the wearer being hidden under a costume which forms an integral part of the mask (as do his own voice, his miming, his dance or his attitude)" (Huet and Savary 1995, 20–21).

14. In the following extract Hazzard-Gordon provides an explanation of the process by which many African customs in French and Spanish slave societies of the New World came to lose their religious meanings: "French and Spanish Catholics introduced their slaves to a pantheon of saints that the Africans came to associate with their own deities and so with their traditional religious practices. Thus, the African theological background to many of these practices (including

dance) might disappear while the practice itself or a version of it survived, eventually relegated by the practitioners to the realm of the secular, magic or folk custom" (1990, 19).

15. For more explanations of these processes, see Ortiz 1981, 252–53, 255–56.

16. I would like to thank Peter Wade for making the suggestions that helped me to develop this part of my argument.

17. Gorer witnessed this dance in Ouanguladougou, the capital of the territory that, at the time he was writing, was known as Upper Volta and in 1984 became Burkina Fasso, whose boundaries are Mali on the north and west side, Niger and Benin on the east, and Togo, Ghana, and the Ivory Coast on the south. See also Huet and Savary for photographs of Yoruba dances performed in animal masks (1995, 132).

18. The association of black female sexuality with fruits is equally evident in nineteenth-century Cuban cigarette lithographs reproduced by Kutzinski. She describes the mulatto women depicted in these in the following way: "The *mulatas* in prints 2, 3 and 4, two of them fruit vendors, are all dressed poorly in both senses of the word. Their faces and bodies bear disfiguring traces of their presumed sexual and materialistic greed, and the symbolic association of exposed breasts with the fruit being sold can hardly be missed." Kutzinski mentions that a possible reason for the association between the erotic body signs of black women and tropical fruits, such as *caimitos, papayas,* and *mameyes,* might be that "female slaves used some of these fruits and plants for contraceptive and related purposes." According to her, these associations "survive even in today's Cuban Spanish" (Kutzinski 1993, 74, 93). Incidentally, the association of black female beauty and sexuality with fruit can be seen in Pablo Picasso's 1901 reworking of Edouard Manet's 1863 painting "Olympia." Picasso chose to make his nude Olympia black instead of white, and whereas in the original a black female servant offers her flowers, in his version a nude *flâneur* offers her a gift of fruit (Gilman 1985, 207, 233).

6. Afrocubanista Poetry and Afro-Cuban Performance

1. As González Echevarría reminds us, in *The Decline of the West* Spengler also divided the historical evolution of culture into the stages of childhood, adolescence and adulthood (1977, 80).

2. On the *libretas,* see also Cuervo Hewitt 1983, 27–28; 1988, 78–79.

3. Some of the stylistic differences between oral and written forms can be found in Eileen Julien's critical review of studies of the oral nature of African novels (1992, 26–42). For example, language that is characterized by parallel phrasing, repetition and antitheses has been considered typical of oral texts. Other principles imputed to oral narrative genres include the presence of the narrator, cyclical time and heroes who transgress societal rules (26–27). Mohamadou Kane sees unity of action, a single dominant character, the motif of the journey and the inclusion of various genres such as proverbs, riddles and tales as primary traits

of the oral tale (31). See Kubayanda 1985, 156, for characteristics of African and African-derived "drum rhythm poetry," which he defines as "poetry for reading aloud" or for "reciting . . . simultaneously accompanied by the beats of the drum."

4. Other strategies include "incorporating cultural memory into habitual patterns of social interaction, movement and body postures, as well as materializing abstract religious concepts by creating icons" (Brandon 1993, 143).

5. Goldberg adopts a similar approach to Bush and Wade in arguing against the assumption on the part of prominent social psychologists that stereotypes are necessarily false generalizations. This, he continues, "is just another version of the usual presumption that stereotyping is inherently irrational" (1993, 122). He posits against this notion that sometimes, "a bare stereotype without any associated or imputed value may reflect the facts rather accurately." In other words, "it is not essential to their nature that they involve factual errors" (1993, 122–26). By contrast, Brookshaw argues that "stereotypes are rooted in prejudice rather than fact" (1986, 3). Williams adopts a balanced view between the two extremes when she argues that stereotypes can have their basis in sociological fact but they often involve "exaggerating observed traits and extending impressions about individuals to the whole class to which those individuals belong" (Williams 2000, 9).

6. By 1931, 31.3 percent of the black population was still illiterate. Nevertheless, this percentage was rapidly decreasing and by 1943 it was down to 25.4 (Castellanos 1990, 356).

7. For Carpentier, the Cuban black's ability to combine cultural practices of different origins was a sign of blacks' capability to adapt to new sociocultural contexts and to create new cultural traditions. Amy Fass Emery interprets this perception of the black on Carpentier's part as "a projection of Western discourse about the colonized Other as a nulity that reflects any desire" (Emery 1996, 35).

8. On *jitanjáforas,* see also Valdés-Cruz 1970, 26–27; Caldera 1989, 53; Hawley (n.d), 217; Feldman Harth 1955, 797.

9. The practice Ortiz referred to as *música de bemba* continues in Cuba nowadays in the *a cappella* compositions of *Vocal Sampling* (*Vocal Sampling* 1994). For use of percussive onomatopoeia by a contemporary rumba ensemble listen to *Conjunto de Clave y Guaguancó*'s "La prueba del ritmo" (*Conjunto de Clave y Guaguancó* 1995). Cuban musician Pello el Afrokán also uses onomatopoeia to explain the rhythms played in *conga* music (Pello el Afrokán 1988).

10. It has often been noted that similar onomatopoeia to those employed in afrocubanista poetry can be found in representations of blacks in Golden Age Spanish literature. For example, in his 1599 *Entremés del platillo* Simón Aguado uses the onomatopoeia "chiqui, chiqui," which are similar to Tallet's reproduction of the sound of shakers in "La rumba" (Feijóo 1986, 17, 66–67). José Juan Arrom provides other examples of similar onomatopoeia in Golden Age Spanish plays (1942, 380–84). See also Feldman Harth 1955, 792–94. As in the case of afrocubanista poetry, Golden Age playwrights may have borrowed these linguis-

tic forms from the black culture of their time. According to Arrom, the presence of blacks in Golden-Age Spain was certainly a common feature of everyday life (1942, 380, 408).

11. For a longer analysis of Guillén's appropriation of the structures of *son* lyrics, see Hidalgo 1999.

12. Transcriptions of the rhythms played on *batá* drums in *bembé* can be found in Amira and Cornelius 1992.

13. Jahn describes Yemayá as being occasionally "desenfrenada" (1970, 77).

14. See, for instance, Jackson 1976, Branche 1998 and 2001, and Davies 2001, 18–19.

15. On Tanco's writings on blacks, see also Paquette 1988, 101, and Ibarra 1967, 13–14.

16. See also Arrufat 1990, 752.

17. The free versification of rumba lyrics can be appreciated in Daniel's transcriptions (1995, 85–90).

18. According to Natalio Galán, this phrase had also been adapted to a *danzonete* by 1929 (1983, 200).

7. The Subversion of Afrocubanista Discourse

1. Ortiz 1981, 533; Piedra 1991, 650; Moore 1997, 49.

2. For a more detailed description of the dances to Changó, Yemayá, and Ochún, see particularly Jahn 1970, 76–79. The dances to all the different orishas are described in Ortiz 1981, 297–352.

3. In relation to this specific episode Adriana Méndez Rodenas argues that the glittering beads worn by the performer around his neck, arms and body suggest that he may have been enacting an *abakuá* ritual, rather than impersonating Changó (Méndez Rodenas 2000, 214).

4. See also Ortiz 1988, 213, 215, 218, 220, and Canizares 1993, 4.

5. A similar phenomenon took place in Brazil with the Afro-Brazilian *umbigada*. This dance form was allowed by Brazilian plantation owners (as opposed to religious practices) on the belief that its erotic qualities were a stimulus to reproduction and, thus, a means of acquiring additional labor. Unbeknown to them, however, the *umbigada* served to maintain African religious traditions by allowing the slaves to perform symbolic dances relating to the orishas (Bastide as cited in Rowe 1991, 123–24).

6. See, for example, Suárez y Romero as quoted in Ortiz 1981, 565–67 and Guirao's transcription of the slave song "Mamá Iné" in his anthology, which was quoted in the fourth chapter (Guirao 1938, 9–10).

7. On the issue of the secret religious meanings of the *comparsas*, see also Cuervo Hewitt 1988, 45.

8. Moore explains that these cabarets constituted a main source of employment for blacks who were generally denied access to higher education. As a result they predominated in them as musicians, singers, and dancers (1997, 183).

9. Ortiz complained in 1935 that "tourists are now offered a '*rumba* on four legs,' monstrous brothel freak, progeny of hungry Africa and the Yankee who pays, and engendered by greed for the dollar. A good subject for the theorists of historical materialism" (1973b, 159).

10. Some legends specifically present Changó as the son of Yemayá, such as those in which he was born to Agayú and Yemayá in the form of an enormous ball of fire that fell from the sky. Others, however, present him as the offspring of Obatalá and Yemmu. In a *patakí* reproduced by Cros Sandoval, Obatalá (in one of his feminine manifestations) gave birth to Changó, and his father was Agayú Solá (Castellanos and Castellanos 1992, 42–43). Some of Lydia Cabrera's informants talk of his human origins: "Changó did a lot of different things: he was a gambler, a soldier, a troublemaker . . . He was a man and a king, Alafín, before turning into a saint and going to heaven" (Cabrera 1975a, 222). It is also worth noting that Yemayá is sometimes considered the mother of all orishas (Castellanos and Castellanos 1992, 54).

11. Kay Boulware also interprets the conclusion of the poem as a metaphor for birth. She argues that under the universal concept of the sea and the waves as a source from which all life must come, Ballagas's use of water imagery functions as a perfect analogy for the woman who is a giver of human life. Consequently, his description of the black dancer's navel as the centre of the cyclone, which is in turn shaped like a belly, implies that she is giving birth to a natural force. From this assumption Boulware goes on to argue that "woman gives life to humans as well as to natural forces. Likewise, her navel becomes the object for perceiving Changó who appropriately is a synecdoche for nature; he is the god of thunder and the son of Yemayá, and husband to Ochún and Oyá—all water goddesses." Boulware also brings attention to the association between women and water present in orishas such as Oshún and Yemayá, but she does not see the poem as specifically symbolizing Yemayá or the birth of Changó (Boulware 1977, 22). In his analysis of this poem, Rogelio de la Torre also overlooks the presence of Yemayá (1977, 80–81).

12. As explained in chapter 6, the *patakíes* are religious short stories of the *Lucumí*.

13. As mentioned earlier, Ortiz referred to a "*rumba* on four legs" as an example of how the "pristine" and "spontaneous" sensuality of Cuban vernacular dances was being corrupted by U.S. tourism (1973b, 159).

14. There exist several versions of this myth of origin but Jorge and Isabel Castellanos provide a summary that includes all the major themes that recur in all of them (1992, 215–17). Other versions can be found in Cabrera 1975a, 276–87; 1975b, 5–6; and Cabrera Infante 1991, 89–90.

15. Sikán's sacrifice is partly the punishment for verbally revealing the secret of her tribe to their sworn enemies the *Efik*. As Conrad James points out, this aspect of the legend of Sikán means that a violent suppression of woman's speech underpins *Abakuá* mythology (personal communication on 8 April 2001).

16. For a description of this drum, which is generally referred to as *quinto*, see León 1984, 155–56.

17. Incidentally, Amira and Cornelius explain that in present day Cuba members of the Conjunto Folklórico Nacional teach *batá* drumming to anyone who is interested, regardless of sex. They also explain that *batá* drumming in New York was initially open to female performers, but that the situation changed when the musicians' interest moved from aural constructs to religious ideology (Amira and Cornelius 1992, 13). Daniel explains that the popularity of Afro-Cuban rumba outside of Cuba has led to the appearance of several female drummers of Afro-Cuban percussion, for example, Carole Steele and Nurudafina Piliabena (Daniel 1995, 131).

18. See also Castellanos and Castellanos 1992, 225. José Piedra writes in relation to this part of Abakuá rituals that "the male representative of culture is often revealed to Sikán as an amphibian appendage (represented musically by a percussion stick) that she can neither readily identify or ever reveal, name, play, or play with" (1991, 658). Curiously, despite the fact that it is the spirit and the voice of Sikán that inhabit *ekue* and the *güin,* José Piedra also argues that *ekue* inhabits Sikán and he wonders whether "the inhabiting act implies for women an intervention or, worse yet, a violation." He is also mistaken when he refers to another Abakuá drum known as *seseribó* as being "silently or stridently 'played' with a stick (phallic inscription) or with a visual image/gesture, cosmetic massage or cosmic message (vaginal inscription)" (Piedra 1991, 657). Attractive as these analogies may seem, the *seseribó* is never played, as its function is strictly symbolic (Castellanos and Castellanos 1992, 225; Cabrera 1975a, 210; León 1991, 9; Ortiz 1996b, 97).

19. It seems that similar images were used by negrista poets from other parts of the Hispanic Caribbean. For example, Dominican poet Manuel del Cabral addressing the female protagonist of one of his poems writes "tu cuerpo mismo el bongó" (your very body is a bongo drum). Piedra argues in relation to this line that the poet perhaps realizes "that he is 'playing' the very woman's body, rather than some intermediary tune, tone, and instrument that belong to her" (1991, 657).

20. Jorge and Isabel Castellanos define *omó* in the following way: "'son' of an orisha or *Lucumí* saint. In *Regla de Ocha* this orisha is considered 'the guardian angel' of the *santero*" (1992, 394).

21. See also Cabrera 1975a, 236, and Jahn 1970, 111–12.

22. *Güelimere* is a religious ceremony of the Regla de Ocha (Castellanos and Castellanos 1992, 396).

23. See Benítez Rojo 1992, 211, for a description of the *solar*. See also De La Fuente 2001, 114–15, and Brock 1998, 28.

24. See León 1984, 151; Alén Rodríguez 1994a, 47; Daniel 1995, 17, 19, 64; and Elio Ruiz as cited in Luis 1994, 42.

25. A *toque* is a liturgical celebration for the orishas using the *batá* drums (Amira and Cornelius 1992, 124).

26. This line refers to a specific feature of *comparsa* dancing. As Emilio Grenet explains, "In all the even bars one off beat is accentuated and the dancers respond to it by slightly raising one leg" (as cited in Mayer Serra 1947, 230).

27. Curiously, the poem's clear allusion to "The Birth of Venus" through this image prefigures the birth of Changó at the end of the poem, which was illustrated earlier. Significantly, Yemayá has been described as a Lucumí Venus (Castellanos and Castellanos 1992, 49).

28. Janheinz Jahn also equates the character in Arozarena's poem to Oshún but does not clearly explain how he arrives at this conclusion (1970, 11–12).

Conclusion

1. A useful outline of Arozarena's work can be found in Arozarena Himely and Pinto 1998. The entire issue of *Afro-Hispanic Review* in which this article is found is dedicated to Marcelino Arozarena and contains two essays by Miriam DeCosta-Willis and Ian Smart, a selection of Arozarena's poems, and translations by various contributors.

2. For an assessment of the relevance of Du Bois's concept in contemporary United States and a comparison of U.S. and Brazilian race relations, see Winant 1999.

3. An example of a recent study that attempts to escape from the essentialism of discourses on *lo cubano* is Fernández and Cámara Betancourt 2000a. These authors see Cuban identity "as marked more by tension and diversity than by harmony or monolithic unity" (2000b, 6).

Bibliography

Acevedo, Javier P. 1935. "Un nuevo libro sobre Martí." *Revista Cubana* 1.1: 156–57.
Acosta, Leonardo. 1991. "The Rumba, the Guaguancó and Tío Tom." In Manuel 1991, 51–73.
Aharonián, Coriún. 1994. "Factores de identidad musical latinoamericana tras cinco siglos de conquista, dominación y mestizaje." *Latin American Music Review* 15.2: 189–227.
Agier, Michel. 1995. "Racism, Culture and Black Identity in Brazil." *Bulletin of Latin American Research* 14.3: 245–64.
Alén Rodríguez, Olavo. 1994a. *De lo afrocubano a la salsa: Subgéneros musicales de Cuba.* Havana: Ediciones Artex.
———. 1994b. "The Afro-French Settlement and the Legacy of Its Music to the Cuban People." In Béhague 1994a, 109–17.
Amira, John, and Steven Cornelius. 1992. *The Music of Santería.* New York: White Cliffs Media Company.
Andreu, Enrique. 1937. "Los 'Spirituals negro song' y su acción étnico social." *Estudios Afrocubanos* 1.1: 76–91.
Animan, Clément. 2003. "El sujeto cultural negro y su 'alter ego' identitario en 'Balada de los dos abuelos' de Nicolás Guillén." In Branche 2003, 87–97.
Aponte-Ramos, Dolores. 2003. "Habladurías sobre la diferencia: La corporalización de la mulata en Nicolás Guillén." In Branche 2003, 73–86.
Arnedo, Miguel. 1997. "The Portrayal of the Afro-Cuban Female Dancer in Cuban Negrista Poetry." *Afro-Hispanic Review* 16.2: 26–33.
———. 2001a. "'Arte Blanco con Motivos Negros': Fernando Ortiz's Concept of Cuban National Culture and Identity." *Bulletin of Latin American Research* 20.1: 88–101.
———. 2001b. "*Afrocubanista* Poetry and Afro-Cuban Performance." *Modern Language Review* 96.4: 990–1005.
Arozarena, Marcelino. 1974. "Nicolás Guillén, antillano domador de sones." In Morejón 1974a, 325–27.

———. 1983. *Canción negra sin color*. Havana: Ediciones Unión.
Arozarena Himely, Georgina, and Celia Pinto. 1998. "Marcelino Arozarena: Abnegado trabajador de la cultura cubana." *Afro-Hispanic Review* 17.1: 3–11.
Arrom, José Juan. 1942. "La poesía afrocubana." *Revista Iberoamericana* 4: 379–411.
———. 1985. *Estudios de literatura hispanoamericana*. Roma: Bulzoni Editore.
Arrufat, Antón. 1990. "El nacimiento de la novela en Cuba." *Revista Iberoamericana* 56.152–53: 747–57.
Augier, Ángel. 1965. *Nicolás Guillén: Notas para un estudio biográfico-crítico*, vol. 1. Havana: Editora del Consejo Nacional de Universidades.
Aviram, Amittai F. 1994. *Telling Rhythm: Body and Meaning in Poetry*. Ann Arbor: University of Michigan Press.
Bachiller y Morales, Antonio. 1924. "Los ojos de cucubá." *Archivos del Folklore Cubano* 1.1: 43–46.
Ballagas, Emilio. 1931. "El mensaje inédito." In Morejón 1974a, 259–61.
———, ed. 1935. *Antología de la poesía negra hispanoamericana*. Madrid: M. Aguilar.
———. 1937. "La poesía en mí." *Revista Cubana* 9.26: 158–61.
———, ed. 1946. *Mapa de la poesía negra americana*. Buenos Aires: Editorial Pleamar.
———. 1973a. "Situación de la poesía afro-americana" [first published in 1946]. In Fernández de la Vega and Pamies 1973, 37–77.
———. 1973b. "Poesía afrocubana" [first published in 1951]. In Fernández de la Vega and Pamies 1973, 78–87.
———. 1984. *Obra poética*. Ed. Osvaldo Novarro. Havana: Editorial Letras Cubanas.
Baquero, Gastón. 1969. *Darío, Cernuda y otros temas poéticos*. Madrid: Editora Nacional.
Bareiro Saguier, Rubén. 1973. "César Vallejo y el mestizaje cultural." In *Séminaire César Vallejo*. Poitiers: Centre de Recherches Latino-Américaines de l'Université de Poitiers.
Barnet, Miguel. 1990a. *Autógrafos cubanos*. Havana: Ediciones Unión.
———. 1990b. "Claves por Rita Montaner." In Barnet 1990a, 78–99.
———. 1990c. "Bola de Nieve: Su universal cubanía." In Barnet 1990a, 11–15.
Barquet, Jesús J. 1992. *Consagración de La Habana (Las peculiaridades del Grupo Orígenes en el proceso cultural cubano)*. Miami: North-South Centre of the University of Miami.
———. 1996. "El Grupo Orígenes ante el negrismo." *Afro-Hispanic Review* 15.2: 3–10.
Barth, Fredrik, ed. 1969. *Ethnic Groups and Boundaries: The Social Organisation of Ethnic Difference*. Oslo: Universitetsforlaget.
Beals, Ralph. 1962. "Acculturation." In *Anthropology Today: Selections*. Ed. Sol Tax. Chicago: University of Chicago Press.

Béhague, Gerard H., ed. 1994a. *Music and Black Ethnicity: The Caribbean and South America*. Miami: North-South Centre of the University of Miami.
———. 1994b. Introduction to Béhague 1994a, v–xii.
Benítez Rojo, Antonio. 1988. "Fernando Ortiz and Cubanness: A Post-modern Perspective." *Cuban Studies* 18: 125–32.
———. 1992. *The Repeating Island*. Durham, NC: Duke University Press.
———. 1998. "Música y nación." *Encuentro de la Cultura Cubana* 8–9: 43–54.
Blanco, Tomás. 1938. "Escorzos de un poeta antillano Luis Palés Matos." *Revista Bimestre Cubana* 42.3: 221–40.
Boti, Regino E. 1932. "La poesía cubana de Nicolás Guillén." In Morejón 1974a, 81–90.
Boulware, Kay. 1977. "Woman and Nature in *Negrismo*." *Studies in Afro-Hispanic Literature* 1: 16–25.
———. 1978. "Nature in Three Negrista Poets: Nicolás Guillén, Emilio Ballagas, Luis Palés Matos." PhD diss., University of California, Berkeley.
Branche, Jerome. 1998. "Ennobling Savagery? Sentimentalism and the Subaltern in *Sab*." *Afro-Hispanic Review* 17.2: 12–23.
———. 1999. "Negrismo: Hibridez cultural, autoridad y la cuestión de la nación." *Revista Iberoamericana* 65.188–89: 483–504.
———. 2001. "Mulato entre negros (y blancos): Writing, Race, the Antislavery Question and Juan Francisco Manzano's *Autobiografía*." *Bulletin of Latin American Research* 20.1: 63–87.
———, ed. 2003. *Lo que teníamos que tener: Raza y revolución en Nicolás Guillén*. Pittsburgh: University of Pittsburgh.
Brandon, George. 1993. *Santería from Africa to the New World: The Dead Shell Memories*. Bloomington : Indiana University Press.
Bremer, Fredrika. 1981. *Cartas desde Cuba*. Havana: Editorial de Arte y Literatura.
Brock, Lisa, and Castañeda Fuertes, Digna. 1998. *Between Race and Empire: African Americans and Cubans before the Cuban Revolution*. Philadelphia: Temple University Press.
Brock, Lisa. 1998. "Introduction: Between Race and Empire." In Brock and Castañeda Fuertes 1998, 1–32.
Brookshaw, David. 1986. *Race and Color in Brazilian literature*. Metuchen, NJ: Scarecrow Press.
———. 1988. *Paradise Betrayed: Brazilian Literature of the Indian*. Amsterdam: Centrum voor Studie en Documentatie van Latijns Amerika.
Bueno, Salvador. 1976. "'La canción del bongó': Sobre la cultura mulata de Cuba." *Cuadernos Americanos* 3: 89–106.
———. 1990. "Itinerario de Alfonso Hernández Catá (1885–1940)." *Revista Iberoamericana* 56.152–53: 933–50.
Bush, Barbara. 1990. *Slave Women in Caribbean Society, 1650–1838*. Bloomington: Indiana University Press.
Cabrera, Lydia. 1975a. *El monte*. Miami: Ediciones Universal.

———. 1975b. *Anaforuana: Ritual y símbolos de la iniciación en la sociedad secreta Abakuá.* Madrid: Ediciones R.

Cabrera, Ramiro. 1926. "El juego del papalote." *Archivos del Folklore Cubano* 2.1: 47–59.

Cabrera Infante, Guillermo. 1991. *Tres tristes tigres.* Barcelona: Seix Barral.

Cairo Ballester, Ana. 1976. *El movimiento de veteranos y patriotas (Apuntes para un estudio ideológico del año 1923).* Havana: Editorial Arte y Literatura.

Caldera, Ermanno. 1989. "Las jitanjáforas del teatro fantástico y anti-hipocóndrico de Monsieur Débout." In *La Chispa '89: Selected Proceedings from the Tenth Louisiana Conference on Hispanic Languages and Literatures,* 53–62. New Orleans: Tulane University.

Cámara Betancourt, Madeleine. 2000. "Between Myth and Stereotype: The Image of the *Mulata* in Cuban Culture in the Nineteenth Century, a Truncated Symbol of Nationality." In Fernández and Cámara Betancourt 2000, 101–15.

Campoamor, Fernando. 1937. "Martí, hombre total." *Revista Cubana* 9.26: 205–12.

Canizares, Raúl. 1993. *Walking with the Night: The Afro-Cuban World of Santería.* Rochester, VT: Destiny Books.

Captain, Yvonne. 1994. "Writing for the Future: Afro-Hispanism in a Global, Critical Context." *Afro-Hispanic Review* 13.1: 3–9.

Cárdenas, Osvaldo, and McGarrity, Gale. 1995. "Cuba." In *No Longer Invisible: Afro-Latin Americans Today,* ed. Pedro Pérez-Sarduy and Jean Stubbs, 77–108. London: Minority Rights Publications.

Carpentier, Alejo. 1929. "Lettre des Antilles." *Bifur* 3: 91–105.

———. 1937. "Un ballet afrocubano." *Revista Cubana* 8.22–24: 145–54.

———. 1961. *La música en Cuba.* Havana: Luz-Hilo.

———. 1964. *Tientos y diferencias (Ensayos).* Mexico City: Universidad Nacional Autónoma de México.

———. 1974. "Carta abierta a Manuel Aznar sobre el meridiano intelectual de nuestra América" [first published in 1927]. *Casa de las Américas* 84: 147–50.

———. 1980a. *Ese músico que llevo dentro,* vol. 2. Havana: Editorial Letras Cubanas.

———. 1980b. "La consagración de nuestros ritmos" [first published in 1922]. In Carpentier 1980a, 528–32.

———. 1980c. "Las nuevas ofensivas del cubanismo" [first published in 1922]. In Carpentier 1980a, 533–37.

———. 1982. *Écue-yamba-ó.* Madrid: Ediciones Alfaguara.

Carrera Damas, Germán. 1977. "Huida y enfrentamiento." In Moreno Fraginals 1977a, 34–52.

Cartey, Wilfred G. 1970. *Black Images.* New York: Teachers College, Columbia University.

Casado, Pablo Gil. 1989. "*Partiendo de la angustia:* Prolegómenos a la utopía del mestizaje, de Manuel Andújar." In *La Chispa '89: Selected Proceedings* from the Tenth Louisiana Conference on Hispanic Languages and Literatures, 153–60. New Orleans: Tulane University.

Castellanos, Jorge, and Isabel Castellanos. 1988. *Cultura afrocubana 1: El negro en Cuba, 1492–1844.* Miami: Ediciones Universal.

———. 1990. *Cultura afrocubana 2: El negro en Cuba, 1845–1959.* Miami: Ediciones Universal.

———. 1992. *Cultura afrocubana 3: Las religiones y las lenguas.* Miami: Ediciones Universal.

———. 1994. *Cultura afrocubana 4: Letras, música, arte.* Miami: Ediciones Universal.

Chacón y Calvo, José María. 1924. "Cuestionario de literatura popular cubana." *Archivos del Folklore Cubano* 1.1: 9–37.

Conjunto de Clave y Guaguancó. 1995. "La prueba del ritmo" [written by Amado Dedeu]. In *Cuba Classics: Rumba*, CD no. 052. London: Tumi Music Ltd.

Cornejo Polar, Antonio. 1978. "El indigenismo y las literaturas heterogeneas: Su doble estatuto socio-cultural." *Revista de Crítica Latinoamericana* 7–8: 7–21.

———. 1980. *Literatura y sociedad en el Perú: La novela indigenista.* Lima: Lasontay.

———. 1994a. *Escribir en el aire.* Lima: Editorial Horizonte.

———. 1994b. "Mestizaje, transculturación, heterogeneidad." *Revista de Crítica Literaria Latinoamericana* 40: 368–71.

———. 1995. "Condición migrante e intertextualidad multicultural: El caso de Arguedas." *Revista de Crítica Literaria Latinoamericana* 42: 101–9.

———. 1997. "Mestizaje e hibridez: Los riesgos de las metáforas: Apuntes." *Revista Iberoamericana* 63.180: 341–44.

———. 1998. "*Indigenismo* and Heterogeneous Literatures: Their Dual Socio-Cultural Logic." Trans. John Kraniauskas. *Journal of Latin American Cultural Studies* 7.1: 15–27.

Coronil, Fernando. 1995. "Transculturation and the Politics of Theory: Countering the Centre, Cuban Counterpoint." Introduction to *Cuban Counterpoint*, by Fernando Ortiz, trans. Harriet de Onís, ix–lvi. Durham, NC: Duke University Press.

Coulthard, G. R. 1962. *Race and Color in Caribbean Literature.* London: Oxford University Press.

Crook, Larry. 1982. "A Musical Analysis of the Cuban Rumba." *Latin American Music Review* 3.1: 92–123.

Cuadra, Pablo Antonio. 1983. "Rubén Darío y la aventura literaria del mestizaje." *Cuadernos Hispanoamericanos* 398: 307–21.

Cuddon, J. A. 1992. *The Penguin Dictionary of Literary Terms and Literary Theory.* London: Penguin Books.

Cuervo Hewitt, Julia. 1983. "Ifa: Oráculo Yoruba y Lucumí." *Cuban Studies* 13.1: 25–40.

———. 1988. *Aché, presencia africana: Tradiciones yoruba-lucumí en la narrativa cubana.* New York: Peter Lang.

Dahl, Anthony G. 1995. "Resolving the Question of Identity: Nicolás Guillén's 'La balada de los dos abuelos.'" *Afro-Hispanic Review* 14.1: 10–17.

D'Allemand, Patricia. 1996. "Urban Literary Production and Latin American Criticism." *Bulletin of Latin American Research* 15.3: 359–69.

———. 1999. "La crítica latinoamericana y sus metáforas: Algunas anotaciones." *Thesaurus* (Boletín del Instituto Caro y Cuervo) 54.3: 827–42.

———. 2000. *Latin American Cultural Criticism: Re-interpreting a Continent.* Lewiston, NY: Edwin Mellen Press.

Daniel, Ivonne. 1995. *Rumba: Dance and Social Change in Contemporary Cuba.* Bloomington: Indiana University Press.

Davies, Catherine. 1997. "Lydia Cabrera, Cuban Writer and Ethnographer." In Smith 1997, 153–55.

———. 2000. "Fernando Ortiz's Transculturation: The Postcolonial Intellectual and the Politics of Cultural Representation." In *Postcolonial Perspectives on the Cultures of Latin America and Lusophone Africa,* ed. Robin Fiddian, 141–68. Liverpool: Liverpool University Press.

———. 2001. Introduction to *Sab,* by Gómez de Avellaneda. Manchester: Manchester University Press, 2001.

Davis, James J. 1988. "Ritmo poético, negritud y dominicanidad." *Revista Iberoamericana* 54.142: 171–85.

de Armas, Emilio. 1997. "Cuba: Nineteenth[-] and Twentieth-Century Prose and Poetry." In Smith 1997, 235–42.

de Costa-Willis, Miriam. 1998. "Marcelino Arozarena's Journey to His Roots." *Afro-Hispanic Review* 17.1: 12–18.

de la Campa, Román. 1996. "Latinoamérica y sus nuevos cartógrafos: Discurso poscolonial, diásporas y enunciación fronteriza." *Revista Iberoamericana* 62: 176–77.

De La Fuente, Alejandro. 2001. *A Nation for All: Race, Inequality and Politics in Twentieth-Century Cuba.* Chapel Hill: University of North Carolina Press.

de la Torre, Rogelio. 1977. *La obra poética de Emilio Ballagas.* Miami: Ediciones Universal.

Delgado, Celeste Fraser, and José Esteban Muñoz. 1997a. *Everynight Life: Culture and Dance in Latin/o America* Durham, NC: Duke University Press.

———. 1997b. "Rebellions of Everynight Life." In Delgado 1997a, 9–32.

Departamento de Turismo del Municipio de la Habana. 1937. "El concierto afrocubano de Gilberto S. Valdés." *Estudios Afrocubanos* 1.1: 139–45.

Deschamps Chapeaux, Pedro. 1971. *El negro en la economía habanera del siglo XIX.* Havana: UNEAC.

Díaz de Ayala, Cristóbal. 1989. "Correspondence on 'Cuba's Bola de Nieve.'" *Latin American Music Review* 10.1: 188–93.

Dodson, Julyanne E. 1998. "Encounters in the African Atlantic World: The African Methodist Episcopal Church in Cuba." In Brock and Castañeda Fuertes 1998, 85–103.

Domínguez, Ivo. 1977. "En torno a la poesía Afro-hispanoamericana." *Cuadernos Hispanoamericanos* 107: 125–31.

Domínguez Alfonso, Aleida, ed. 1969. *Índices de las revistas cubanas*. Havana: Biblioteca Nacional José Martí.

Duany, Jorge. 2000. "Reconstructing Cubanness: Changing Discourses of National Identity on the Island and in the Diaspora during the Twentieth Century." In Fernández and Cámara Betancourt 2000, 17–42.

Duno Gottberg, Luis. 2003a. "Los imaginarios sosegantes de la nacionalidad: Nicolás Guillén y la ideología del mestizaje." In Branche 2003, 147–65.

———. 2003b. *Solventando las diferencias: La ideología del mestizaje en Cuba*. Madrid: Iberoamericana.

Duque, Félix. 1992. "La conciencia del mestizaje: El inca Garcilaso y sor Juana Inés de la Cruz." *Cuadernos Hispanoamericanos* 504: 7–31.

Eli Rodríguez, Victoria. 1994. "Cuban Music and Ethnicity: Historical Considerations." In Béhague 1994a, 91–108.

Ellis, Keith. 1983. *Cuba's Nicolás Guillén: Poetry and Ideology*. Toronto: University of Toronto Press.

———. 1988. "Images of Black People in the Poetry of Nicolás Guillén." *Afro-Hispanic Review* 7.1–3: 19–22.

———. 1997. "Motivos para elegir el son: Claves en la prosa de Guillén." *La Gaceta de Cuba* (July/August): 34–37.

———. 1998. "Nicolás Guillén and Langston Hughes: Convergences and Divergences." In Brock and Castañeda Fuertes 1998, 129–67.

Embales, Carlos. 1995. "Pim pam pum y blen blen blen." In *Cuba Classics: Rumba*, CD no. 052. London: Tumi Music Ltd.

Emery, Amy Fass. 1996. *The Anthropological Imagination in Latin American Literature*. Columbia: University of Missouri Press.

Eriksen, Thomas Hylland. 1993. *Ethnicity and Nationalism: Anthropological Perspectives*. London: Pluto Press.

Espinosa Delgado, Magaly. 1995. "Cultural Studies: A View from the Caribbean." *Journal of Latin American Cultural Studies* 4.2: 231–40.

Esténger, Rafael. 1927. "El poema de las narices." *Revista de Avance* 4 (30 April): 82–83.

Feal, Rosemary Geisdorfer. 1988. "*Black Literature and Humanism in Latin America*, by Richard L. Jackson." *Afro-Hispanic Review* 7.1–3: 60–62.

Feijóo, Samuel, ed. 1961. *Teatro bufo: Siete obras*, vol. 1. Havana: Universidad Central de las Villas.

———. 1977. "Influencia africana en Latinoamérica: Literatura oral y escrita." In Moreno Fraginals 1977a, 185–214.

———. 1986. *El son cubano: Poesía general*. Havana: Editorial Letras Cubanas.
———. 1987. *El negro en la literatura folklórica cubana*. Havana: Editorial Letras Cubanas.
Feldman Harth, Dorothy. 1955. "La poesía afrocubana." In *Miscelanea de estudios dedicados a Fernando Ortiz*, vol. 2, 791–815. Havana: Sociedad Económica de Amigos del Pais.
Fernández, Damián J., and Madeleine Cámara Betancourt, eds. 2000a. *Cuba, the Elusive Nation*. Gainesville: University Press of Florida.
———. 2000b. "Interpretations of National Identity." In Fernández and Cámara Betancourt 2000a, 1–13.
Fernández Retamar, Roberto. 1954. *La poesía contemporánea en Cuba (1927–1953)*. Havana: Orígenes.
———. 1981. *Para el perfil definitivo del hombre*. Havana: Letras Cubanas.
Fernández Robaina, Tomás. 1990. *El negro en Cuba*. Havana: Editorial de Ciencias Sociales.
———. 2003. "La prosa de Guillén en defensa del negro cubano." In Branche 2003, 123–46.
Fernández de la Vega, Óscar. 1977. "Origen del negrismo lírico antillano desde tres perspectivas." In *Homenaje a Lydia Cabrera*, ed. Reinaldo Sánchez and José A. Madrigal, 131–38. Miami: Ediciones Universal.
Fernández de la Vega, Oscar, and Alberto N. Pamies, eds. 1973. *Iniciación a la poesía afro-americana*. Miami: Ediciones Universal.
Ferrer, Ada. 2000. "Rethinking Race and Nation in Cuba." In Fernández and Cámara Betancourt 2000, 60–76.
Figueroa Berríos, Edwin. 1985. "Raices folklóricas en la poesía de Luis Palés Matos." *Estudios Hispánicos* 12: 179–88.
Finn, Julio. 1988. *Voices of Négritude*. London: Quartet Books.
Fornet, Ambrosio. 1967. *En blanco y negro*. Havana: Instituto del Libro.
Galán, Natalio. 1983. *Cuba y sus sones*. Valencia: Pre-textos.
García Canclini, Néstor. 1995a. *Culturas híbridas: Estrategias para entrar y salir de la modernidad*. Buenos Aires: Editorial Sudamericana.
———. 1995b. *Consumidores y ciudadanos: Conflictos multiculturales de la globalización*. México DF: Editorial Grijalbo.
Gates, Henry Louis, Jr. 1984. "The Blackness of Blackness: A Critique of the Sign and the Signifying Monkey." In *Black Literature and Literary Theory*, ed. Henry Louis Gates Jr., 285–328. New York: Methuen, 1984.
Gilman, Sander L. 1985. "Black Bodies, White Bodies: Toward an Iconography of Female Sexuality in Late Nineteenth-Century Art, Medicine and Literature." *Critical Inquiry* 12: 205–42.
Gilroy, Paul. 1993. *The Black Atlantic: Modernity and Double Consciousness*. London: Verso.
Goldberg, David Theo. 1993. *Racist Culture: Philosophy and the Politics of Meaning*. Oxford: Blackwell.

Gómez García, Carmen. 1998. "Cuban Social Poetry and the Struggle against Two Racisms." In Brock and Castañeda Fuertes 1998, 205–48.

González Contreras, Gilberto. 1973. "La poesía negra" [first published in 1936]. In Fernández de La Vega and Pamies 1973, 111–16.

González Echevarría, Roberto. 1977. *Alejo Carpentier: The Pilgrim at Home.* Ithaca, NY: Cornell University Press.

González Pérez, Aníbal. 1987. "Ballad of Two Poets: Nicolás Guillén y Palés Matos." *Callaloo* 10.2: 285–301.

González-Pérez, Armando. 1990. "Incursión en el maravilloso mundo mágico-religioso de la poesía afrocubana." *Revista Iberoamericana* 56: 1323–37.

Gorer, Geoffrey. 1949. *Africa Dances—A Book About West-African Negroes.* London: John Lehman.

Graham, Joseph F. 1992. *Onomatopoetics: Theory of Language and Literature.* Cambridge: Cambridge University Press.

Graham, Richard, ed. 1996a. *The Idea of Race in Latin America.* Austin: University of Texas Press.

———. 1996b. Introduction to Graham 1996a, 1–5.

Guillén, Nicolás. 1969. *Antología Mayor.* Ed. Andrés B. Consuelo. Havana: Ediciones Huracán.

———. 1990. *Summa poética.* Ed. Luis Íñigo Madrigal. Madrid: Ediciones Cátedra.

Guirao, Ramón. 1934. *Bongó: Poemas negros.* Havana: Ucar, García y Cía.

———, ed. 1938. *Órbita de la poesía afrocubana, 1928–37.* Havana: Ucar, García y Cía.

Habibe, Frederick Hendrik. 1985. *El compromiso en la poesía afroantillana de Cuba y Puerto Rico.* Curaçao: University of Curaçao.

Hall, Stuart. 1992. "The Question of Cultural Identity." In *Modernity and Its Futures,* ed. Stuart Hall, David Held, and Tony McGrew, 274–326. Cambridge: Polity Press.

Hanchard, Michael. 1999. *Racial Politics in Contemporary Brazil.* Durham, NC: Duke University Press.

Hanna, Judith Lynne. 1977. "To Dance Is Human." In *The Anthropology of the Body,* ed. John Blacking, 211–32. London: Academic Press.

———. 1984. "Black/White Non Verbal Differences." In *Non Verbal Behavior: Perspectives, Applications, Intercultural Insights,* ed. Aaron Wolfgang, 373–410. Lewiston, NY: C. J. Hoegrefe.

Harper, Peggy. 1969. "Dance in Nigeria." *Ethnomusicology* 13: 280–95.

Hawley, D.C. N.d. "Elementos onomatopéyicos y jitanjafóricos en la poesía hispanoafricana de América." In *Ensayos de literatura europea e hispanoamericana,* ed. Felix Menchacatorre, 215–22. Universidad del País Vasco: Servicio Editorial.

Hays, H. R. 1944. "Nicolás Guillén y la poesía afrocubana." In Morejón 1974a, 91–99.

Hazzard-Gordon, Katrina. 1990. *"Jookin": The Rise of Social Dance Formations in African-American Culture*. Philadelphia: Temple University Press.

Helg, Aline. 1995. *Our Rightful Share: The Afro-Cuban Struggle for Equality, 1886–1912*. Chapel Hill: University of North Carolina Press.

———. 1996. "Race in Argentina and Cuba, 1880–1930." In Graham 1996, 37–69.

Herskovits, Melville. 1966. *The New World Negro*. Ed. Frances Herskovits. Bloomington: Indiana University Press.

Hidalgo, Narciso, J. 1999. "Arquitectura rítmica y son en los *Motivos de son*." *Monographic Review* 15: 145–60.

Hoag, Charles K. 1987. "*Sensemayá*: A Chant for Killing a Snake." *Latin American Music Review* 8.2: 172–84.

Hoetink, H. 1967. *The Two Variants in Caribbean Race Relations*. London: Oxford University Press.

Howard, Philip A. 1998. *Changing History: Afro-Cuban Cabildos and Societies of Color in the Nineteenth Century*. Baton Rouge: Louisiana State University Press.

Huet, Michael, and Claude Savary. 1995. *Africa Dances*. London: Thames and Hudson.

Ibarra, Jorge. 1967. *Ideología Mambisa*. Havana: Instituto del Libro.

———. 1990. "La herencia científica de Fernando Ortiz." *Revista Iberoamericana* 56: 1339–51.

Ibítókun, Benedict M. 1993. *Dance as Ritual Drama and Entertainment in the Gèlèdé of the Kétu-Yorùbá Subgroup in West Africa (A Study in Traditional African Feminism)*. Ilé-Ifè, Nigeria: Obáfémi Awólóò University Press.

Ichaso, Francisco. 1927. "El prejuicio en nuestra evolución musical." *Revista de Avance* 15 (June 1927): 161–62, 175.

Iznaga, Diana. 1989. *Transculturación en Fernando Ortiz*. Havana: Editorial de Ciencias Sociales.

Jackson, Richard L. 1976. *The Black Image in Latin American Literature*. Alburquerque: University of New Mexico Press.

———. 1978. "Racial Identity and the Terminology of Literary Blackness." *Revista Chicano Riqueña* 5: 43–48.

———. 1984. "The *Afrocriollo* Movement Revisited." *Afro-Hispanic Review* 3.1: 5–9.

———. 1988a. "Afro–Hispanic Literature: Recent Trends in Criticism." *Afro-Hispanic Review* 7.1–3: 32–35.

———. 1988b. *Black Literature and Humanism in Latin America*. Athens: University of Georgia Press.

———. 1995. *Black Writers and the Hispanic Canon*. New York: Twayne Publishers.

Jacobs, Glenn. 1988. "Cuba's *Bola de Nieve*: A Creative Looking Glass for Culture and the Artistic Self." *Latin American Music Review* 9.1: 18–49.

Jacques, Geoffrey. 1998. "Afro-Cuban Music and Twentieth-Century American

Culture." In *Between Race and Empire: African Americans and Cubans before the Revolution*, ed. Lisa Brook and Digna Castañeda Fuentes, 249–65. Philadelphia: Temple University Press.

Jahn, Janheinz. 1968. *Neo-African Literature—A History of Black Writing*. New York: Faber & Faber.

———. 1970. *Muntú: Las culturas de la negritud*. Madrid: Ediciones Guadarrama.

Jarnés, Benjamín. 1929. "Raza, grillete." *Revista de Avance* 20 (January): 8–9, 30.

Jenkins, Richard. 1986. "Social Anthropological Models of Inter-Ethnic Relations." In Rex and Mason 1986a, 170–86.

Jensen, Larry R. 1988. *Children of Colonial Despotism: Press, Politics and Culture in Cuba, 1790–1840*. Florida: University Presses of Florida.

Jiménez, Luis A. 1993. "Facts and Poetry: Afro-Cuban Folklore in José Zacarías Tallet's 'La rumba.'" *Diaspora* (Southern Arkansas University) 2.2: 26–40.

Johnson, Lemuel A. 1971. *The Devil, the Gargoyle and the Buffoon: The Negro as Metaphor in Western Literature*. New York: Kennikat Press.

Joset, Jacques. 1987. "El mestizaje lingüístico y la teoría de los dos mediterraneos en la obra de Alejo Carpentier." *La Torre* (Universidad de Puerto Rico) 1: 251–63.

Julien, Eileen. 1992. *African Novels and the Question of Orality*. Bloomington: Indiana University Press.

Kaliman, Ricardo J. 1994. "Unseen Systems: Avant-Garde Indigenism in the Central Andes." In *Regionalism Reconsidered: New Approaches to the Field*, ed. David Jordan, 159–83. New York: Garland Publishing.

———. 1995. "Cultura imaginada y cultura vivida: Indigenismo en Los Andes centromeridionales." *Revista de Crítica Literaria Latinoamericana* 42: 87–99.

———. 1998. "What Is 'Interesting' in Latin American Cultural Studies." *Journal of Latin American Cultural Studies* 7.2: 261–72.

Kloe, Donald R. 1977. *A Dictionary of Onomatopoeic Sounds, Tones and Noises in English and Spanish*. Detroit, MI: Blaine Ethridge Books.

Klor de Alva, J. Jorge. 1995. "The Post-colonization of the (Latin) American Experience: A Reconsideration of 'Colonialism,' 'Post-colonialism,' and 'Mestizaje.'" In *After Colonialism: Imperial Histories and Postcolonial Displacements*, ed. Gyan Prakash, 241–75. Princeton, NJ: Princeton University Press.

Knight, Alan. 1996. "Racism, Revolution and *Indigenismo*." In Graham 1996, 71–113.

Knight, Franklin. 1970. *Slave Society in Cuba during the Nineteenth Century*. Madison: University of Wisconsin Press.

———. 1977. "The Social Structure of Cuban Slave Society in the Nineteenth Century." In *Comparative Perspectives on Slavery in New-World Plantation Societies*, 259–66. New York: New York Academy of Sciences.

Kubayanda, Josaphat B. 1974. "A Study of Modern Spanish 'Negrista' Poetry in Latin America, with Special Reference to the Poetry of Nicolás Guillén." Master's thesis, University of London.

———. 1982. "The Linguistic Core of Afro-Hispanic Poetry: An African Reading." *Afro-Hispanic Review* 1.3: 21–27.

———. 1985. "Polyrhythmics and African Print Poetics: Guillén, Cesaire and Atukwei Okai." In *Interdisciplinary Dimensions of African Literature: Selected Papers from the 1982 Conference of the African Literature Association*, 155–69. Washington, DC: Three Continents Press.

Kutzinski, Vera M. 1987. *Against the American Grain: Myth and History in William Carlos J. Williams, Jay Wright, and Nicolás Guillén*. Baltimore, MD: John Hopkins University Press.

———. 1993. *Sugar's Secrets: Race and the Erotics of Cuban Nationalism*. Charlottesville: University Press of Virginia.

Lamar Schweyer, Alberto. 1931. "La musa mulata." In Morejón 1974a, 255–58.

Lamore, Jean. 1987. "La mulata en el discurso literario y médico francés del siglo diecinueve." *La Torre* (Universidad de Puerto Rico) 1: 297–318.

Lazo, Raimundo, ed. 1985. *José Martí: Sus mejores páginas*. México DF: Editorial Porrúa.

Le Riverend, Julio. 1978. "Ortiz y sus contrapunteos." Introduction to *Contrapunteo cubano del tabaco y el azúcar*. In Ortiz 1978, ix–xxxii.

Leal, Rine. 1980. *Breve historia del teatro cubano*. Havana: Editorial Letras Cubanas.

———. 1982. *La selva oscura: De los bufos a la neocolonia*, vol. 2. Havana: Editorial Arte y Literatura.

León, Argeliers. 1984. *Del canto y el tiempo*. Havana: Editorial Letras Cubanas.

———. 1991. "Notes Towards a Panorama of Popular and Folk Musics." In Manuel 1991, 3–23.

Lewis, Marvin A. 1983. *Afro-Hispanic Poetry 1940–1980: From Slavery to "Negritud" in South-American Verse*. Columbia: University of Missouri Press.

Lezcano, José Manuel. 1991. "African-Derived Rhythmical and Metric Elements in Selected Songs of Alejandro García Caturla and Amadeo Roldán." *Latin American Music Review* 12.2: 173–86.

Lienhard, Martín. 1992. *La voz y su huella: Escritura y conflicto étnico-cultural en América Latina*. Lima: Editorial Horizonte.

———. 1994a. "Sociedades heterogéneas y 'diglosia' cultural en América Latina." In *Lateinamerika denken: Kulturtheorische Grenzgänge zwischen Moderne und Postmoderne*, ed. Birgit Scharlau, 93–104. Tübingen: Gumter Narr Verlag.

———. 1994b. "Oralidad." *Revista de Crítica Literaria Latinoamericana* 40: 363–74.

———. 1996. "El fantasma de la oralidad y algunos de sus avatares literarios y etnológicos." *Les Langues Neó-Latines* 11.297: 19–33.

———. 1997. "Of Mestizajes, Heterogeneities, Hybridisms and Other Chimeras: On the Macroprocesses of Cultural Interaction in Latin America." *Journal of Latin American Cultural Studies* 6.2: 183–200.

———. 1999. "Kalunga o el recuerdo de la trata esclavista en algunos cantos afro-americanos." *Revista Iberoamericana* 65.188–89: 505–17.
López Morales, Humberto. 1967. "La lengua de la poesía afrocubana." *Español Actual* 7: 1–3.
López Segrera, Francisco. 1989. *Cuba: Cultura y sociedad*. Havana: Editorial Letras Cubanas.
Losada, Alejandro. 1977. "Rasgos específicos de la producción literaria ilustrada en América Latina." *Revista de Crítica Literaria Latinoamericana* 6: 7–36.
Luis, William. 1990. *Literary Bondage: Slavery in Cuban Narrative*. Austin: University of Texas Press.
———. 1994. "Cultura afrocubana en la Revolución: Entrevista a Elio Ruiz." *Afro-Hispanic Review* 13.1: 37–45.
———. 1998. "Cuban Counterpoint, Coffee and Sugar: The Emergence of a National Culture in Fernando Ortiz's *Cuban Counterpoint: Tobacco and Sugar* and Cirilo Villaverde's *Cecilia Valdés*." *Palara* 2 (Fall): 5–16.
———. 2001. *Culture and Customs of Cuba*. London: Greenwood Press.
———. 2003. "En busca de la cubanidad: El negro en la literatura y la cultura cubana." In *Heterotropías narrativas de identidad y alteridad latinoamericana*, ed. Carlos A. Jáuregui and Juan Pablo Dabove, 391–415. Pittsburgh: Instituto Internacional de Literatura Iberoamericana.
Madrigal, Íñigo. 1990. Introduction and notes to Guillén 1990, 15–45.
Malinowski, Bronislaw. 1978. Introduction to Ortiz 1978, 3–10.
Mansour, Mónica. 1973. *La poesía negrista*. México DF: Ediciones Era.
Manuel, Peter. 1985. "The Anticipated Bass in Cuban Popular Music." *Latin American Music Review* 6.2: 249–61.
———. 1987. "Marxism, Nationalism and Popular Music in Revolutionary Cuba." *Popular Music* 6.2: 161–78.
———, ed. 1991. *Essays on Cuban Music: North-American and Cuban Perspectives*. Lanham, MD: University Press of America.
———. 1994. "Puerto-Rican Music and Cultural Identity: Creative Appropriation of Cuban Sources from *Danza* to Salsa." *Ethnomusicology* 38.2: 249–80.
Mañach, Jorge. 1931. "Sóngoro cosongo." In Morejón 1974a, 251–54.
Mariátegui, José Carlos. 1968. *Siete ensayos de interpretación de la realidad peruana*. Lima: Empresa Editora Amauta.
———. 1985. *Siete ensayos de interpretación de la realidad peruana*. Lima: Empresa Editora Amauta.
Marinello, Juan. 1933. *Poética: Ensayos en entusiasmo*. Madrid: Espasa Calpe.
———. 1937. "Hazaña y triunfo americanos de Nicolás Guillén." In Morejón 1974a, 283–91.
———. 1969. "Notas sobre la Revista de Avance." In Domínguez Alfonso 1969, 11–18.
———. 1977. "Sobre el vanguardismo en Cuba y en la América Latina." In *Los*

vanguardismos en la América Latina, ed. Óscar Collazos, 211–24. Barcelona: Ediciones Península.

———. 1998. "Carta negra" [first published in 1929]. *La Gaceta de Cuba* 4: 11.

Martí, Oscar R. 1989. "Sarmiento y el positivismo." *Cuadernos Americanos* 1.13: 142–54.

Martí, José. 1985a. "Nuestra América" [first published in 1891]. In Lazo 1985, 87–93.

———. 1985b. "Mi raza" [first published in 1893]. In Lazo 1985, 52–53.

———. 1985c. "El 'manifiesto de Montecristi': El partido revolucionario a Cuba" [first published in 1895]. In Lazo 1985, 67–72.

Martínez, Juan A. 1994. *Cuban Art and National Identity: The Vanguardia Painters, 1927–1950.* Gainesville: University Press of Florida.

Martínez Furé, Rogelio. 1979. *Diálogos imaginarios.* Havana: Editorial Arte y Literatura.

———. 1991. "Tambor (Drum)." In Manuel 1991, 27–47.

———. 2000. "A National Cultural Identity? Homogenizing Monomania and the Plural Heritage." In Pérez Sarduy and Stubbs 2000, 154–61.

Mason, John. 1992. *Orin Orisa: Songs for Selected Heads.* Brooklyn, NY: Yoruba Theological Archministry.

Matamoros, Miguel. 1992. "Frutas del caney." In *Semilla del son: Trío Matamoros.* Madrid: Animal Tour Producciones, RCA.

Matibag, Eugenio. 1996. *Afro-Cuban Religious Experience: Cultural Reflections in Narrative.* Gainesville: University Press of Florida.

Mayer Serra, Otto. 1947. *Música y músicos de Latinoamérica.* México DF: W. M. Jackson.

Méndez Rodenas, Adriana. 1999. "Tropics of Deceit: Desire and the Double in Cuban Antislavery Narrative." *Cuban Studies* 28: 83–99.

———. 2000. "Bondage in Paradise: Frederika Bremer's Travels to Cuba and the Landscape of National Identity." In Fernández and Cámara Betancourt 2000, 200–223.

———. 2002. *Cuba en su imagen: Historia e identidad en la literatura cubana.* Madrid: Editorial Verbum.

Miller, Marilyn. 2003. "Palomas de vuelo popular: Los poemas de Guillén más allá de la hoja blanca." In Branche 2003, 244–69.

Moliner, María. 1960. *Diccionario del uso del español.* Madrid: Editorial Gredos.

Montejo Arrechea, Carmen. 1998. "*Minerva*: A Magazine for Women of Color." In Brock and Castañeda Fuertes 1998, 33–48.

Moore, Robin Dale. 1994. "Representations of Afro-Cuban Expressive Culture in the Writings of Fernando Ortiz." *Latin American Music Review* 15.1: 32–54.

———. 1997. *Nationalizing Blackness: Afrocubanismo and Artistic Revolution in Havana, 1920–1940.* Pittsburgh: University of Pittsburgh Press.

Morales, Jorge Luis. 1976. *Poesía afroantillana y negrista.* Río Piedras: Editorial Universitaria.

Moraña, Mabel, ed. 1998. *Indigenismo hacia el fin del milenio: Homenaje a Antonio Cornejo-Polar.* Pittsburgh: Instituto Internacional de Literatura Iberoamericana.

Morejón, Nancy, ed. 1974a. *Recopilación de textos sobre Nicolás Guillén.* Havana: Casa de las Américas.

———. 1974b. "Conversación con Nicolás Guillén." In Morejón 1974a, 31–61.

———. 1982. *Nación y mestizaje en Nicolás Guillén.* Havana: Ediciones Unión.

Moreno Fraginals, Manuel, ed. 1977a. *Africa en América Latina.* Mexico DF: Siglo XXI.

———. 1977b. "Aportes culturales y deculturación." In Moreno Fraginals 1977a, 13–33.

———. 1978. *El ingenio,* vol. 2. Havana: Editorial de Ciencias Sociales.

———. 1996. *Cuba/España, España/Cuba: Historia común.* Barcelona: Grijalbo Mondadori.

Moulin, Sylvie. 1987. "El bongó del Caribe: Apuntes sobre los poemas negros de Luis Palés Matos." *Confluencia: Revista Hispánica de Cultura y Literatura* 3.1: 105–11.

Mullen, Edward. 1987. "*Los negros brujos:* A Re-examination of the Text." *Cuban Studies* 17: 11–29.

———. 1988. "The Emergence of Afro-Hispanic Poetry: Some Notes on Canon Formation." *Hispanic Review* 56: 435–53.

———. 1998. *Afro-Cuban Literature: Critical Junctures.* Westport, CT: Greenwood Press.

Neira Betancourt, Lino Arturo. 1991. *Como suena un tambor abakuá.* Havana: Editorial Pueblo y Educación.

Noble, Enrique. 1958. "Introducción al tema de la mulata en la poesía negrista." *Cuadernos Hispanoamericanos* 99: 383–86.

Onions, C. T., ed. 1966. *The Oxford Dictionary of English Etymology.* Oxford: Clarendon Press.

Orihuela L., Carlos. 1996. "La heterogeneidad negrista en la literatura peruana: El caso de *Monólogo desde las tinieblas* de Antonio Galvez Ronceros." In *Asedios a la heterogeneidad cultural: Libro de homenaje a Antonio Cornejo Polar,* ed. José Antonio Mazzotti and U. Juan Zeballos Aguilar, 379–94. Philadelphia: Asociación Internacional de Peruanistas.

Orovio, Helio, ed. 1969. *Órbita de José Zacarías Tallet.* Havana: UNEAC.

———. 1992. *Diccionario de la música cubana biográfico y técnico.* Havana: Editorial Letras Cubanas.

———. 1994. *Música por el Caribe.* Santiago de Cuba: Editorial Oriente.

Orozco, Román, and Natalia Bolívar. 1998. *Cubasanta: Comunistas, santeros y cristianos en la isla de Fidel Castro.* Madrid: Ediciones El Pais.

Ortiz, Arturo. 1983. "El mestizaje cultural en majestad negra de Palés Matos." *Journal of the Pacific North-West Council on Foreign Languages* 4: 126–33.

Ortiz, Fernando. 1924a. *Glosario de afronegrismos.* Havana: Imprenta El Siglo XX.

———. 1924b. "Personajes del folklore afrocubano." *Archivos del Folklore Cubano* 1.1: 62–75.

———. 1924c. "La fiesta afrocubana del 'Día de Reyes.'" *Archivos del Folklore Cubano* 1.2: 146–65.

———. 1924d. "Cataurito de cubanismos." *Archivos del Folklore Cubano* 1.2: 174–75.

———. 1934. "La poesía mulata: Presentación de Eusebia Cosme, la recitadora." *Revista Bimestre Cubana* 34: 205–13.

———. 1937. "Luis Palés Matos, *Poemas afroantillanos*." *Estudios Afrocubanos* 1.1: 156–59.

———. 1938. "Dos nuevos libros del folklore afrocubano." *Revista Bimestre Cubana* 42.3: 307–20.

———. 1939. "La cubanidad y los negros." *Estudios Afrocubanos* 3.1–4: 4–15.

———. 1947. *El Huracán: Su mitología y sus símbolos*. México DF: Fondo de Cultura Económica.

———. 1965. *La Africanía de la música folklórica de Cuba* [first published in 1950]. Havana: Editorial Universitaria.

———. 1973a. *Los negros brujos* [first published in 1906]. Miami: Ediciones Universal.

———. 1973b. "Los últimos versos mulatos" [first published in 1935]. In Fernández de La Vega and Pamies 1973, 156–71.

———. 1973c. "Más acerca de la poesía mulata: Escorzos para su estudio" [first published in 1936]. In Fernández de La Vega and Pamies 1973, 173–202.

———. 1974. *El engaño de las razas* [first published in 1946]. Havana: Editorial de Ciencias Sociales.

———. 1978. *Contrapunteo cubano del tabaco y el azúcar* [first published in 1940]. Caracas: Biblioteca Ayacucho.

———. 1981. *Los bailes y el teatro de los negros en el folklore de Cuba* [first published in 1951]. Havana: Editorial Letras Cubanas.

———. 1984. *La clave xilofónica de la música cubana* [first published in 1946]. Havana: Editorial Letras Cubanas.

———. 1986a. *Los negros curros*. Havana: Editorial de Ciencias Sociales.

———. 1986b. *Entre cubanos: Psicología tropical* [first published in 1913]. Havana: Editorial de Ciencias Sociales.

———. 1988. *Los negros esclavos* [first published in 1916]. Havana: Editorial de Ciencias Sociales.

———. 1991a. *Estudios etnosociológicos*, ed. Isaac Barreal Fernández. Havana: Editorial de Ciencias Sociales.

———. 1991b. "Los factores humanos de la cubanidad" [first published in 1949]. In Ortiz 1991a, 10–30.

———. 1991c. "La música sagrada de los negros yorubas en Cuba" [first published in 1937]. In Ortiz 1991a, 82–96.

———. 1991d. "La secta conga de los matiabos de Cuba" [first published in 1937]. In Ortiz 1991a, 102–22.

———. 1991e. "La religión en la poesía mulata" [first published in 1937]. In Ortiz 1991a, 141–75.

———. 1991f. "La transculturación blanca de los tambores de los negros" [first published in 1952]. In Ortiz 1991a, 176–201.

———. 1991g. "Cómo eran los indocubanos" [first published in 1935]. In Ortiz 1991a, 31–43.

———. 1992. *Los cabildos y la fiesta afrocubanos del Día de Reyes* [first published in 1921 under the title *Los cabildos afrocubanos*]. Havana: Editorial de Ciencias Sociales.

———. 1995. *Cuban Counterpoint: Tobacco and Sugar.* Durham, NC: Duke University Press.

———. 1996a. *Los instrumentos de la música afrocubana,* vol. 1 [first published in 1952]. Madrid: Editorial Música Mundana Maqueda.

———. 1996b. *Los instrumentos de la música afrocubana,* vol. 2 [first published in 1952]. Madrid: Editorial Música Mundana Maqueda.

Ortiz Herrera, María Fernanda. 1996. *"In Memoriam."* In Ortiz 1996a, xi–xiv.

Otero, Lisandro. 1990. "Del Monte y la cultura de la sacarocracia." *Revista Iberoamericana* 56.152–53: 723–31.

Pallas, Rosa. 1973. *La poesía de Emilio Ballagas.* Madrid: Playor.

Palmié, Stephan. 1993. "Ethnogenetic Processes and Cultural Transfer in Afro-American Slave Populations." In *Slavery in the Americas,* ed. Wolfgang Binder, 337–63. Würzburg: Konigshausen and Neumann.

———. 1995. "Against Syncretism: 'Africanizing' and 'Cubanizing' Discourses in North-American Orisha Worship." In *Counterworks. Managing the Diversity of Knowledge,* ed. Richard Fardon, 73–104. London: Routledge.

Paquette, Robert. 1988. *Sugar Is Made with Blood: The Conspiracy of La Escalera and the Conflict between Empires over Slavery in Cuba.* Middletown, CT: Wesleyan University Press.

Pello el Afrokán. 1988. "Toque la conga: Método." In *Congas por barrio.* Havana: Areito/Egrem LP LD-4471.

Peñalver Moral, Reynaldo. 2000. "Under the Streetlamp: A Journalist's Story." In Pérez Sarduy and Stubbs 2000, 41–48.

Pereda Valdés, Ildefonso, ed. 1936. *Antología de la poesía negra americana.* Santiago, Chile: Ercilla.

———. 1970. *Lo negro y lo mulato en la poesía cubana.* Montevideo: Ediciones Ciudadela.

Pérez, Louis A. 1988. *Cuba: Between Reform and Revolution.* New York: Oxford University Press.

Pérez Firmat, Gustavo. 1989. *The Cuban Condition.* Cambridge: Cambridge University Press.

———. 1999. *My Own Private Cuba: Essays on Cuban Literature and Culture.* Boulder, CO: Society of Spanish and Spanish-American Studies.
Pérez Sarduy, Pedro, and Stubbs, Jean, eds. 2000a. *Afro-Cuban Voices on Race and Identity in Contemporary Cuba.* Gainesville: University Press of Florida.
———. 2000b. "Introduction: Race and the Politics of Memory in Contemporary Black Consciousness." In Pérez Sarduy and Stubbs 2000a, 1–38.
Phaf, Ineke. 1999. "El 'Cuaderno' de Nancy Morejón: La Habana 1967–1993." *Revista Iberoamericana* 65.188–89: 535–51.
Piedra, José. 1985. "From Monkey Tales to Cuban Songs: On Signification." *Modern Language Notes* 100: 361–90.
———. 1991. "Poetics for the Hip." *New Literary History* 22: 633–75.
Powell, Richard J., and Roger Malbert. 1997. "Rhapsodies in Black: Art of the Harlem Renaissance." Guide to the exhibition "Rhapsodies in Black: Art of the Harlem Renaissance" shown at the Hayward Gallery of London from 19 June to 17 August 1997.
Pratt, Mary Louise. 1992. *Imperial Eyes: Travel Writing and Transculturation.* London: Routledge.
Pryor Rice, Argyll. 1966. *Emilio Ballagas: Poeta o poesía.* México DF: Ediciones de Andrea.
Raby, D. L. 1975. "The Cuban Pre-revolution of 1933: An Analysis." Occasional Papers, no. 18. University of Glasgow.
Radillo, Teófilo. 1939. *Resonancias.* Havana: Editorial Guaimaro.
Rama, Ángel. 1982. *Transculturación narrativa en América Latina.* Mexico DF: Siglo XXI Editores.
Ramos, José Antonio. 1937. "Cubanidad y Mestizaje." *Estudios Afrocubanos* 1.1: 92–113.
Revista de Avance. 1927. "'1927': Exposición de arte nuevo." *Revista de Avance* 5 (15 May): 112–13.
Rex, John, and David Mason, eds. 1986. *Theories of Race and Ethnic Relations.* Cambridge: Cambridge University Press.
Rex, John. 1986. "The Role of Class Analysis in the Study of Race Relations—A Weberian Perspective." In Rex and Mason 1986, 64–83.
Ripoll, Carlos. 1964. "La *Revista de Avance* (1927–1930): Vocero de Vanguardismo y Pórtico de Revolución." *Revista Iberoamericana* 30: 261–82.
———. 1968. *La generación del 23 en Cuba y otros apuntes sobre el vanguardismo.* New York: Las Americas Publishing Company.
Robbins, James. 1990. "The Cuban *Son* as Form, Genre and Symbol." *Latin American Music Review* 11.2: 182–200.
Roig de Leuchsenring, Emilio. 1924. "Los velorios." *Archivos del Folklore Cubano* 1.1: 47–51.
———. 1935. *Historia de la Enmienda Platt. Una interpretación de la realidad cubana.* Havana: Editorial de Ciencias Sociales.

RoseGreen-Williams, Claudette. 1992. "Representations of Afro-Caribbean Folklore in Spanish Caribbean Poetry." *Interamerican Review of Bibliography* 42.1: 121–31.

———. 1993. "The Myth of Black Female Sexuality in Spanish Caribbean Poetry." *Afro-Hispanic Review* 12.1: 16–23.

Rowe, William. 1996. *Hacia una poética radical: Ensayos de hermeneútica cultural*. Lima: Mosca Azul Editores.

Rowe, William, and Vivian Schelling. 1991. *Memory and Modernity: Popular Culture in Latin America*. London: Verso.

Royce, Anya Peterson. 1977. *The Anthropology of Dance*. Ontario: Fitzhenry & Whiteside.

Rubila Lagos, Marcela. 1993. "Maldita yo entre las mujeres: El mestizaje como elemento transgresor." *Acta Literaria* 18: 171–82.

Ruiz del Vizo, Hortensia. 1972. *Poesía negra del Caribe y otras áreas*. Miami: Ediciones Universal.

R.V., J (sic), ed. 1893. *Décimas cubanas y canciones y guarachas modernas*. Havana: Establecimiento Tipográfico de Canalejo y Xiqués.

Salazar, Adolfo. 1938. "La obra musical de Alejandro García Caturla." *Revista Cubana* 11.31: 5–43.

Santí, Enrico Mario. 2002. *Fernando Ortiz: Contrapunteo y transculturación*. Madrid: Editorial Colibrí.

Schmidt, Friedhelm. 1995. "¿Literaturas heterogéneas o literatura de la transculturación?" *Nuevo Texto Crítico* 7.14–15: 193–99.

Schwartz, Rosalie. 1977. *The Displaced and the Disappointed: Cultural Nationalists and Black Activists in Cuba in the 1920s*. Ann Arbor, MI: UMI Dissertation Services.

———. 1998. "Cuba's Roaring Twenties: Race Consciousness and the Column 'Ideales de una raza,'" In Brock and Castañeda Fuertes 1998, 104–19.

Scott, Rebecca J. 1985. *Slave Emancipation in Cuba: The Transition to Free Labor, 1860–1899*. Princeton, NJ: Princeton University Press.

Sexteto Habanero. 1992. *Las raíces del son* [all recordings made between 1925 and 1931], CD no. 009. Switzerland: Tumbao Cuban Classics.

Skidmore, Thomas E. 1996. "Racial Ideas and Social Policy in Brazil, 1870–1940." In Graham 1996a, 7–36.

———. 1998. *Black into White: Race and Nationality in Brazilian Thought*. Durham, NC: Duke University Press.

Smart, Ian Isidore. 1990. *Nicolás Guillén: Popular Poet of the Caribbean*. Columbia: University of Missouri Press.

Smith, Colin. 1988. *Collins Spanish-English, English-Spanish Dictionary*. Barcelona: Grijalbo.

Smith, Verity, ed. 1997. *Encyclopedia of Latin American Literature*. London: Fitzroy Dearborn.

Smorkaloff, Pamela Maria. 1997. *Readers and Writers in Cuba: A Social History of Print Culture, 1830s–1990s.* New York: Garland Publishing.

Sociedad de Estudios Afrocubanos. 1937a. "La Sociedad de Estudios Afrocubanos Contra los Racismos: Advertencia, comprensión y designio." *Estudios Afrocubanos* 1.1: 3–6.

———. 1937b. "Estatutos de la Sociedad de Estudios Afrocubanos." *Estudios Afrocubanos* 1.1: 7–8.

———. 1937c. "Miembros de la Sociedad de Estudios Afrocubanos." *Estudios Afrocubanos* 1.1: 9–10.

Sociedad del Folklore Cubano. 1924a. "Actas de la 'Sociedad del Folklore Cubano.'" *Archivos del Folklore Cubano* 1.1: 47–51.

———. 1924b. "Esta revista cubana." *Archivos del Folklore Cubano* 1.1: 5–8.

Stolcke, Verona. 1992. *Racismo y sexualidad en la Cuba colonial.* Madrid: Alianza Editorial.

Stubbs, Jean. 1995. "Social and Political Motherhood of Cuba: Mariana Grajales Cuello." In *Engendering History: Caribbean Women in Historical Perspective,* ed. Verene Shepherd, Bridget Brereton, and Barbara Bailey, 296–317. Kingston, Jamaica: Ian Randle Publishers.

Suárez Solís, Rafael. 1935. "Poesía negra." *Revista Cubana* 1.1: 155–56.

Tallet, José Z. 1927. "Tedium Carnis." *Revista de Avance* 14 (30 October): 42.

Thomas, Ena V. 1990. "Black Images in the Poetry of Palés Matos." *Afro-Hispanic Review* 9.1–3: 30–33.

Thomas, Hugh. 1971. *Cuba or the Pursuit of Freedom.* London: Eyre & Spottiswoode.

Thompson, Robert Farris. 1974. *African Art in Motion.* Berkeley: University of California Press.

Tieles Ferrer, Cecilio. 1994. *Espadero, lo hispánico musical en Cuba.* Barcelona: Agil Offset.

Trelles, Carlos M. 1924. "Notas bibliográficas acerca del folklore cubano." *Archivos del Folklore Cubano* 1.2: 103–11.

Turner, Victor. 1986. *The Anthropology of Performance.* New York: PAJ Publications.

Urfé, Odilio. 1977. "La música y la danza en Cuba." In Moreno Fraginals 1977a, 215–37.

Uslar Pietri, Arturo. 1967. "El mestizaje y el nuevo mundo." *Revista de Occidente* 17: 13–29.

Valdés-Cruz, Rosa E. 1970. *La poesía negroide en América.* New York: Las Americas Publishing Company.

Vasconcelos, José. 1958. *Obras completas.* México DF: Libreros Mexicanos Unidos.

Verma, Gajendra K. 1984. "Introduction: Multicultural Education: Problems and Issues." In *Race Relations and Cultural Differences: Educational and Interpersonal Perspectives,* ed. Gajendra K. Verma and Christopher Bagley, 1–11. New York: St. Martin's Press.

Vianna, Hermano. 1999. *The Mystery of Samba: Popular Music and National Identity in Brazil*. Chapel Hill: University of North Carolina Press.
Vilanova, Manuel. 1977. "Mestizaje y marginación: El laberinto de la identidad en América Latina." *Cuadernos Hispanoamericanos* 320–21: 285–99.
Villanueva Callado, Alfredo. 1982. "Fili-Mele: Símbolo y mujer en la poesía de Luis Palés Matos e Iván Silén." *Revista Chicano-Riqueña* 10.4: 47–54.
Vitier, Medardo. 1937. "Lineamientos de la literatura hispanoamericana." *Revista Cubana* 9.26: 131–57.
Vocal Sampling. 1994. "Congo Yambumba" (written by Jesús Pérez). In *Una forma más*, CD no. 9362-45751-2. New York: Sire.
Wade, Peter. 1991. "The Language of Place, Race and Nation in Colombia." *América Negra* (Bogota) 2: 41–66.
———. 1993. *Blackness and Race Mixture: The Dynamics of Racial Identity in Colombia*. Baltimore, MD: John Hopkins University Press.
———. 1995. "Black Music and Cultural Syncretism in Colombia." In *Slavery and Beyond: The African Impact on Latin America and the Caribbean*, ed. Darién J. Davis, 121–46. Wilmington, DE: SR Books.
———. 1997. *Race and Ethnicity in Latin America*. London: Pluto Press.
Williams, Brackette F. 1991. *Stains on My Name, War in My Veins: Guyana and the Politics of Cultural Struggle*. Durham, NC: Duke University Press.
Williams, Claudette M. 2000. *Charcoal and Cinnamon: The Politics of Color in Spanish Caribbean Literature*. Gainesville: University Press of Florida.
Williams, Lorna V. 1982. *Self and Society in the Poetry of Nicolás Guillén*. Baltimore, MD: John Hopkins University Press.
———. 1995. "The Emergence of an Afro-Cuban Aesthetic." *Afro-Hispanic Review* 14.1: 48–57.
Wilson, Leslie N. 1979. *La poesía afroantillana*. Miami: Ediciones Universal.
Winant, Howard. 1999. "Racial Democracy and Racial Identity: Comparing the United States and Brazil." In Hanchard 1999, 98–115.
Wright, Ann. 1988. "Intellectuals of an Unheroic Period of Cuban History, 1913–1923. The 'Cuba Contemporánea' Group." *Bulletin of Latin American Research* 7.1: 109–22.
Young, Ann Venture. 1977. "The Black Woman in Afro-Caribbean Poetry." In *Blacks in Hispanic Literature*, ed. Miriam De Costa Willis, 137–42. Port Washington, NY: Kennikat Press.
———. 1982. "Black Women in Hispanic American Poetry: Glorification, Deification and Humanization." *Afro-Hispanic Review* 1.3: 23–27.
———. 1987. *The Image of Black Women in Twentieth Century South-American Poetry*. Washington, DC: Three Continents Press.
Zielina, María, 2003. "Descubriendo al otro a partir de sí mismo." In Branche 2003, 99–118.

Index

Abakuá, 27, 28, 39, 58, 62, 63, 64, 115, 143, 146, 151–52, 155, 159–60, 186n3, 187n15, 188n18
Abela, Eduardo, 1, 58–59
abolitionism, 119, 137–38, 182n1
Acosta, Agustín, 32
Acosta, Leonardo, 127
acculturation, 9, 70–71, 77–78, 177–78n3, 178n5
African culture, 50, 73–74, 79, 93, 108, 115, 120, 123–24, 137–38, 144, 175n9, 183n13, 184–85n3
africanización perpetua, 8, 42
Afro-Cuban, category of, 48–50, 84
Afro-Cuban culture: and Afro-Cuban identities, 47–50; collective practices in, 50; dance in, 73–74, 116–19, 135–37, 142–47, 162; discourses against, 26, 28–30, 51, 67, 79–85, 138; heterogeneity of, 48–50, 92–93, 115–16; music in, 50, 73–74; musical instruments in, 118–19, 154–56; non-written media in, 126–29, 130, 133–34, 140, 145, 185n4; orality in, 123–26; repression of, 26–28, 51; sexist notions in, 116–17, 151–56
afrocubanista: category, 55, 171n1; music, 1, 8, 44, 52, 59, 67, 81–82, 143, 174n3; painting, 1, 2, 28, 30, 31, 58, 88–89, 92, 104, 107, 111, 182n4, 184n18
Afro-Hispanism, 8–18, 57, 79, 104
ajiaco. See under Ortiz, Fernando
anthropology, 3, 4–5, 8, 17, 49, 68, 69, 70–71, 77–78, 178n4
Apollinaire, Guillaume, 31, 88
Archivos del Folklore Cubano, 87–88, 101, 134

Arguedas, José María, 4, 78, 176n21
Arozarena, Marcelino, 7, 12, 37, 54, 109, 114, 118–19, 120, 134–35, 140, 156–61, 163–64, 168–69, 175n17, 189n28, 189n1
Arredondo, Alberto, 8, 44, 46–47, 51, 52, 172n1
Arrom, José Juan, 6, 172n16, 185–86n10
Augier, Ángel, 46, 52, 55–56, 57
authenticity, concept of, 3, 15, 17, 55, 57–58, 168, 171n12

Babalú Ayé, 133, 158
Ballagas, Emilio, 9, 37, 53, 54, 58, 60, 61, 72, 73, 76, 80, 86, 108, 112–13, 118–19, 128, 130, 135–37, 139, 148–49, 150, 155–56, 157, 161–62, 163, 172n15, 179n1, 182n4, 182n6, 183n12, 187n11
Baquero, Gastón, 8, 16, 42, 44, 46, 51, 52
Barth, Fredrick, 4–5, 49, 174n7
Bartmann, Sarah, 107–8
Batista, Fulgencio, 33
Benítez Rojo, Antonio, 13, 24, 36, 60, 66, 127, 149, 150–51, 169, 171n11, 173n3, 188n23
Black Cubans: and Cuban politics, 21–28, 34, 38–40; discrimination against, 8, 21–23, 26–28, 45–46, 47–48, 49, 50–51, 53, 56; elitism amongst, 51–52, 175n11; literacy amongst, 22, 128, 172n1; political mobilization of, 23–24, 38; role in Wars of Independence, 21, 38, 51; social and cultural differences amongst, 44–48, 52, 54, 55–56
bongó drum, 1, 12, 14, 34, 46, 74, 86, 132, 133, 156, 158, 188n19

Boti, Regino, 30, 35, 175n12
Boulware, Kay, 121, 149, 161, 187n11
bozal dialect, 44, 98, 179–80n6
Branche, Jerome, 141, 171n5, 171n8, 186n14
Brandon, Richard, 50, 126, 127, 164, 177n28, 185n4
Brazil, 8, 11, 78, 162, 173nn8–9, 174n4, 176n26, 178n6, 182n2, 186n5, 189n2
Bremer, Fredrika, 142, 143, 145, 146
brujería, 27, 29, 47, 101
Brull, Mariano, 129
Bueno, Salvador, 7, 48–50, 84

cabildos de nación, 25–26, 27, 46, 47, 48, 49, 50, 88, 90, 130, 131, 142, 143, 173n4
Cabrera, Lydia, 1, 2, 25, 87, 147, 149, 152, 157, 180n6, 187n10
Carbonell, Walterio, 47
Carpentier, Alejo, 1, 34, 46, 52, 55, 58, 59–60, 62–63, 86, 128, 182n4, 185n7
Cartey, Wilfred G., 128
Castellanos, Israel, 28, 29, 30, 87
Castellanos, Jorge and Isabel, 7, 47, 48, 82–83, 152, 172n1, 180n6, 187n14, 188n20
Cendrars, Blaise, 31, 88, 173n9
Chacón y Calvo, José María, 88, 101, 180n8
Changó, 115, 136, 145, 147, 149–51, 153, 155, 158, 162, 183n12, 186nn2–3, 187nn10–11, 189n27
Club Atenas, 46, 51
comparsas, 46, 48, 90, 143, 146, 179n2, 186n7
Congo, 27, 90–91, 133, 176–77n28, 179–80n6
Cornejo Polar, Antonio, 3, 57, 171n6
Coronil, Fernando, 40, 67, 79, 177n1, 178nn4–5
Cosme, Eusebia, 75
Coulthard, G. R., 15, 31, 112, 119, 128

D'Allemand, Patricia, 14, 171n3, 178n7
Daniel, Yvonne, 114, 115, 116, 135, 136, 145, 147, 152, 186n17, 188n17
danzón, 78
de Andrade, Oswald, 78
décimas, 55, 88, 94–95, 96–97, 99

de la Concepción Valdés, Gabriel (Plácido), 45, 47, 71
de la Cruz, Sor Juana Inés, 63
De La Fuente, Alejandro, 22, 23, 24, 33, 37, 38, 39, 40, 68, 157
de Lauria, Roger, 1
del Monte, Domingo, 45, 119, 137–38
del Valle, Gerardo, 1
diablito, 28, 62, 105, 143, 146
Día de Reyes, 26, 46, 63, 90, 142–43
Duno Gottberg, Luis, 29, 38–39, 67, 79, 84

ejército permanente, 39
Enríquez, Carlos, 1, 107, 111
Escalera conspiracy, 45, 99
Esténger, Rafael, 86, 154, 156, 163, 182n5
Estudios Afrocubanos, 2
ethnicity, 3, 17, 100, 174n7; Afro-Cuban, 49–50, 129, 164, 174–75n8; Cuban, 5, 37; emic/etic definition of, 4–5, 49, 174–75n8
exteriority, concept of, 3, 54–58

Feijóo, Samuel, 62, 94, 95, 130, 185n10
folklore, 11, 42, 63, 80, 86, 87–88, 89, 90, 92, 93, 94, 95, 96, 99, 100–102, 141
Frobenius, Leo, 31

García Caturla, Alejandro, 1, 81, 176n24
García Márquez, Gabriel, 4, 78
Gates, Henry Louis, Jr., 151
Gattorno, Antonio, 1, 104
Gilman, Sander L., 107–8, 110
Gilroy, Paul, 57–58, 169
Golden Age Spanish literature, 128, 185–86n10
Gómez Kemp, Rafael, 60, 80
González Contreras, Gilberto, 34, 43, 80
González Echevarría, Roberto, 40, 184n1
Gris, Juan, 31
guaracha, 61–62, 64, 88, 94, 95, 96, 176n27, 180n9, 181n11
Guillén, Nicolás, 5–6, 7, 9, 12, 13–14, 35, 37, 46, 52, 53–54, 55–57, 61–62, 63, 74–75, 76, 80, 82, 84, 86, 95, 121, 130, 132, 134, 151, 163, 168–69, 171nn9–11, 175n12, 176–77n28, 179n10, 182n6, 182n9, 186n11
Guirao, Ramón, 1, 2, 34–35, 37, 38, 39–40, 43, 54, 65, 80, 86–102, 129–30, 133–34, 140, 148, 149, 156, 157, 160,

163, 172n15, 182n4, 182n6; *Bongó: poemas negros,* 53, 86, 175n14; *Órbita de la poesía afrocubana,* 2, 34–35, 65, 86–102, 131

Habibe, Frederick Hendrick, 1, 112
Haiti, 24, 98
Harlem Renaissance, 12, 31
Helg, Aline, 21, 22, 23–24, 26, 27, 45, 47, 51, 174n14
Hernández Catá, Alfonso, 60, 139, 140, 153–54, 182n4
Herskovits, Melville, 49, 71, 77, 178n5
heterogeneity, 48–50, 82, 92–93, 102, 169–70
Hottentot Venus. *See* Bartmann, Sarah
Hughes, Langston, 111–12, 175n12
hybridity, 35, 36, 142, 169, 177n1

identity: black, 9, 11, 17, 85, 128–29, 174n4; Cuban, 7, 13, 15, 30, 35–37, 39, 48, 66, 67, 68, 69, 70, 72, 75, 76, 79, 81–85, 88, 101, 140, 142, 164, 168–69, 172n15, 177n1, 179n12, 189n3
indigenismo, 3, 17, 35, 43, 57, 87, 171n6, 172n17, 175n8, 175–76n19

Jackson, Richard L., 8–9, 11–12, 31, 42–43, 55–58, 103, 168, 171n12
Jesús María neighborhood, 52, 53, 59, 175n12
jitanjáforas, 127–28, 129–30, 131, 185n8
Johnson, Lemuel, 63

Kubayanda, Josephat Bekunuru, 58, 112–13, 134, 183n12, 185n3
Ku Klux Klan, 39
Kutzinski, Vera, 16, 40, 73, 97, 104, 107, 116, 118–19, 141, 171n13, 172n15, 177n28, 184n18

Lachatañeré, Rómulo, 1, 138
Lamar Schweyer, Alberto, 6, 35
Landaluce, Víctor Patricio, 92
León, Argeliers, 115–16, 121, 176n27, 179n4, 188n16
Lewis, Marvin, 9, 10, 11, 15, 43, 57–58, 73
Liberation Army, 21
libretas, 126, 128
Lienhard, Martín, 3, 4, 77, 126, 128–29, 138, 175n8

Lima, Lezama, 84, 179n12
Lipchitz, Jacques, 40
Lorca, Federico García, 54, 92
Loveira, Carlos, 30
Lucumí, 27–28, 50, 64, 126, 135, 138, 144, 145, 146, 157, 160, 161, 188n20, 189n27

Maceo, Antonio, 39, 150
Machado, Gerardo, 28, 32–33, 39–40, 60, 142–43, 174n10
Malinowski, Bronislaw, 71, 77, 78, 178nn4–5
Mansour, Mónica, 10, 135
Manuel de Céspedes, Carlos, 33
Manzano, Juan Francisco, 86, 93, 101
Marinello, Juan, 43, 65, 105, 182n4
Martí, José, 34, 36, 68–69, 174n15
Martínez Furé, Rogelio, 126, 127, 128, 154
Martínez Villena, Rubén, 32
Méndez Rodenas, Adriana, 67, 103, 137, 182n1, 186n3
Mendieta, Carlos, 33
mestizaje, 8–10, 16, 69, 82–83, 103, 141, 169, 179n10
Moore, Robin Dale, 26, 28, 50, 53, 58, 60, 64, 67, 79, 94, 96, 98, 101, 134, 143, 147, 173n5, 186n8
Morejón, Nancy, 7, 82, 179n10, 182n1
Moreno Fraginals, Manuel, 44, 116, 146
Mullen, Edward, 12, 29, 58, 73, 90, 93–94, 172n15

Ñáñigo. *See* Abakuá
negrista poetry, 11–12, 15, 43, 128, 167
Négritude, 11, 15, 31, 109
Noble, Enrique, 6
Novás Calvo, Lino, 146–47

Ochún, 145, 186n2, 187n11
onomatopoeia, 130–31, 133, 139, 154, 156, 185nn9–10
Orovio, Helio, 59
Ortiz, Fernando, 8, 13–14, 25, 33, 37, 42, 50, 52, 58, 60, 63–64, 65–85, 87, 91–92, 93, 95, 96, 99, 100, 105–11, 118, 120, 129, 142, 143–44, 145–46, 147, 148, 161, 162, 164, 165, 173–74n10, 175n16, 187n9; and *ajiaco* metaphor, 70, 82, 172n15; and

Ortiz, Fernando (*continued*)
biological determinism, 29, 72, 75, 123–25; and concept of race, 68–69, 71–72, 73, 75; and concept of "transculturation," 66–67, 70–71, 75, 76–79, 172n15, 177n3, 178n5; criticism on, 66–67, 177n1; and cultural evolutionism, 67, 80–82, 84–85, 123–25; and positivism, 29
Oshún. *See* Ochún

Palo, 48, 126
pataki, 138, 149, 157, 161, 163, 187n10
Pedroso, Regino, 11–12, 32
Pérez Firmat, Gustavo, 13, 30, 66–67
Picasso, Pablo, 31, 40, 88, 184n18
Pichardo, Esteban, 142, 177n29
Pichardo, Francisco Javier, 32
Pichardo Moya, Felipe, 32
Piedra, José, 151, 152, 188nn18–19
Plácido. *See* de la Concepción Valdés, Gabriel
Portuondo, José Antonio, 54, 125, 163, 182n6
postmodernist thought, 70, 83, 179n11
primitivism, 15, 31, 39, 43, 88–89, 95

race: concept of, 4–5, 68–69, 72, 73, 82, 94; in Cuba, 4, 5–6, 23, 24, 37, 45, 69
racial categories, 4, 54
racism, 8, 17, 119; amongst Cubans, 21–23, 24, 45, 51, 52, 62, 96–99, 111, 116; in nineteenth-century Cuban abolitionism, 119, 137–38; in nineteenth-century European discourse, 107–9, 117
Radillo, Teófilo, 86, 125, 148, 151, 182n6
Rama, Ángel, 3–4, 78, 178n5
Regla neighborhood, 52, 59
Revista de Avance, 59, 104, 107, 182n4
Reyes, Alfonso, 129
Roa Bastos, Augusto, 4, 78
Rodríguez, Arsenio, 179n6
Rodríguez Méndez, José, 86
Roig de Leuchsenring, Emilio, 33–34, 87, 101
Roldán, Amadeo, 1, 59, 81
RoseGreen-Williams, Claudette, 13, 104, 107, 110, 111, 119, 141
Rulfo, Juan, 4, 78
rumba, 1, 46, 48–49, 64, 74–75, 79, 83, 111–12, 114, 115–17, 127, 130, 133, 134, 136–37, 140, 142, 143, 145, 147–48, 151, 152–54, 156–58, 162; *columbia*, 118; *guaguancó*, 112, 152, 153; *vacunao*, 64, 112, 114, 120, 150, 153

samba, 162, 176n26
San Martín, Grau, 33, 173n10
Santería (or Regla de Ocha), 50, 64, 74, 120, 126–27, 148, 149, 150, 154–55, 160, 174–75n8, 188n20, 188n22
Sexteto Habanero, 131, 132, 140
Singer, Milton, 129
Singerman, Berta, 59, 176n24
slavery, 7, 9; abolition of, 26, 53; in Cuba, 25–26, 28, 36, 60, 83, 116, 137–38, 146, 154, 162
Sociedad de Estudios Afrocubanos, 36–37, 65
Sociedad del Folklore Cubano, 87–88, 94, 100–101
sociedades de color, 26
solar, 59, 116, 127, 157, 176n26, 188n23
son, 46, 48–49, 60, 101, 131, 132, 143, 147, 179–80n6, 186n11
Spengler, Oswald, 31, 40–41, 67, 184n1
stereotypes, 53, 128, 185n5
Stolcke, Verona, 111
Stravinsky, Igor, 31, 52
Suárez y Romero, Anselmo, 137, 138, 142, 186n6
syncretism, 79, 174–75n8

Tallet, José Z., 2, 12, 55, 59, 104–5, 107, 112, 114, 119, 120, 130, 131, 132–33, 134, 135, 140, 150, 152–53, 162, 163, 176n24, 182n4, 183n12, 185n10
Tanco y Bosmeniel, Félix, 137
teatro bufo, 62, 64, 92, 94, 95, 97–98, 179n3, 181n12; *negrito* figure in, 92, 97–98, 182n13
transculturation. *See* Ortiz, Fernando: and concept of "transculturation"
Trío Matamoros, 121

United States: influence on Cuban culture, 31, 33–34; occupation of Cuba, 21–22, 23, 31–34, 37, 173–74n10

Valdés, Gilberto, 1
Valdés Cruz, Rosa E., 7, 10

Valls Díaz, Jaime, 1, 110, 137
Villaverde, Cirilo, 110, 137, 182–83n10

Wade, Peter, 5, 17, 29, 49, 54, 70, 100, 128, 184n16
War of Independence, 21, 38, 51

whitening, 37, 47, 97
Williams, Claudette M., 108

Yemayá, 64, 135–36, 145, 149–50, 157, 161, 186n13, 186n2, 187nn10–11, 189n27
Young, Ann Venture, 103, 119, 120–21

New World Studies

Vera M. Kutzinski, *Sugar's Secrets: Race and the Erotics of Cuban Nationalism*

Richard D. E. Burton and Fred Reno, editors, *French and West Indian: Martinique, Guadeloupe, and French Guiana Today*

A. James Arnold, editor, *Monsters, Tricksters, and Sacred Cows: Animal Tales and American Identities*

J. Michael Dash, *The Other America: Caribbean Literature in a New World Context*

Isabel Alvarez Borland, *Cuban-American Literature of Exile: From Person to Persona*

Belinda J. Edmondson, editor, *Caribbean Romances: The Politics of Regional Representation*

Steven V. Hunsaker, *Autobiography and National Identity in the Americas*

Celia M. Britton, *Edouard Glissant and Postcolonial Theory: Strategies of Language and Resistance*

Mary Peabody Mann, *Juanita: A Romance of Real Life in Cuba Fifty Years Ago*, Edited and with an introduction by Patricia M. Ard

George B. Handley, *Postslavery Literatures in the Americas: Family Portraits in Black and White*

Faith Smith, *Creole Recitations: John Jacob Thomas and Colonial Formation in the Late Nineteenth-Century Caribbean*

Ian Gregory Strachan, *Paradise and Plantation: Tourism and Culture in the Anglophone Caribbean*

Nick Nesbitt, *Voicing Memory: History and Subjectivity in French Caribbean Literature*

Charles W. Pollard, *New World Modernisms: T. S. Eliot, Derek Walcott, and Kamau Brathwaite*

Carine M. Mardorossian, *Reclaiming Difference: Caribbean Women Rewrite Postcolonialism*

Luís Madureira, *Cannibal Modernities: Postcoloniality and the Avant-garde in Caribbean and Brazilian Literature*

Elizabeth M. DeLoughrey, Renée K. Gosson, and George B. Handley, editors, *Caribbean Literature and the Environment: Between Nature and Culture*

Flora González Mandri, *Guarding Cultural Memory: Afro-Cuban Women in Literature and the Arts*

Miguel Arnedo-Gómez, *Writing Rumba: The Afrocubanista Movement in Poetry*

www.ingramcontent.com/pod-product-compliance
Lightning Source LLC
Chambersburg PA
CBHW011717220426
43662CB00019B/2411